# THE
# WEEK
# FRANCE
# FELL

# NOEL BARBER

# THE WEEK FRANCE FELL

STEIN AND DAY/*Publishers*/New York

First published in the United States of America, 1976
Copyright © 1976 by Noel Barber
All rights reserved
Printed in the United States of America
Stein and Day/*Publishers*/Scarborough House,
Briarcliff Manor, N.Y. 10510

Library of Congress Cataloging in Publication Data

Barber, Noël.
    The week France fell.

    1.   World War, 1939-1945—France—Chronology.
I.   Title.
D761.B33 1976        940.53'44        75-34398
ISBN 0-8128-1921-7

*For Budge and Marcina Patty*

# Contents

4              CONTENTS

# List of Illustrations

## MAPS

Acknowledgements for the plates are due to: Associated
Newspapers for 1, 2*a*, 2*b*, 3*a*, endpapers; Popperfoto for 3*b*,
5*b*; Imperial War Museum for 4*a*, 5*a*; Collection Viollet for
4*b*; Musée de la Guerre, Vincennes, for 8.

The map on page 14 is reprinted from Winston S. Churchill, *The Second World War*, vol. II, *Their Finest Hour*
(Cassell, 1949).

# Acknowledgements

My most grateful thanks are due to the many people who
have helped me over the years with the research for this
book.

In France, Reynaud's *chef de cabinet* Roland de Margerie,
who kept careful notes during that eventful week, was
unstinting with his time and help; his frankness was equally
helpful. I did not know Reynaud well, but we did have many
talks during a cruise we took with friends among the Greek
islands, and I found him forthright and honest in his answers
to all my questions. I must also thank Geoffroy de Courcel,
de Gaulle's aide in those days, and now Director of Political
Affairs at the Quai d'Orsay. I went to Paris especially to see
him, and the time was very well spent.

Jean-Noël Jeanneney, grandson of Jules Jeanneney who
figures in this book, was helpful in dozens of ways, and so
were the directors of two organisations: the Centre Information de la 2ème Guerre Mondiale and the Société des Amis
de Paul Reynaud. That wonderful lady Madame Tabouis has,
in her eighties, a memory as sharp as a razor.

Much of my research in France consisted of retracing the
steps of the French Government, and everywhere I received
much help. The Marquis Armand de Cosnac, then as now the
owner of the Château du Muguet, which became the French
army headquarters, was kindness itself when I arrived
unannounced. So were the government officials in Tours and
Bordeaux, who went to great pains to track down witnesses
working there in 1940.

In the United States, Freeman Matthews, a great gentleman of American politics, and ex-ambassador to Vienna, even allowed me to take back to England the only copy of his private papers dealing with the days when he was at the American Embassy, in Paris, Tours, Bordeaux, recording events hour by hour. I am deeply indebted to my old friend John Barron, the author of *KGB*, for opening State Department files for me during my many weeks of research in Washington. I would also like to thank the authorities at the University of Virginia for help during my stay in Charlottesville, where Roosevelt made what was perhaps his most historic speech of the war.

In Britain I have to thank the Foreign Office and the Public Record Office for their patience and understanding.

There is one more and very different group of people without whose help this book would not have been possible; the 'ordinary' people, caught up in the tide of that terrible week, but these I cannot thank individually in print. Nor do I need to, for I count most of them as personal friends.

Indeed, in a way this is very much a 'family' book, for it was to my friends in France that I first turned for help, and those who read about them in the pages that follow might like to know that for eight of the ten years I lived in France I worked daily with Jimmy Ashworth, and spent six weeks at Portofino with Harold King of Reuter; he was so well informed that de Gaulle always referred to him as 'mon ami King'. I spent Christmas in New York with Ivan Foxwell; I even drove to Calcutta in a land-rover with Dynevor Rhys (and it is only due to his tolerance and understanding that we remain good friends to this day!). It was in France that I met the 'long-legged Italian' whom Jimmy Ashworth drove to Tours after their blind date at the Ritz in Paris; and Zena Marshall first outlined her story over dinner at our house.

To all of them and many more, my most grateful thanks. But these must be shared with my two devoted and patient researchers in Paris, Joan Smyth and Susan Whittinghill, who did me an immense service, not only by tracing individuals, but in making appointments for me and checking facts. My thanks also to Anthony Davis for his research in London, and to Donald Dinsley for his diligence at the London Library.

I should only add that any conclusions reached from the facts given to me by my friends are my own.

N.B.

# THE
# WEEK
# FRANCE
# FELL

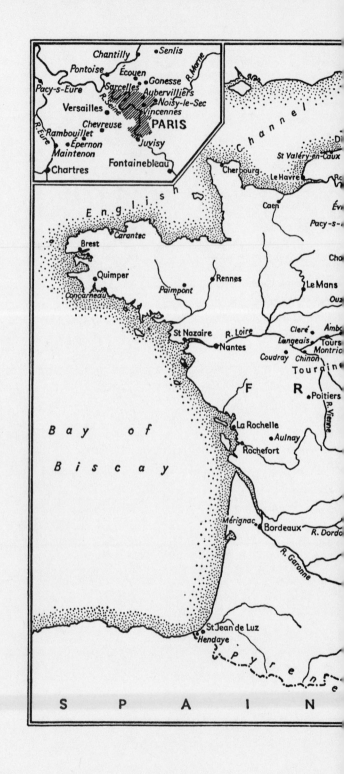

Chantilly
Senlis
R. Morne
Pontoise
Écouen
Gonesse
Pacy-s-Eure
Sarcelles
Aubervilliers
Noisy-le-Sec
Versailles
Vincennes
R. Seine
Chevreuse
PARIS
Rambouillet
R. Eure
Épernon
Juvisy
Maintenon
Chartres
Fontainebleau

E n g l i s h   Channel

Di
St Valéry-en-Caux
Cherbourg
Le Havre
Ro
Caen
Év
Pacy-s-
Carantec
Cho
Brest
Rennes
Le Mans
Quimper
Paimpont
Ou
Concarneau
Cleré
Amb
St Nazaire
R. Loire
Langeais
Tours
Nantes
Montric
Coudray
Chinon
Tourain
F
R
Poitiers
R. Vienne
Bay   of
La Rochelle
Aulnay
Biscay
Rochefort

Mérignac
Bordeaux
R. Dordo
R. Garonne

St Jean de Luz
Hendaye
Pyrene

S   P   A   I   N

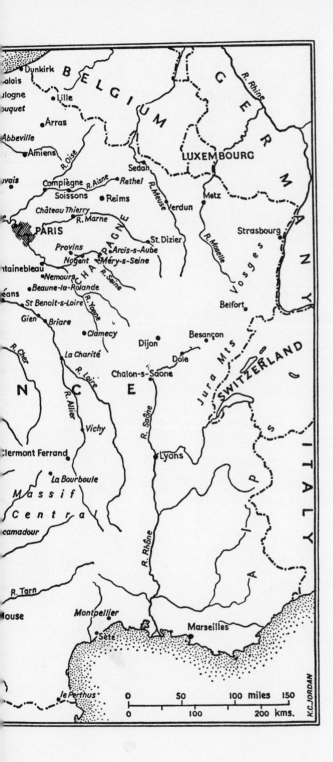

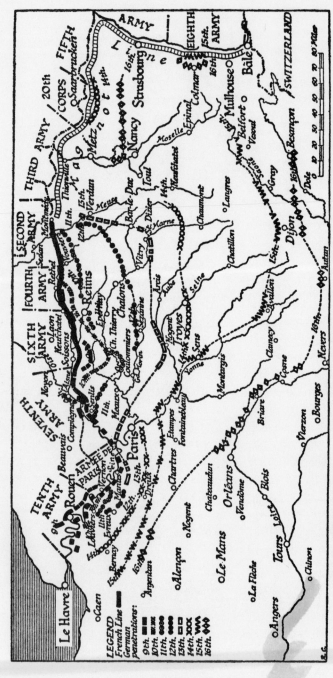

THE LAST STAND OF THE FRENCH ARMY — June 1940

# Monday, 10 June

## 1. *Paris – the people*

LITTLE more than a month ago, the chestnuts were bursting into leaf on the boulevards as Paris sang its favourite tune of the moment, 'J'Attendrai'. The Duke of Windsor and King Zog of Albania were the honoured guests at a charity gala in the Marigny Theatre, while the Académie Française, perfecting its new dictionary, was arguing whether the wing of a chicken was a limb or a muscle. Staff officers of General Joseph Georges' headquarters near the German lines were playing bridge far into the night, while General Georges Boris, Inspector-General of Artillery, reassured senior officers at Metz that new, improved guns would be ready by next spring. That same night, Major-General Erwin Rommel, in charge of a Panzer division, scribbled a note to his wife in Germany: 'Dearest Lu, We're packing up at last. Let's hope not in vain. . . .'

Next morning the storm broke. General Boris heard the boom of the guns and asked where the manœuvres were being held.

'They are not manœuvres,' his aide replied. 'That, *mon général*, is the start of the German offensive.'

In that month, Hitler's tanks changed the face of Europe; half-forgotten names leapt into the headlines again – Sedan, Ypres, Dunkirk, Arras, Verdun. Before France could catch its breath Holland fell, bombed into submission by the Stukas. Belgium capitulated. The British were driven into the sea.

Over the fair countryside of France, thousands of uprooted men, women and children – some in cars, some on cycles, some driving their cattle before them – headed for Paris, then the south. All believed, as the people of Paris believed even when the enemy was at the gates, that the invincible French Army remained to hold aloft the banner of freedom.

No matter that each dawn posed a new threat as German tanks roamed freely north of Paris. France would hold. Pétain, the hero of Verdun, had rallied to the cause. Weygand had assumed command of the armies. And if the worst came to the worst, then the beleaguered capital would echo the promise of the great Clemenceau and fight before Paris, in Paris, behind Paris.

Perhaps the peerless June weather helped to foster the sense of illusion, even when distant gunfire could be heard in the capital; the hot sun seemed particularly benevolent after a brutal winter, the worst in living memory.

The city had the appearance of a stage set. On this Monday, 10 June, the pavement cafés on the boulevards were as crowded as ever, a kaleidoscope of gaily flowered dresses, of men fighting for places at the minuscule tables, ordering a *vin rouge* or a *bière de pression*; yet the roads were so empty that they gave the city a nostalgic turn-of-the-century character like an old sepia postcard unearthed from a dusty drawer. One almost expected to hear the clatter of a pony and trap.

An occasional taxi-driver sped along the Champs Élysées with the verve of a racing driver who has no competition. An occasional ancient car – most of the rich had already left – rumbled up the avenue, always in the direction of the Étoile, to join the queue leaving the gates of the city for an unknown destination. Most were piled high with the pathetic belongings of fleeing families, with that symbol of flight: a mattress on the roof as a rudimentary precaution against aerial machine-gunning.

There were some strange sights. A farmer who had fled from Holland was resting near the Invalides, his cows and his flock of sheep contentedly cropping the grass. To Roger

Langeron, head of the Paris police, they gave the city the atmosphere of a fairground.

Sometimes, in a burst of excitement, a sad-faced child refugee forgot all he had passed through and became a tourist for a few seconds as he saw the Concorde or the Étoile for the first time and cried, 'I know this place. Our teacher told us about it.'

But to most Parisians still left in the city the Dutch and the Belgians, passing like a frieze, excited no more than the tolerant sympathy reserved for people from another world, the world of uprooted, small nations; mighty France, though reeling under massive blows, could never be defeated.

It was impossible; France possessed not only the Maginot Line but the finest army the world had ever known, the army of Revolution, of Austerlitz, of Verdun, the army that last time had stood for more than four years against German might, the army of glory that Lavisse once described as 'one of the most perfect instruments of war history has ever seen'. It was more than an army, it was the heart of the nation; it epitomised the very greatness of France. France might have changed, its politicians might be muddlers, dishonest even, but now more than ever people believed in the words of Anatole France, that the French Army 'is all that is left of our glorious past. It consoles us for the present and gives us hope for the future.'

The heat shimmered and danced along the beautiful broad avenues, and though many shops were shuttered, and two million people had already fled, the city bore few traces of war. Near the new Pont des Beaux Arts two formal gardens of flowers had just been planted on the embankment. In the symmetrical courtyards of the Louvre, in the gardens by Notre-Dame, men – brown and sweating though stripped to the waist – uprooted the early spring flowers and filled the beds with geraniums from loaded trucks.

On the Left Bank the bookstalls were open, and down by the *quai* – the dome of Les Invalides shining in the sun – a man in uniform calmly set up his easel and started painting. Below him a barge loaded with refugees sailed up the Seine.

In the rue de la Paix, a photograph of King Leopold of the
Belgians had been taken out of the window of Cartier to
mark their displeasure at the Belgian surrender. In its place
stood a framed photograph of Queen Mary. A few yards away
in the Place Vendôme there was still an excellent range of
summer ties at Charvet, though the sandbags round the base
of the Napoleon column had collapsed and burst open.

Each evening the theatres were filled. Cocteau had a new
comedy at the Bouffes, while the latest production of *Cyrano
de Bergerac* drew packed houses at the Comédie Française.
So did the Guignol in the Luxembourg, where images of
Hitler and Goering strutted across the stage every evening.

Theatregoing was still preceded by champagne at the Ritz
bar, which had been newly decorated for the season, and
after the play one could stroll through moderately well-lit
streets to supper at those *boîtes* still open. One had to choose
carefully, for behind the scenes life was not so normal. There
were three meatless days a week, three days when restaurants
could not serve hard liquor (though there was always champagne, of course), three days without pastries, and enterprising hostesses spent hours calculating the permutations to suit
their more demanding guests. But, even though Parisians
had just received the cards for their slender rations in the
coming winter, it seemed far away, and in the meantime one
could always eat at home, for though coffee and sugar were
(officially) scarce there was more than enough food, and a
woman could find anything she wanted in the market.

It was not complacency that made the people of Paris sit
at the cafés discussing the war with the detachment of non-
participants; it was the result of a myth carefully fostered in
the corridors of power. True, many Frenchmen had died in
the fearful carnage to the north and east; but every mother
in Paris whose son fought on those 'distant' fronts knew that
he was fighting to save a France that would go on for ever.

The mood came from the top. Throughout this Monday
every effort was made in government departments to keep up
normal appearances. In the Élysée Palace and the Premier's
office in the rue St Dominique, slow-moving *huissiers* carried

messages on silver platters up or down stairs as though this day were a day like any other, not the day when the Government was about to flee the capital and the armed retreat was accelerating into a rout – not the day when Italy was about to declare war. When General de Gaulle – newly transferred from the battlefield of arms to the more sinister battlefield of politics – went to see President Lebrun to receive his credentials as Under-Secretary for Defence, he found that 'at the top of the State the tragedy was being played as though in a dream'.

Yet all was hidden, and a curious hiatus seems to have hung over Paris on this Monday morning, an interlude of inactivity, even boredom, so that when one sifts through documents, studies books of the period, talks to people who were there, a vagueness clouds all answers. 'No, the office wasn't open – at least I don't think so.' 'We went to Fouquet's for a drink, and I remember the sun was very hot.'

Not one in ten thousand realised that the Germans had crossed the River Aisne, and were attacking south of Soissons, while a Panzer division was moving on Rouen. Instead, most Parisians seem to have been caught up in the euphoric conviction, fostered by daylong broadcasts, that somehow the French line would hold and Paris would be saved. The French radio – or at least its 'official spokesman' – was apparently convinced that the age of miracles had not passed. It was pleasant to agree with him. Even the imminent entry of Italy into the war seemed, if anything, to stiffen morale, to make neighbours say to one another, 'Well, at least we'll beat the hell out of them.'

In a city bewildered by total lack of communication between leaders and citizens, one rumour chased another. All were 'good' rumours. The Americans had declared war. The British had landed ten more divisions. The Germans north of Pontoise had fallen into a huge French trap and three Panzer divisions had been decimated. 'The remnants are in full retreat,' the buxom cashier at Fouquet's announced smugly.

With all news gagged by the Ministry of Information at the

Hôtel Continental, with every radio broadcast extolling non-existent French victories, was it any wonder that the people of Paris could not see the truth? Instead one and all lifted their glasses in the glorious sunshine, and echoed the toast that was proclaimed on thousands of posters all over the city: *Chantons quand même!* – 'Let's sing all the same!'

Many people were firm in their determination to 'stick it out'. Mrs Etta Shiber, a New York widow in her forties, who had lived the past three years in Paris, announced firmly, 'I'm a neutral American, and I'm not going to let the Germans tell me what to do.'

Mrs Shiber shared a five-roomed apartment on the sixth floor of a modern building in the rue Balny d'Avricourt near the Arc de Triomphe with Madame Kitty Beaurepos, an Englishwoman separated from her French husband, and Madame Beaurepos was inclined to agree.

'All the same, I'll fill up the tank of the car – just in case,' she decided.

Dynevor Rhys, a tall, gangling American with a domed forehead, and a face that lit up in sudden wide smiles, had lived in his fifth-floor apartment at 15 rue du Cherche Midi, on the Left Bank, since 1921, when he decided to study art in Paris. He remembers looking round the L-shaped room, with its divan bed discreetly hidden – a perfect bachelor establishment – and thinking, 'It's not our war – and Roosevelt has promised it never will be. Besides, I've got a business to run.'

Over the years Rhys, who was now forty-five, had turned from art to photography, finally opening a photographer's studio in the rue du Suresne near the Madeleine, in 1933 – the year Roosevelt became President and Hitler became Chancellor. He now had an international reputation and a staff to consider.

Among those who worked for Rhys was thirty-eight-year-old Iris Schweppe, a naturalised British subject whose German father was dead but whose mother still travelled on a German passport. Iris Schweppe had worked in Paris for seventeen years and she and her mother shared a tiny apartment in the dormitory suburb of Vaucresson, midway between Paris and Versailles. Her reason for staying was dictated by simple economics – she was the sole provider and, so long as Dynevor Rhys stayed in business, she would stay. 'They won't touch the women,' she said.

Many people had already gone, but many who remained faced the same dilemma as Iris Schweppe. They had to work for a living. Why throw up a livelihood to bolt to – where?

Others were making last-minute preparations. Early in the day Colonel Thomas, the French press liaison spokesman, had called journalists to the Clock Room in the Quai d'Orsay, and warned them off the record that the Government was leaving for Tours that night. He delivered an even worse blow: all Paris newspapers would cease publication after today. As soon as the news was telephoned to the Paris *Daily Mail* in the narrow rue du Sentier off the Grands Boulevards, the staff prepared to leave for Tours in the hope of publishing a makeshift edition on the presses of a local paper. Jimmy Ashworth, the advertising manager – a Yorkshireman of thirty-nine from Hebden Bridge, who swore better in French than many Parisians – had already filled three cars with petrol for just such an emergency. Ashworth – married to a French girl who had borne him a son and daughter – was the sort of man that every city throws up, friendly alike to policemen and pimps, a man who could always be relied upon to find a room in a hotel already booked up, or a seat on the Golden Arrow or the Train Bleu when trains were full.

Henri Malherbe, the chief cashier, filled two small sacks with petty cash. A Frenchman of scrupulous honesty – with a Gauloise forever dangling at his lips – he insisted on the cash being counted before witnesses, then sealed. None of the linotype operators had come in so early in the day, except one. Without warning, Charles Vallotton arrived with three *baguettes* of bread, a satchel of food and four bottles of red wine.

'I'm staying here in case the Boches arrive,' he announced. 'I've got one last thing to do before I leave Paris.'

These were people who had to go, like most journalists.
Arved Arenstam, a Latvian who was chief political correspondent for a number of newspapers in the Baltic states,
arranged a farewell dinner for twelve. His housekeeper had
no problems obtaining food, for one could eat like a king at
home and, as Arenstam noted tartly in his diary, 'Officialdom
does not peer into domestic saucepans.'

Others were not so sure. Arthur Koestler noticed 'the melt-
ing away of the town, as if infected with consumption', and
when he travelled by Métro was conscious of the uneasy,
suspicious glances of other passengers, worried about fifth
columnists, 'the dim candles of fear lit behind their eyeballs'.
Gordon Waterfield of Reuter news agency toured the city
that morning and discovered that 'where there should have
been tremendous defensive activity, there was listlessness.
Bewildered people took the easy way out and still trusted
the government'. Though he found the centre of Paris
orderly, the roads leading from the capital were blocked, and
he had a shock when he drove along the straight Avenue des
Grandes Armées and the Avenue Foch. Every fifty yards or
so a green Paris bus had been parked crossways – presumably to prevent German troop-carrying planes from landing.

To those who had to leave, there were hurried family
partings and the agony of deciding what treasures should be
left behind. Élie Bois, editor of the *Petit Parisien* for over
twenty years and on friendly terms with many political
leaders – he had seen Reynaud that very morning – was
preparing to publish in Tours, and remembers thinking, 'Let
me take a good look at this. Perhaps we shall never see it
again.'

Among those who left Paris on Monday was the writer
André Maurois, a captain in the Army, who had been ordered
to fly to America for a propaganda lecture-tour. He planned
first to fly to London where he would board a ship, and very
early that morning a government minister telephoned him
and advised him to send his wife to the south.

As soon as he had digested the news, Maurois leant out of
the window of his apartment, gazed over the pale blue skies

at the Fort of Mount Valerian 'looking in the mist like a
Florentine convent'. Below, the concierge was watering the
begonias in her small garden, and a workman whistled a military tune as he mended a tap.

Maurois, too, found it hard to believe that he might never
see Paris again and on an impulse he and his wife decided
to visit – 'perhaps for the last time' – the corners of Paris
they loved, the Invalides, the Quais, the Place Dauphine.
'The city had never been more beautiful. The sky was pure
blue, the air was soft.' They went into a shop and found the
salesgirls alert and obliging, 'though one sensed tears in
everyone's eyes'. Many others were making similar 'pilgrim-
ages', and they, too, were near to tears, 'but I heard not a
single word of despair'.

Maurois and his wife were close friends of Dr Thierry de
Martel, the most eminent brain-surgeon in France, and
Director of the American Hospital, who had vowed more
than once to take his life if ever the Germans reached Paris.
Unknown to Maurois, de Martel had that morning asked
William C. Bullitt, the American ambassador, whether he
should stay or leave. Bullitt had begged him to stay, insisting
that if the worst came to the worst every man would be
needed, especially doctors.

Yet, shortly after Maurois had set off for London, de Martel
telephoned Madame Maurois and asked her whether they
intended to remain in Paris.

'André has been sent on a mission to London,' she told
him, 'and I am leaving tomorrow at dawn.'

'I am going too,' said de Martel, adding mysteriously, 'but
for a much longer voyage.' De Martel, it seems, had not yet
made up his mind.

Neither had Jimmy Ashworth, the French-speaking
Yorkshireman, whose many problems included a strange
request to meet a French countess, who had been given his
name by her husband fighting at the Front. He left the Paris
*Daily Mail* and set off on foot for the Ritz bar. As he turned
the corner out of the rue du Sentier and strolled along the
Boulevard des Italiens, he saw that Pillot, the shoe shop, was

still open – and stocked with goods. He bought six pairs of shoes for his children. At the corner of the rue Lafitte he caught a glimpse of Sacré Cœur in the distance, a bright white against the cloudless blue sky. A few yards further on a street vendor was doing a roaring trade selling porcelain dogs with one leg cocked over a copy of *Mein Kampf.* Ashworth was early and stopped for a drink at a brasserie where he was a regular customer. The long, thin head-waiter, who had been left in charge by the owner, said the Germans would be in Paris within a week, but did not seem unduly concerned. 'I was a prisoner in the last war. Les salauds! We know how to deal with them.'

Ashworth finished his beer, picked up his package of shoes and set off for the rue Cambon entrance to the Ritz to meet the unknown countess.

## 2.  *The politicians*

Paul Reynaud, the sixty-two-year-old French Premier, was born in Barcelonnette, in the Alps. The son of a textile manufacturer who made a fortune in Mexico, Reynaud practised first as a lawyer, then entered politics in 1919, becoming French Finance Minister in 1930. Like Churchill in Britain, he repeatedly warned France of the dangers of Nazi aggression; he opposed appeasement at Munich.

A man with a first-class mind, he was short and dapper, with many of the characteristics that are associated with short men: he was aggressive, but his surface confidence hid an inferiority complex, and he was susceptible to flattery. But he did have one certain attribute: great courage. His friend Maurois called him 'a little fighting cock'. His enemies nicknamed him 'Mickey Mouse'.

During the morning de Gaulle arrived at the Ministry of Defence in the rue St Dominique. Though as premier Reynaud's proper office was the Hôtel Matignon, he was also

Minister of Defence and much preferred the eighteenth-century *hôtel particulier* in the rue St Dominique which reeked of history – and particularly of that other short man who led France, Napoleon.

Roland de Margerie, Reynaud's *chef de cabinet*, worked on the ground floor in a room which had once been planned and decorated for Napoleon's mother, 'Madame Mère', as she was known. De Gaulle had his office next door, Reynaud on the first floor. All overlooked a charming, enclosed garden.

When de Gaulle arrived, he found Bullitt, the American ambassador, in Reynaud's study. Perhaps naïvely de Gaulle assumed that Bullitt had called to 'bring some encouragement for the future from Washington. But no. He had come to say goodbye.' Against the express wishes of President Roosevelt, Bullitt had decided to remain in Paris. To de Gaulle, Bullitt's refusal to travel with the Government meant that 'the United States no longer had much use for France', and he could hardly bring himself to be polite to him. But, then, even his prime minister and mentor Reynaud, who had been a friend since 1934 of the 'outlandish, relatively obscure' Colonel Charles André Joseph Marie de Gaulle, once said frankly, 'He has the character of a stubborn pig.'

De Gaulle, who at fifty was the youngest general in the French Army, had only been appointed a minister the previous week – on the night of 5–6 June – after leading one of the few successful French tank attacks of the war near Abbeville.

Reynaud had long been an admirer of this tall, long-nosed, prickly, withdrawn, intensely patriotic son of a professor, who at St Cyr – the Sandhurst or West Point of France – was nicknamed 'le grand asperge' and who had been wounded three times in the First World War before being taken prisoner and making five escape attempts.

As far back as 1934 when they met, Reynaud, then a deputy, was advocating the need for a modern, attacking army, instead of relying on the outmoded defence plans of French military leaders. And when de Gaulle wrote his 'revolutionary' book on warfare, *Towards a Professional Army*

(1935), Reynaud was one of the first to buy a copy. Few others followed his example, for only 700 copies were sold in France, and de Gaulle was lambasted by almost every military critic for suggesting a doctrine of attack diametrically opposed to the defensive ideas of the High Command which were based on the Maginot Line. However, there were foreign sales, by order of ex-Corporal Hitler.

Hitler was so enthralled by its line of thought, which coincided with German military thinking, that he ordered all his chief advisers – among them Keitel, Rundstedt and Guderian – to read it. They were equally fascinated and, unlike the French, profited from de Gaulle's concept of self-contained mechanised divisions with their own air support and infantry back-up; within three years the first German Panzer division paraded through the streets of Berlin. Ironically it incorporated many of the theories in an obscure French book which cost fifteen francs.

As soon as Bullitt left, the two men started to draft a speech Reynaud planned to make that night. It was not easy. The man who had become Prime Minister of France on 21 March was in a foul temper; as always when he was edgy, he could not control a nervous mannerism – a jerking movement of his head from right to left. What was on his mind was far removed from anxieties about the continuing German advance.

In fact Reynaud's bad temper stemmed from a mundane experience shared by millions of lesser mortals: the Prime Minister of France had started the day with a blazing row with his mistress, the Countess de Portes, a woman who shared his small 'bachelor' apartment in the Place du Palais Bourbon, behind the Assembly, while her husband was gallantly fighting at the Front and Madame Reynaud was circumspectly rolling bandages and preparing comforts for the troops at the Reynauds' family home.

Reynaud and Hélène de Portes had been lovers for ten years. In her late forties, she had a somewhat angular face, a large mouth and a rather sallow complexion. But she was an elegant, fashionably dressed woman who wore her dark curly hair brushed upwards in the style of the day, though Élie Bois, who knew both Reynaud and his mistress well, noted that her 'features and eyelids bore traces of the fatigues of an eventful life'.

Behind her back she was called 'la porte acôté', a nickname that was double-edged. She *was* the 'side door' that had to be used by anyone who wanted to see Reynaud, but *acôté* was also a snobbish term, so that to her enemies she was 'a little *acôté*' – 'a little ordinary'. The fact that the two openly shared a flat led to many diplomatic embarrassments. When 'Monsieur et Madame Reynaud' were invited to dinner, the anxious hostess could never be certain which lady would turn up. Robert Murphy, the American diplomat, remembers the occasion when both ladies arrived for dinner at the American embassy, though only one had been invited.

The most powerful woman in France, she exercised a malign influence on the destinies of her country. Reynaud was so besotted by her that he even dyed his hair to look younger and at times allowed her to sit at his desk and take charge of conferences. Even when Reynaud was deciding that the Government must evacuate Paris, Pierre Lazareff, the editor of *Paris-Soir*, found her seated at the Premier's desk presiding over a meeting of government officials. As Lazareff watched 'aghast, absolutely tongue-tied', she stepped into the next room and Lazareff heard her say, 'Are you all right, Paul? Just relax – we are working.'

Others had similar experiences. When André Maurois, a close friend of Reynaud's, criticised an appointment, Reynaud replied, 'It wasn't my choice, it was hers.'

'That's no excuse,' retorted Maurois. 'Ah,' sighed Reynaud, 'you don't know what a man who has been hard at work all day will put up with for the sake of an evening's peace.'

Even Bullitt seemed to come under her spell. When Vincent Sheean, the journalist and author, arrived at the American embassy by appointment, he had not been with the ambassador more than a couple of minutes before a secretary announced that the Countess de Portes was on the telephone.

Bullitt took the call, 'and the lady – in what seemed a remarkably brief conversation – summoned him to her apartment to have chocolate with her . . . apparently this happened quite often'.

Bullitt was under no illusion about the dangerous role played by Madame de Portes. He had already told Roosevelt that it was the Countess who had persuaded Reynaud to dismiss Daladier and to install Paul Baudouin, a defeatist, as Under-Secretary for Foreign Affairs. He wrote to Roosevelt, 'The people of France who are fighting with an absolute selflessness deserve better at this moment than to be ruled by a prime minister's mistress – not even a king's. In the end she will be shot. Meanwhile, she will rule the roost.'

Bullitt had also described to Roosevelt an extraordinary interlude when the President was discussing American policy with Reynaud. On the way to Reynaud's private study in his apartment Reynaud told her, in front of Bullitt, that he was expecting a telephone call from the President and that she must on no account come into the room. She took no notice. As soon as the phone rang she walked right in as Roosevelt was talking. As Bullitt wrote to the President, 'When he ordered her out of the room, [she] refused to go. I thought you would like to know that there is still some continuity in French life, and that the mistress of the ruler again directs the State as she has since time immemorial.'

No one has ever really succeeded in analysing the reason for her power over the diminutive Reynaud. Perhaps one unnamed Frenchman came near to the truth when he told Harold Nicolson, the British diplomat, that 'she made him feel tall and grand and powerful. Had Reynaud been three inches taller, the history of the world might have been changed.'

That morning there had been a quarrel and Élie Bois, to whom Reynaud often confided his woes, discovered that it had been of a ridiculous nature, almost bordering on farce. Though Hélène de Portes knew all about the arrangements for leaving Paris, she suddenly insisted that she could never leave, and that anyone who did so was a coward and a traitor.

'You can't go, Paul!' she cried furiously. 'You can't run away. I'm not afraid of the Germans.'

Incredibly it was (according to Bois after talking to Reynaud) nothing less than a trick. The Countess – so violently anti-British that Hitler had once sent an emissary to woo her favours – had no intention of remaining in Paris; but she wanted Reynaud to persuade her to leave 'against her will'.

Élie Bois asked himself, 'Was it a deliberate device calculated to hasten on the request for an armistice already decided upon? Was it a mere feminine trick, the coquetry of a woman who puts a high price on her presence and wants to be entreated?'

Whatever the reason, it left Reynaud miserable. Curtly he told de Gaulle to help him to write his speech, but now there was another interruption. This time it was seventy-two-year-old General Maxime Weygand, who had replaced Gamelin as Army Commander-in-Chief on 19 May. Weygand had been born in Belgium. He had been Chief of Staff to Foch in the First World War; but he was now a worn-out shadow of a once-great military leader, a little sparrow of a man, with small, bitter eyes set in a face that seemed stretched like parchment ready to crack. Lord Lloyd, the British Colonial Secretary, had found him only the previous week 'a crumpled, broken little man, completely finished and filled with vague but bitter recriminations', while one Frenchman summed him up as looking like an aged, retired jockey. He disliked the British, despised de Gaulle, hated politicians, feared revolution. And now, having been asked to lead an army that was virtually beaten when he was appointed, he was extending his 'duties' into forbidden territory – he was dabbling in politics. His interference was already profoundly weakening Reynaud's resolve to fight.

Almost before the secretary announced that Weygand was waiting in an ante-room, the General burst into the Prime Minister's study. Reynaud looked up, astonished, from his papers.

'But I was sent for!' cried Weygand.

'Not by me,' said Reynaud shortly.

'Then it's a misunderstanding,' Weygand said rather lamely, 'but it's a useful mistake for I have something important to say.' Obviously Weygand had decided to come and see the Prime Minister without an invitation. He sat down now, drew out a document and said, 'Things have reached the point where everyone's responsibilities must be clearly established. That's why I have put my opinion on paper and am handing you this note.'

Reynaud was working against time to compose the vital broadcast, but he listened as Weygand barked that the battle was lost, France must capitulate.

'But surely there are other prospects?' interrupted de Gaulle, who remembered later the mocking tone in which Weygand asked him, 'Have you anything to suggest?'

With a touch of the imperiousness that aggravated so many people all through his life de Gaulle retorted loftily, 'The Government has not suggestions to make, but orders to give. I am sure it will give them.'

Weygand was not to be deterred, and of course there was nothing untruthful in the dark tale of military defeats he unfolded. One disaster had followed another. Almost the last French reserves had been thrown into the battle, and only a wide expanse of flat countryside, admirably suited to tanks, lay between the German Panzers and the capital. Weygand was already moving his headquarters from Paris to Briare, a town of 5000 people on the Loire, east of Tours.

Weygand, having committed his thoughts to paper, thrust his note under Reynaud's nose. The tired premier's eyes lit on one sentence: 'The events of the past two days make it my duty to warn the prime minister that the final breaking up of our lines may occur at any moment.'

Talk of surrender was already in the air. As de Gaulle later put it, 'one tried to think that there was still a front, an active command ... [but] in fact, in the midst of a nation prostrate and stupefied, behind an army without faith and without hope, the machinery of power turned over in irremediable confusion'.

Weygand now launched another bitter attack – this time on Churchill. It contained a criticism shared by every French leader, including both Reynaud and de Gaulle. With France fighting to the last gasp, said Weygand, what was Britain – who had already extricated her expeditionary forces at Dunkirk* – doing to help? Britain had the fighter aircraft to strafe the German Army, but where were they? 'In Britain, safe,' sneered Weygand.

In fact they were not in Britain, but attacking German troop formations. That, however, was not the point. The argument went deeper. Fighters with their limited flying time could only operate really effectively over the German lines if they were based in France. No one disputed that. The bulk of Britain's few remaining fighters were based in Britain, so that each time they flew a sortie – and they were flying in every hour of daylight – they used up so much fuel crossing the Channel that they could only operate over the Germans for a few minutes.

'I want them based on French airfields,' cried Weygand. 'We know it could mean the difference between victory and defeat.'

Churchill had been obdurate. He was fearful that, if he agreed, British planes would be destroyed on the ground by the onrushing Germans. He regarded the remaining British fighter planes as his last line of defence and refused to commit them to French airfields. Only the previous day de Gaulle had been in London and broached the question of more air support for the French Army, but, in his words, 'My pressing demand that at least part of Britain's air support should be moved to the airfields south of the Loire met with a categorical refusal from Mr Churchill.'

---

* In the last week of May and the first week of June 338,226 British and Allied troops were evacuated from Dunkirk; 2300 guns, 7000 tons of ammunition, 90,000 rifles, 8000 Bren guns, 400 anti-tank rifles and 120,000 vehicles were lost.

Weygand's insistence and Churchill's refusal pinpointed the totally different attitudes of the French and British to the war. Weygand – and many French leaders – believed that war was an affair to be settled between opposing troops in the field of battle, and that civilian suffering would only occur in fighting areas. They wanted fighters for the battle area, but were not enthusiastic when Churchill offered to bomb any industrial targets chosen by the French, for that would have invited reprisals. (When Clare Boothe was in a shelter during an early raid on Paris, one Frenchwoman turned to her and cried, 'This isn't the life for us. Why can't the Germans let our soldiers fight the war?')

The British saw the war in a very different light – as an air war from which civilians could not hope to escape. They had been told that Hitler would wreak a merciless revenge by bombing Britain. Baldwin had said, 'The bomber will always get through,' and it was a phrase that haunted most people – including Churchill. The Committee for Imperial Defence had estimated that when the Germans launched their air attacks on London 600,000 people would be killed and more than a million injured. 50,000 papier-mâché coffins were stored in the country areas, which were unlikely to be bombed, and a million 'instant burial forms' had been printed. To Churchill, Britain's only hope lay in its few remaining fighters. He was certainly hesitant about the decision he had to make. He was intensely pro-French and he might indeed have wavered and split the British fighter defence force – which would have been disastrous – had he not received a blunt warning from Sir Hugh Dowding, the Commander-in-Chief of Fighter Command, that if any fighter aircraft were sent to France he would not assume responsibility for the defence of Britain. It was more than a warning. It was an ultimatum by a man for whom Churchill had a deep respect.

One more decision had to be made. With the Germans barely half an hour's car drive from the capital, should Paris be defended or declared an open city?

Weygand was adamant that it would be useless to fight, and handed a formal note to Reynaud which declared categorically, 'The city of Paris is an open town, but it is placed within a broad zone of armies whose front is about thirty kilometres distant from the capital. In order that Paris should preserve its character of an open town, it is my intention to avoid any defensive organisation around the city.'

Reynaud was torn. Paris was already outflanked. He knew that 'we were no longer able to prevent the investment and siege of the city'. Still hoping to escape if necessary to north Africa, and fight on from there, Reynaud felt he could not countermand Weygand's orders and offer the population of Paris to massacre, 'though [as he wrote later] I knew the people of Paris too well to feel the slightest doubt that they would not be ready to sacrifice everything for the welfare of the country'. Would they? It was by no means certain, and one wonders whether Reynaud *really* believed this at the time, or wrote it when basking in the warm glow of liberation.

The decision to declare Paris an open city was not taken lightly. Reynaud in fact had told Élie Bois only on Sunday that 'We shall fight before Paris, *in* Paris, behind Paris.' But, when Bois saw Reynaud again on Monday, Reynaud admitted that Paris would not be defended after all.

There were two diametrically opposed schools of thought, each equally understandable. The traditional French revolutionaries wanted to defend Paris street by street, *quartier* by *quartier*, so that with fire and sword they would, as Élie Bois felt, 'rouse the dulled soul of the country and set free in the world, and particularly in America, a current of love and help in favour of France'. Inevitably the 'revolutionaries' compared the Paris of 1940 with the besieged capital that held out in the winter of 1870–1 until the heroic defenders had eaten the last dog, cat and rat. Men like Jimmy Ashworth said bluntly, 'If Warsaw could fight for thirteen days – to prove they could fight – then Paris must fight too. If we decide not to defend our capital, then that means the defenders of Warsaw were wrong to fight.'

Against them was ranged the powerful argument used by Weygand that enemy explosives in 1870 were not powerful enough to destroy Paris and bore no relationship to modern aerial attack and bombardment, which in 1940 would reduce the city to rubble in a week. (Needless to say, Weygand received a great deal of backing from the curators of historic buildings.) Weygand also insisted that it was not cities that fought wars, but armies, and even if a capital were occupied, the Army could remain intact and fight elsewhere. From a military point of view Weygand was right, for the heroic resistance in Warsaw made little difference to the outcome of the war in Poland (though the defence of Stalingrad much later did change the course of the war).

One wonders why Reynaud did not make the historic decision himself. As prime minister he had every right to do so, but time after time the French leaders, with an eye to future judgements, preferred to let others make difficult decisions. So Reynaud took refuge in asking Weygand point blank, 'Will Paris be defended?' Weygand immediately handed the Prime Minister his answer in writing: 'Paris is an open city. . . .'

Whatever the rights and wrongs of this decision, they pale before the monumental blunder which Weygand now committed – an oversight which added to the ordeal and agony of the people of the capital. For, incredible though it may seem, after the decision had been made, Weygand did not tell the commander of the city for two days. The confusion over the future of the capital was total. On this Monday, General Pierre Hering, in command of the city's forces, received the order to command Weygand's newly created 'Army of Paris' with, presumably, the express purpose of defending the capital. Not a word was mentioned about the decision taken not to fight for Paris. Immediately Hering started drafting a statement he would issue to his forces and the police, telling them, 'The capital will be defended to the last.'

At the same time, printers rushed out handbills ready to

be posted over the city, 'Citoyens! Aux armes!' The people did not officially learn the truth for two more days.

## 3. *The trains that never ran*

Now the capital was on the brink of panic, largely because nobody really knew anything. Because of Weygand's stupid forgetfulness, most people were convinced that fighting would erupt in the city within a few days, though in fact the likelihood was remote. And even before the handbills were distributed, anyone could see that the politicians were preparing to bolt – without an official explanation. It was not difficult to draw conclusions.

But why did the politicians keep their plans for departure secret? And why did those who must have known of the decision to declare Paris an open city not spread the word? It seems that they were so absorbed in making their last-minute arrangements that nobody thought of telling anyone. In all probability they assumed that the news would become common knowledge within hours.

The stark evidence of the Cabinet's intention to flee was there for people to see. Quick-witted Parisians did not need to tax their powers of deduction unduly as they watched clerks at the Ministry of Marine in the Place de la Concorde hurriedly filling up trucks with files of paper; but nobody expected the Government to share the fate of the people. The journalists, who were in less of a rush, had time to tell their friends the significant fact that no Paris newspapers would be printed on the morrow. Somehow the draft text of General Hering's 'fight to the last' proclamation was leaked to an evening paper, which warned its readers to prepare to fight. At the same time the radio's official spokesman cried that, 'Should the Germans reach Paris, we shall defend every stone, every clod of earth, every lamp-post, every building, for we would rather have our city razed to the ground than fall into the hands of the Germans.'

As they digested this, the dulled sensibilities of a hitherto gagged city suddenly awoke to the fact that the Germans were approaching Pontoise. Had another town been mentioned it might not have meant so much. But Pontoise had a special significance for thousands of Parisians. At one time or another they had crossed the Seine at Pontoise, and admired the long line of beautiful, grey-roofed houses on the crest of the hill behind as they drove to the Channel coast.

Then came the posters, suddenly it seemed, appearing all over the city, as though daubed on the walls and urinals by thousands of invisible, fleet-footed bill-stickers. (In truth very few appeared, and the message probably spread more by word of mouth, but everyone was soon insisting, with the same pride the British later reserved for bomb stories, that they had seen one.)

'Citoyens! Aux armes!' The cry, ringing with the clash of battle, had a fearful sound to it. It conjured up an image of siege, the drawbridge being raised, the inexorable clang of the portcullis being lowered; in short, to the French with their sense of history, Paris in 1870. The instant reaction was fear, and the rush to escape began.

It is not until now that one begins to sense a change of pace in Paris, a mood of urgency previously missing. Until this moment the people had talked about the war almost as though it were a theoretical exercise; they had been concerned with its problems without relating them to their own lives. Suddenly they awoke to find that a horrible nightmare had become reality.

Had the people of Paris been warned, had the Government thought to educate them by the simple process of telling them the truth, the effects might have been less traumatic.

Until now Dynevor Rhys, like so many people in Paris, had felt no real sense of impending disaster; his main worry centred round buying raw materials for his photographic studio so that his small staff could be kept working. Bad news, he remembers, was not actually hidden from the citizens of Paris 'but the impact was so slight it never seemed to sink in'.

No one seemed to realise that the German Panzer divisions almost encircled Paris. Like nine out of ten people in the capital, Rhys was convinced that every French setback was temporary, that the Germans would be stopped at a point previously determined for strategic reasons by the Allies.

Paris, it is true, seemed empty, and when he walked from the rue du Cherche Midi to the rue du Suresne he did not see a single car, and at the Concorde he looked up the broad sweep of the Champs Élysées: nothing was moving – not a car, not a taxi, not a bus, not even a pedestrian. Only when he was near the office, walking the few yards along the rue Royale, did he for the first time face up to reality. At the corner of the Madeleine one of the posters calling people to arms had been stuck on the wall.

Dynevor Rhys's reaction was typical: 'If the Germans are going to fight in the streets of Paris, my business will go bust, and there's no place for a neutral American.' Rhys walked quickly to the rue Cambon branch of the Chase Bank opposite the 'back door' to the Ritz bar, and withdrew a large sum in notes. As he returned to his studio, he saw a queue stretching out of a side street into the Boulevard des Malesherbes. It consisted almost entirely of women, and each carried a dog or cat. They were waiting patiently for the vet to put down the pets they could not take with them.

Once at the studio he managed to get a message through to Iris Schweppe at Vaucresson, telling her the business would be closed until further notice, and that he would set off on foot for Vaucresson as soon as possible. In his office Rhys found a knapsack and on an impulse walked round to Hédiard, the exotic general grocery store founded by an English colonel. There, behind the Madeleine, he bought a few simple provisions – more, really, for old Mrs Schweppe than for himself – and at the last minute picked up two fat grapefruit and put them in his pack.

While Rhys was waiting for his banknotes in the rue Cambon Jimmy Ashworth was entering the Ritz on the opposite side of the street. Ashworth, who had an eye for a pretty

girl, was delighted to find that his blind date turned out to
be with a stunning-looking long-legged Italian of seventeen.
As she was the only woman alone in the bar he had no hesitation in approaching her.

She was, it transpired, a Florentine married only a few
months previously to the French Count de Gelabert who was
fighting 'somewhere in France'. She lived in a four-roomed
apartment in the rue de la Boëtie, and was expecting their
first baby. That morning she had found a scribbled note from
her husband Gabby which had been pushed through the
letter box. The envelope bore no stamp. There was no indica-
tion of how the message had reached her, but she had recognised Gabby's handwriting immediately, and the gist of the
message was brutally clear: Gabby warned her not to believe
what the radio told her. Things were going from bad to
worse at the Front, and she must get back to her mother in
Italy as quickly as she could, have the baby and wait.

'The note gave me your name and telephone number,' she
added. 'That's why I'm here.'

'Gabby's right.' Ashworth had met her husband several
times. 'What's more, you're going to be in even worse trouble
when Italy declares war; that will be later today.'

Jimmy Ashworth had already made plans to leave for
Tours and help to publish the Paris *Daily Mail* from there. He
promised her a lift. 'The others are leaving earlier,' he said,
'but I can't. I've got something to do first.'

Until this moment it had never occurred to the Countess
that Ashworth was anything but a Frenchman. But now he
explained that his five-year-old daughter Jenny was an infant
musical prodigy, and he was trying desperately to raise cash
for her to continue piano tuition with Marguerite Long,
perhaps the greatest teacher in Paris, for the next four years.
'When the war's over,' he said, 'you'll hear Jenny playing in
concert halls over the world.'*

Only when Marguerite de Gelabert asked innocently why

---

* He was right. Among other successes, Jenny played concertos with the
Hallé and London Symphony orchestras after the war. Since Jenny and her
mother were French, there would be no question of internment.

he had to pay four years in advance did Ashworth reply airily, 'Oh, the moment the Germans see me I'll be arrested and interned with all the other 7000 Britishers who live in Paris.'

He arranged to pick her up at her apartment. And as the waiter poured out the last of the champagne Ashworth raised his glass and echoed the toast that had swept Paris. 'Don't worry – *Chantons quand même!*'

There was panic at the stations, as Jean Chamby quickly discovered. Chamby, who was forty, worked for a French news agency and was under no delusions. He lived with his beautiful Jewish wife, who painted under her first name of Ginette, in the rue des Sts-Pères on the Left Bank (like Dynevor Rhys, up five flights of rickety, twisting stairs without a lift). The reason for Chamby's visit to the railway stations was twofold: to write a story for his news agency, but also to sound out the possibility of getting his wife away to the south.

He made for the Gare d'Austerlitz, near the Seine, southeast of the Île de la Cité. Separated only by the river from the Gare de Lyon, it had a direct southbound line. One look told Chamby it was hopeless to try to cut a way through the milling crowds; the streets were blocked for hundreds of yards with people trying to scramble inside for non-existent trains. Yet, if he could somehow get inside, he was a good friend of the assistant stationmaster.

Leaving his car, he forced his way – passing an ominous sign, 'Rendezvous for lost people' – until he found a back door leading into a goods yard. The grey iron door was locked and bolted, but nearby were some packing-cases. With an effort he lugged one across to the door, climbed on it, and hoisted himself on top of the gate, which he remembers had spikes at each end, but none in the middle – 'typical French logic'. Once over, he made for the stationmaster's office, a glass watchtower perched high above the platforms.

Henri Deschamps, the assistant stationmaster, seemed pleased enough to see Chamby, who will never forget the moment he walked into his office. Deschamps was crying bitterly. 'Look at them, look at the children.' He kept on pointing down to the platforms. 'They will die.' And then more quietly, 'What stupidity – what irony. The children here are starving because their parents insist they stay in this suffocating prison of a station – yet outside there's enough food in Paris to feed them all.'

There seemed to be thousands of children. They looked like old dwarfs, Chamby thought; but the very old were just as pathetic, for they could do nothing but be led like children.

After Deschamps had calmed down, Chamby asked him if any more trains would be leaving that day. Deschamps said that maybe one would leave the next day, 'but it won't be able to carry a tenth of these people'.

Would there be room for his wife? Chamby asked, and again the stationmaster shrugged his shoulders. He would be on duty, he would make sure she had a place, but she would never be able to get into the station.

'No one can get through that crowd,' he said. 'Even a woman would be lynched if she tried to jump that queue.'

Chamby pointed out that Deschamps had got through.

'My uniform,' replied Deschamps with a sudden dignity.

And that was how the plan was born. When Jean Chamby climbed back over the gate half an hour later, he clutched a precious parcel under his arm. It contained a porter's uniform, the smallest in Deschamps' locker of spares. Small enough, Chamby hoped, to fit Ginette.

Cecily Mackworth, a tall English brunette living in Paris, spent almost the entire day at the Gare d'Austerlitz. She was one of twenty volunteer nurses who were trying to look after 5000 refugees a day arriving from Belgium and Holland. Though she wore a uniform, Miss Mackworth had never nursed anyone in her life, but she and the others contrived to erect a makeshift rest-centre and dispensary, together with a mobile canteen, though all they could offer the refugees were meat-paste sandwiches and buckets of water flavoured with cola. For the babies there were very limited quantities of dried milk.

Looking back on that terrible Monday, she remembers, 'I

can still feel the glare of the sun on concrete, and smell the railway carriages which had become like red hot cages after people had been locked in there for fourteen hours.'

Until this Monday, Cecily Mackworth had believed in the myth of the Maginot Line and 'the inviolability of the capital'. But then the news was released that the Germans were south of Beauvais, twenty-five miles from the Place de l'Opéra. That morning, when she arrived to start her shift at the Gare d'Austerlitz, she found the streets blocked for half a mile. A gendarme, seeing her uniform, told her the railway lines south of Paris had been blown up, but the crowd refused to believe it. While he was trying to force a passage for the British nurse to reach the station, a rumour swept the crowd that the Germans had actually reached Paris and were massacring the population.

As Cecily Mackworth stood there helpless, 'the mob seethed forward determined to break down the station gates. Women screamed and fainted and I could see that children were being trampled underfoot.'

The gendarme, watching some men trying to wrench out the iron railings, shrugged his shoulders and told her, 'They'll calm down in a minute. They won't believe there isn't going to be another train.'

He finally took Cecily Mackworth round to the back entrance to a goods yard. Inside, the platforms were covered with people, most of them trying to shield their heads from the burning sun with newspapers. Each train was jammed full, with eighteen or twenty people to a carriage. The heat got worse. The stationmaster gave her an orange for lunch, but when a child saw it she cried so bitterly that 'I had to give it away'. In the next railway carriage a woman gave birth to a baby.

Arved Arenstam, the Balkan journalist, was at the station at the same time. The woman next to him fainted, and he saw two small children trodden underfoot, before a gendarme ordered all babies to be handed over to the police. Arenstam himself passed seven babies over the heads of the crowd. Others did the same until most children were grouped around a table on one platform waiting until their mothers could get through and join them.

To Clare Boothe, the American writer, who had arrived from Belgium, 'they came off the trains with their bewildered faces, white faces, faces beaten out of shape by the Niagara of human tears that flowed down them'.

It was just as bad at the Gare Montparnasse, and among those who helped there was a beautiful blonde American actress, Drue Tartière, who had joined the staff of Radio Mondiale, and was broadcasting daily to the United States. As Drue Leyton – before she married French actor Jacques Tartière in 1939 – she had played in several 'Charlie Chan' films in Hollywood, and on the Broadway and London stages. Now, with Jacques in the Army, all her spare time was spent helping refugees in the 'large, grey dismal station' at Montparnasse, where she remembers seeing 'grandmothers holding dead babies in their arms, women with parts of their faces shot away, and the insane women who had lost their children, their husbands, and all reason for living'. She found 'the stench, the filth and the grief that filled the Gare Montparnasse almost unbearable'.

Among the trains arriving from Belgium that afternoon was one that had taken several days to travel from Brussels. Its ultimate destination was Bordeaux.

Tucked into one corner of a crowded carriage was an eleven-year-old English schoolgirl from Skeffington in Leicestershire. She had wide eyes, a beautifully shaped face below curly black hair; she was dressed inappropriately in a thick Harris tweed suit. On her lap sat her white Pekinese named Ming Phoo, but nicknamed Gussy. A label round the girl's neck proclaimed her to be 'Mlle Zena Marshall'. Zena was attending a school near Antwerp when Hitler attacked Belgium, though she was staying with her grandparents when the school was bombed and most of the girls died. For a week her Belgian grandmother tried to telephone Zena's mother, then finally decided they must try to get her to England.

In Brussels, they put her into a carriage in which a priest

was already seated. It seemed an extra precaution. Like so many trains, this one seemed to meander aimlessly across the French countryside, diverted time and again. (On one train taking a group of British soldiers to Brittany to embark for England, the soldiers at one time actually saw the Atlantic in the distance, but ended up at Belfort on the Swiss frontier.)

For days and nights the little girl sat and slept clutching Gussy, and guarding the pigskin suitcase her mother had given her for her birthday, and into which she had packed her 'treasures' – her Catholic prayer-book, a statue of the Virgin Mary, and a double-decker Rowney paint-box. Her grannie had packed a few tins of sardines and a bottle of red wine. As to the wintry attire in the suffocating heat – 'I couldn't bear to leave my Harris tweed behind, but there was no room in the suitcase so I had to wear it.'

Eleven people had settled down to the strange communal life of an overcrowded, creaking, ancient railway carriage. Opposite Zena sat the young, benign priest, who smiled regular encouragement and nodded approvingly when Zena – who quickly became 'la petite anglaise' – showed him her prayer-book and statue, both given to her when she was confirmed. Next to her was a handsome blond youth who looked eighteen or nineteen, and she remembers that he had startling blue eyes. He immediately undertook the role of 'protector' – jumping up at the innumerable stops where occasionally it was possible to find bread or water. Sometimes he even took the well trained but suffering Gussy for a badly needed walk to the nearest lamp-post. For leaving your seat, even to stretch your legs, was a hazard which only the toughest survived. At every stop, scores of people were ready to fight for your place. At one small wayside halt Zena did get out for a walk, but then could not get back through the door. 'Blue Eyes' was behind her, lifted her up easily, and pushed her through the window.

In Paris she did not dare to leave the carriage. Though she had no idea at which station the train stopped – nor that it was delayed in Paris because of bomb damage on the line further south – she remembers the baking heat, the Red Cross

nurses who came round with 'watery powdered milk', the
platforms crowded with other children, mostly crying. And
there was a horrible moment when two women tried to force
their way into the carriage. Catching sight of Zena's dog, one
screamed, 'This train is to save human beings, not animals.'

The woman tried to wrench the door open, and the blond
boy started to get out of his seat. Gently the priest waved him
back and through the window talked to the woman quietly,
smilingly patting Zena on the head, presumably as he
explained that she was a lost little girl and the dog was causing no trouble. The woman left. The blond boy – who seemed
to have an inexhaustible supply of cheese – took a small piece
out of his knapsack, cut it in two with a huge jack-knife,
and offered her half. She chewed it and fell asleep on his
shoulder.

Zena could not know that her grandparents had managed
to telephone her mother with the news that they had put
Zena on a train to Bordeaux via Paris, reassuring her by
adding, 'There's a nice priest in the same carriage and he has
promised to look after Zena'; or that Zena's mother then
pulled every string until she gained permission to go to Paris.

Nor could Zena know that for hours her mother had
haunted the Gare d'Austerlitz and the Gare de Lyon, waiting,
searching, hoping to find her daughter, and that as the train
rumbled out of the station, her mother was only a few yards
away, trying to reach the platform, struggling in vain to force
her way through the hostile, panic-stricken crowds.

4.   *Rome, London, Washington*

As though the rout of French arms was not enough to bear,
war with Italy now became certain. For some time it had
been clear that Mussolini was preparing to profit from German successes, and it was only a question of fixing the date,
though the United States had tried every possible way to

prevent Italy entering the war. Bullitt had even suggested to Roosevelt that he should invite the Pope to take refuge in America, thinking, as he cabled the President, 'that nothing could have a greater restraining influence on Mussolini than a genuine fear that the Pope might leave Rome'.

The French had also tried to avert war by buying off Mussolini in a series of diplomatic manœuvres with the highly sinister Italian ambassador to Paris, Signor Guariglia, whose role in the capital was curious to say the least of it, for even as Italy was poised to strike he was meeting important French leaders and being told French state secrets.

Behind the scenes the Countess de Portes had been using the Count de Paris (a young, ineffectual but hopeful royalist) and the pro-Fascist Anatole de Monzie, in an effort to appease the Italians. De Monzie was so hated by Reynaud that the two were not on speaking terms; yet the Countess had insisted on his remaining in the Cabinet. He had lasted until 5 June when an exasperated Reynaud finally dismissed him while his mistress was at the theatre.

Hélène de Portes wanted to come to terms with Italy as much as she did with Germany, and thought she could win the day because of the prevailing French (and to a lesser degree British) opinion; both countries had plied Mussolini with coal, iron, petroleum, food, in the hope of keeping him out of the war. To the Countess de Portes, the Italian ambassador was the key figure – and, on at least two occasions when Reynaud was known to be occupied, de Monzie took Guariglia round to Reynaud's private apartment behind the Assembly to discuss with the Countess the prospects of concessions, particularly in Tunisia.

The intrigue was to no avail. Finally Count Ciano, the Italian Foreign Minister, cynically told François-Poncet, the French ambassador, 'Even if you offered me all Tunisia immediately, it would be no good. The die is cast. Italy is entering the war.'

So Churchill's twenty-five-day-old prophecy to Roosevelt that Mussolini would soon strike and collect his share of the 'loot of civilisation' came true. The Italian press raged. So did Ciano: 'Italy cannot remain absent from the terrible struggle which will forge the destinies of the world.'

On Monday afternoon Ciano informed the British and French ambassadors to Rome that Italy would consider itself at war with the two countries from 10 a.m. the following day. François-Poncet reached the door of Ciano's office, turned and said, 'You too will find the Germans are hard masters.' Ciano was even more put out by the attitude of Sir Percy Lorraine, the British ambassador, who, he remembers, 'received my communication without batting an eyelid or changing colour'. But what really infuriated Ciano was Sir Percy's last words as he reached the door. Looking at the Italian Foreign Minister with ill-concealed distaste he said, 'I have the honour to remind Your Excellency that England is not in the habit of losing her wars.'

From the balcony of Rome's Palazzo di Venezia, from which he had made a hundred rabble-rousing speeches, Mussolini thundered, 'We have entered the lists against the plutocrats and reactionary democracies of the west which have always barred the path of the Italian people. Our conscience is absolutely clear. The world is witness to the fact that Italy has done all that is humanly possible to avoid war. But that has all been in vain.'

What Mussolini did not tell the people in that historic speech was his real purpose in declaring war. This he had made clear to Marshal Badoglio a few days previously, declaring frankly, 'I need a few thousand dead to be able to sit down at the peace table as a belligerent.'

Italy's entry into the war meant that huge new forces faced the Allies – an army of a million men, 4000 planes, a navy totalling 700,000 tons. It presaged an ominous spread of the fighting later to the Balkans, the Mediterranean, north Africa. There lay the danger.

Poor Reynaud. One setback after another was testing the fortitude of this dapper little man who was fighting not only an enemy without, but sinister influences within, ranging from a modern caricature of Madame de Pompadour, intriguing with foreign diplomats, to a bitter army commander and a senile Marshal Pétain who hated what he called 'the moral rottenness of French political life'.

In his broadcast that evening Reynaud told the French people, 'We are in the sixth day of the greatest battle in history. Nothing will weaken our will to fight for our land and our liberty. Signor Mussolini has chosen this moment to declare war on us. How can this action be judged? France has nothing to say. The world looking on will judge. In the course of her long and glorious history France has been through worse trials. At such times she has always astonished the world. France cannot die.'

Next he drafted a cable to Roosevelt, even managing to inject into it a touch of sardonic humour. He cannot have expected that one phrase in the brief cable would so excite the President's imagination that it would soon be known all over the world. 'What really distinguished, noble and admirable persons the Italians are, to stab us in the back at this time,' cabled Reynaud.

Because of the time difference, the message reached the President as he was about to leave with his wife and son to make a speech to the university of Virginia in Charlottesville, and Roosevelt immediately seized on the phrase 'stab us in the back'. He told Sumner Welles he intended to include it in his speech. Welles begged him not to. It would jeopardise American–Italian relations, and it might be wise to keep them 'open'. At first Roosevelt agreed, but on the way he changed his mind and finally did use the stinging, scathing phrase in one of his greatest foreign-policy speeches: 'On this tenth day of June, 1940, the hand that held the dagger struck it into the back of its neighbour.'

Roosevelt went on to make a promise to the free world. 'We will pursue two obvious and simultaneous courses,' he declared. 'We will extend to the opponents of force the material resources of this nation. . . . All roads leading to the accomplishment of these objectives must be kept clear of obstruction. We will not slow down or detour. Signs and signals call for speed – full speed ahead.'

Reynaud was 'elated' at Roosevelt's declaration. Churchill

cabled his congratulations on the 'grand scope of your declaration' (while wondering privately 'about the Italian vote in
the forthcoming US elections').

And so, in the curious way that old and hackneyed saws
sometimes do ring true, good came out of Mussolini's evil,
for Roosevelt might never have gone so far had he not been
so angry. The Charlottesville speech contained implications
that marked a great turning-point in the war. To the hard-
pressed French, the words might have sounded empty, but
to the free world it was a clarion call that would lead to Lend-
Lease, to the gigantic United States war production, 'without
which', as even Stalin later admitted at Tehran, 'our victory
would have been impossible'.

In London, where *Gone with the Wind* was playing to packed
houses, Winston Churchill sat alone in the Cabinet Room at
10 Downing Street, brooding on the latest news from France.
He was sitting there motionless when Major-General Sir
Edward Spears arrived. Though he had been sent for, Spears
knew better than to interrupt a man who 'does not like his
train of thought to be broken into until he has reached a
conclusion'.

Spears, who spoke French fluently, was Churchill's personal representative with the French Government and had
flown over to report. Churchill was not long in reaching his
'conclusion'. Playing with his multi-circled ring, he looked
at Spears without speaking for a moment then, drumming his
fingers on the table, growled, 'The news is bad. We will fly
to Paris immediately.'

'But you can't.' Spears was horrified. 'The Germans have
crossed the Seine. They may be in Paris in two hours' time.
They may actually be fighting in Paris, though I don't think so.'

Churchill 'looked startled', and Spears had the impression
that he had not fully realised the gravity of the situation.
Spears suggested they should meet Reynaud somewhere
south of Paris, and Churchill agreed. He ordered the Foreign
Office to telephone the British ambassador in Paris and
arrange a meeting-place.

It was not so easy. Until the Monday morning, communication, though almost always delayed, had been possible, but now there was no answer from Paris. All the telephone lines were dead; 'perhaps they were cut,' thought Spears. No one knew where Reynaud was, and Spears had the feeling (wrong, but only by an hour or two) that the French cabinet had already left Paris. Time after time Churchill demanded, 'Where is the French Government?' Nobody knew. Churchill was keenly conscious of the fact that 'Pétain had already made up his mind the war was lost', and that it was neither right nor wise to leave Reynaud alone to face 'this disastrous situation'. Spears felt much the same, that 'every pressure would be put on him [Reynaud] to throw up the sponge now that Paris was directly threatened'.

As though to aggravate the bad news, the brilliant sunshine of the previous few days in London had given way to 'a darkness in the air'. The day was so gloomy that the sunset and blackout came almost as a relief when Spears made his way to Admiralty House later in the day to dine with the Churchill family. After the other guests had gone he stayed on, and no sooner were the two men alone than Churchill posed a blunt question: 'What will happen to the Navy if France drops out of the war?'

'It will follow the admirals, I suppose,' Spears replied, 'and the admirals will follow Darlan.' But, as Spears remembered, 'I really could not imagine France out of the war.'

Churchill persisted. What about the sailors, the actual men of the fleet? They were 'the salt of the earth, simple and unsophisticated'. And the officers? Ah! That was a different matter. To Spears they were 'a closed caste, a law unto themselves'. Hatred of Britain was 'a canker eating into their collective souls' and if 'Love God and hate the Englishmen' was not their motto, then it should have been.

Spears stayed with Churchill far into the night, trying to console him, for he found the Prime Minister 'profoundly unhappy' as he sat at his desk, hunched up, dressed in black, his face paler than usual under a strong light with a green shade, the bad news coming in almost every time the door opened to admit a messenger.

'For the first and only time in my experience I heard words akin to despair pass his lips,' Spears remembered that night. 'Several times, hands flat on the table, his eyes fixed on the blotting paper between them, he said that we were losing everywhere, in every field, owing to the lack of preparation and lack of planning.' To Spears, 'there seemed to be nothing, no fingerhold to which even his courage could fasten in the slimy mess of incompetence revealed in France' – or, for that matter, 'the cheerful inefficiency of our amateur attempts to cope with the grim reality of a robot war'.

How long they stayed together neither remembered, but finally the Foreign Office managed to make contact with France. The Embassy hoped to be in Tours in the morning. No one knew exactly where Reynaud was, but the Foreign Office did know that Weygand was establishing his new military headquarters at Briare, about fifty miles south-east of Orléans. Pétain was already on his way there.

'That's all we need to know,' grunted Churchill. 'We fly to Briare tomorrow.'

Meanwhile a first-class row was blowing up in Washington between President Roosevelt and Cordell Hull, his Secretary of State. The subject of the argument was William Bullitt, the American ambassador in Paris. Hull insisted that Bullitt should accompany Reynaud to Tours. The President refused to give Bullitt an actual order, though he had advised him to leave Paris with the Government; consequently Bullitt decided to stay.

'Bill' Bullitt was rich and pampered. He was contemptuous of the bureaucratic machinery (particularly his own State Department). He had never married. He was in many ways a good diplomat, but he was vain, flamboyant and impulsive, sides to his character which his fellow diplomat George F. Kennan felt 'tended to limit what he was able to accomplish'.

A sophisticated, good-looking extrovert of great charm, he captivated Roosevelt when the two men first met in 1932, a year before Bullitt became ambassador to the Soviet Union, where he spent three years before being transferred to Paris. In France he was immediately at home. French political leaders (including the Countess de Portes) responded to the infectious charm of a rich ambassador who spoke their language fluently, was unencumbered with a wife and quickly made it clear that he infinitely preferred the French to their dull-witted neighbours across the Channel. Indeed he thoroughly disliked the British. Kennan remarked: 'It was an animus which found a certain justification in the well-known deficiencies of British policies in those years, but it was carried further than the situation warranted.' Bullitt was flawed chiefly by his egotism and his misplaced idealism. Perhaps he had never read the *New York Times* of 1 February 1931, which contained the acerbic warning, 'There is nothing the matter with Americans except their ideals.'

Much to Cordell Hull's displeasure, Bullitt enjoyed a special relationship with the President – so 'special' that President and ambassador often bypassed the State Department, communicating directly, using a secret code known only to the two men, so that, according to Cordell Hull, 'at times the State Department remained in the dark as to what Bullitt was thinking and doing'. But, as Hull had already discovered, Roosevelt 'liked the dramatic side of foreign affairs'.

Some time before the Germans attacked France Bullitt had discussed with Roosevelt the possibility of his remaining in Paris if ever the Germans took the city, and Roosevelt had given him an offhand assent, probably thinking very little of an eventuality that he scarcely believed would happen.

Bullitt, however, cherished a romantic dream. If the French Government fled from Paris he would remain behind, a symbol of freedom (as he thought), a man who preferred to stay, to suffer, to die if necessary, in his beloved Paris rather than bolt for safety.

With his sense of French history, he knew that during the Terror of the French Revolution the American Gouverneur Morris had remained in Paris, and that in the siege of Paris in 1870–1 Minister Elihu Washbourne had stayed at his post eating horse-meat. When in 1914 the Germans again threatened the capital, Myron T. Herrick, the American ambassador, had also refused to leave. So Bullitt saw himself as the 'saviour of the soul of Paris' by electing to remain in the capital under the swastika. He would, he hoped, carve his name in the history books as the man who felt so deeply for Paris that he preferred to remain there rather than follow a government that fled.

Bullitt would have been horrified had anyone suggested that his decision would contribute to the downfall of the country he loved; nor did he take into account the fact that he was making an empty gesture. He would not suffer in Paris as the French would. He was a neutral; he was a diplomat. He would not starve, nor be brutally arrested without warning, or undergo any of the humiliations of an occupied nation. Living the special esoteric life of the diplomat, with servants at his bidding, Bullitt would be no more a part of occupied Paris than an African delegate to the United Nations is a part of New York.

Cordell Hull was still adamant and, though Roosevelt was loath to break his 'gentleman's agreement' with Bullitt, Hull had managed, on Sunday, 9 June, to persuade the President to draft a message to the ambassador. It read:

On the assumption that all or most of the foreign Chiefs of Mission follow the French Government to its temporary capital, I have reached the conclusion that it would be preferable to alter the plans we had previously agreed upon, and have you do likewise. In the first place I doubt if the German military officials would co-operate with you in trying to ease the general situation. More important, however, I consider it highly desirable that you be in direct contact with the French Government in the event of certain contingencies arising. In order to forestall any possible criticism of a last-minute change in your announced plans, you may inform the French Government that you are leaving Paris with the other Chiefs of Mission at my express request.

It was never sent. Instead Roosevelt telephoned – and Bullitt immediately took advantage of his 'special relationship' to refuse. Hull was furious and demanded to see Roosevelt immediately. Angrily he told the President that he thought Bullitt should go with the French Government.

'It seems to me that his influence with the German authorities in Paris will be very small,' he told Roosevelt. 'His strong anti-Nazi sentiments are well known to the German government. On the other hand, his influence with the French might be decisive.' Hull argued from strength. When Roosevelt said that even Churchill's pleas were having very little effect on French morale, Hull retorted that the French Government was angered with Churchill following Dunkirk and Churchill's refusal to send British planes to France.

'On the other hand,' he added, 'our influence with Reynaud and his cabinet ministers is of the highest. I feel that with Bullitt at Reynaud's side we have a reasonable chance of inducing the French cabinet to continue the fight with the fleet and colonies.'

Roosevelt took the point and again telephoned personally to Bullitt, telling him that he agreed with Hull's assessment. The conversation was again couched as a suggestion rather than an order, and it is faintly possible that Bullitt might have changed his mind had not Roosevelt introduced a naïve note.

'Bill,' he said, 'you'll be killed if you stay in Paris, and I don't want you killed. I want you back here. If the Communists don't get you before the Nazis come in, the Nazis will kill you. They hate you worse than anyone.'

Bullitt's self-importance was inflated by this ridiculous suggestion. It would ill become an American diplomat to run away from danger, he retorted. Roosevelt, after some hesitation, refrained from giving the actual order.

Hull still persisted, finally persuading Roosevelt to sign a much stronger cable, reading in part: 'It is strongly recommended that if all foreign Chiefs of Mission follow French Government to its temporary capital, you should do likewise.' Even then, Roosevelt, probably secretly admiring his swashbuckling ambassador, refused to give the formal order, but added, 'Because it is impossible here to know last-minute developments or the wishes of the French Government, I must rely on your discretion and assume you will make your decision in the best interests of the United States and humanity.'

Even his colleagues in the embassy tried to make Bullitt change his mind. H. Freeman Matthews, a counsellor known affectionately to all as 'Doc' Matthews, felt like others that Bullitt might 'at one or two critical moments have succeeded in giving the necessary push to swing the scales', for he believed that now more than ever 'the French Government would need his advice and encouragement ... in the dark days after its departure from Paris'. Yet Bullitt refused to heed their advice and, as Matthews recorded later, 'chose to remain in the capital on the quixotic theory that an ambassador should not run away from his post. From the tenth of June he was consequently helpless to do anything.'

Bullitt assured the President that he proposed to send Anthony J. Drexel Biddle to Tours in his place. Biddle had been ambassador to Poland but was now an out-of-work 'refugee' in France. Bullitt described him as 'a man of great experience', which was not true, and forbore to add that Biddle was hardly on the same intimate terms with French political leaders as he was.

So Bullitt remained to face the Germans. Nothing, nobody could sway his decision, which did the gravest harm to the cause of France. For, as Cordell Hull later wrote, 'If Bullitt had maintained contact with the French Government, it is possible, if not probable, that the Government would have taken the fleet, gone to north Africa, and continued the fight from there.'

Meanwhile, Roosevelt had returned from Charlottesville, in great spirits. Harry Hopkins was waiting for him, together with his personal physician, Rear-Admiral Ross T. McIntire, who took the President to his medical office in the White House basement and sprayed his throat, which often irritated Roosevelt after a long speech. Hopkins congratulated Roosevelt on 'standing up' to Welles, and Roosevelt was delighted that he had 'for once said exactly what I think of an evil action'.

As soon as the small party returned upstairs, the President was handed a cable from Reynaud. He read it carefully and showed it to Hopkins. It was a passionate appeal for a declaration of support 'by all means short of an expeditionary force'. Reynaud hoped the United States would declare itself a non-belligerent ally. Pledging resistance at all costs, he cabled Roosevelt, 'Today the enemy is almost at the gates of Paris. We shall fight in front of Paris; we shall fight behind Paris; we shall shut ourselves up in one of our provinces and, if we should be driven out, we shall go to north Africa and if necessary to our possessions in America.'

The State Department had already seen the telegram, and everyone advised Roosevelt to take no action until he studied possible implications the following morning.

In fact Roosevelt took three days to reply. True, there was nothing tangible he could do at this late stage, for above all he had to be careful to avoid what Tolstoy once called 'the irrevocable act', even though he had realised from the moment the Germans attacked the Low Countries – if not before – that American enterprise must back France and Britain. Yet he faced opposition from isolationists, from many who believed that if France fell Britain would negotiate for peace. He needed not only the backing of the American people – and this was often divided – but also Congress where legislation was concerned. Worse still, Roosevelt was in the last year of his second term as President and, as his friend (and speech-writer) Robert Sherwood put it, 'It is one of the classic weaknesses of our American constitutional system that a President who is approaching the end of his tenure of office can exercise little authority in the conduct of foreign affairs.'

Yet the delay was tragic. Theodore Draper, the historian, was not alone in criticising the delay of 'three days in which more decisive and daring American support might have given Reynaud a powerful talking point if nothing else'.

Reynaud had penned the appeal to Roosevelt many hours earlier as the Cabinet prepared to leave Paris, with pillars of smoke, like Indian signals, marking government buildings when documents were being burned. But the appeal had been delayed, for when it came to transmitting the message Reynaud discovered that the great exodus from Paris had already started, at least among the lower echelons of his staff. He could find no clerks to code or transmit the message. They had already decamped. He telephoned Bullitt, who arranged to despatch the message after some delay.

By then the French Cabinet had taken to the road. Reynaud asked de Gaulle to share his car. The Countess de Portes followed in another. Though Reynaud made gallant attempts to keep up last-minute appearances, the final nocturnal departure bore all the hallmarks of near-panic. By now eight million refugees clogged the highways south of the capital, most of them without shelter, begging for food and water, desperate to keep one pace ahead of the Germans. Few had any place to go – except in the general direction of the south. They stopped only when the traffic jams prevented further progress, or when they dived for ditches at the sound of enemy aircraft.

In the midst of this confusion were the government cars, and few of those forcing a passage through the refugees had any real idea of what to expect in Tours, a city with a fortieth of the population of Paris. 'Everything was confusion, uncertainty, disintegration. By leaving Paris, the government had become like a lost tribe.'

As de Gaulle and Reynaud drove past the Porte de Châtillon, the lanky general watched the cars 'buffeting each other', the long line of fugitives, and then suddenly a convoy of luxurious white-tyred American cars sweeping along the road, with militiamen on the running-boards, and motorcyclists surrounding the procession. It was the *corps diplomatique* on its way to the châteaux of Touraine.

To everyone this day held a different significance. Bullitt felt that Reynaud, on his last day in Paris, displayed magnificent courage, and cabled Roosevelt, 'There is no question whatsoever about Reynaud's determination and the determination of the French Army to make the end of France as noble as her past.' Alexander Werth, a British war correspondent to whom France was a second home, watched 'a mass of troops, tired, demoralised-looking, all without rifles, drifting into Paris'. Yet, as he cabled his paper, 'Paris in its anguish is strangely calm and beautiful.'

De Gaulle thought rather differently. Recalling 'this day of agony', he realised that 'the evidence of the collapse was there for all to see . . . at certain moments, even, you could have believed that a terrible sort of humour spiced the fall of France'.

General Weygand presided at a last frugal dinner in the great vaulted hall of his fortress headquarters at Vincennes, where 'in the times of illusion there had been plenty of gay talk', but as he and his staff drove through the sombre Forest of Vincennes to his military train, waiting in a siding to take him to Briare, there were only 'dark thoughts in my soul'. At least the military party did not have to grapple with the traffic on the roads. Instead, as General André Beaufre of H.Q. staff remembers, 'We carried our misery away in sumptuous drawing-room cars.'

By contrast General Rommel, commanding the 7th Panzer Division, wrote to his wife that same night: 'Our successes are extraordinary. We had never imagined the war in the west would turn out like this.'

Nothing, it seemed, could check the German advances. In the north they were chasing the last remnants of French troops trying to reach the Channel. In Champagne they had broken through west of Rethel. Across the River Aisne they were well south of Soissons. They had crossed the Seine at several points. Pontoise, thirty-two kilometres from Paris, was in danger of falling. Like two steel claws, the German Panzers, tearing down the Seine and the Marne, were encircling the heart of France.

# Tuesday, 11 June

## 1. *Exodus*

ALL through the night the Government drove south. The only thing its members knew was that the 'centre of government' would operate from the local prefecture in Tours. Other than that, none had any real inkling of what lay ahead.

In fact the decision to establish the Government in Tours was a compromise. De Gaulle and Reynaud believed that the French Army should retreat to the Breton peninsula, and hold out until British shipping could transport hundreds of thousands of Frenchmen to north Africa. To Weygand the idea of a 'Breton redoubt' was 'preposterous'. The French Army, he said, might only be able to hold out for two or three days.

In the end, still hoping to go to Brittany later, but hedging his bet, Reynaud compromised and decided on Tours, a hundred miles south-west of Paris and almost midway between Bordeaux and Brittany. De Gaulle accepted the compromise because it was easy to go from Tours to Brittany; Weygand accepted it because Tours was on the way to Bordeaux.

To minimise the danger of aerial attack (one reason for leaving Paris) the government departments were scattered over a vast area in Touraine. The British ambassador was lodged in a château at Cleré; the Foreign Ministry was at Langeais, the Ministry of Finance at Chinon. Reynaud him-

self was to take over the Château de Chissay, above the
River Cher, midway between Tours and Amboise, which
boasted only one antiquated hand-operated telephone
(though it did have a hundred rooms).

When the first ministers arrived at dawn, cold and hungry
and tired, they found 300 coded telegrams awaiting them at
the post office in Tours. They lay in piles, unattended to
because the cipher clerks who had left Paris earlier professed
themselves 'too tired to deal with them'.

When Sir Ronald Campbell, the British ambassador, saw
Paul Baudouin and M. Charles-Roux, the Secretary-General
to the Foreign Office, neither had heard any developments
or news since leaving Paris. Charles-Roux (ex-ambassador to
the Vatican) also had only one telephone. It was linked to
the exchange in the nearest village where the local operator
– like most others in the area – insisted on taking the usual
two hours for lunch, and warned him that the exchange
closed down each evening at six.

In fact, on this Tuesday, Charles-Roux's only source of
information came from a portable field-radio which the
British ambassador had thoughtfully brought along with him.
And, when the President of France finally arrived at the
Château de Candé, Baudouin found him 'entirely isolated,
without news from the prime minister or Supreme Headquarters, depressed and overwhelmed'. No wonder Campbell
quickly reached the conclusion that the move to Tours was
'merely a stage on the road'. The question was – would the
next move be to Brittany or Bordeaux?

One by one the government chiefs arrived in the overcrowded provincial city – leaders totally cut off from the
French people, the Army, from reality itself. Disunited,
desperate, surrounded by the evidence of panic that appeared
round every street corner, these men held in their shaky
hands the destiny of France.

There was just one oasis of efficiency, the United States
temporary embassy in the Château de Candé (where the
Duke of Windsor and Mrs Simpson had been married). In
stark contrast to the lack of amenities in other temporary

headquarters, Candé was a haven of luxury, thanks to American foresight. The embassy had arranged with its owner to prepare the château for just such an emergency as this, so that while other embassies wrestled impotently with ancient hand-cranked telephones Candé had a telephone in every one of its twenty rooms, and even its own internal switchboard. When Freeman Matthews arrived, he was greeted by the owners' impeccable English butler James, who had been left behind to help.

Reynaud did not reach Tours that morning. By dawn he and de Gaulle, inching their way southwards, were at Orléans. Neither had slept on the way, but at least their sleeplessness seemed to have produced one important decision, thanks to the persuasive powers of de Gaulle. He had finally tied down the wavering Prime Minister to take action on the Breton redoubt – the last toehold from which French troops might be embarked for north Africa. Reynaud issued de Gaulle with the necessary orders – if only verbal – to prepare for a government move to Brittany, and indeed suggested that he should fly the following day to Britain to arrange for the necessary shipping.

After a hastily summoned and dishevelled Prefect of Police at Orléans had found the two men some coffee and *croissants*, they went for a few moments into separate offices to make two vital telephone calls.

De Gaulle telephoned North-Eastern Army headquarters, to announce that the Government would be installed at Quimper in Brittany. Hearing a faint 'When?' on the bad line, he shouted, 'Perhaps tomorrow.' Then he tried to telephone Georges Mandel, Minister of the Interior, at the Prefecture in Tours without success. He did not get hold of Mandel until later in the day, when he arranged with him to requisition hotels and châteaux in and around Quimper and set up the various government departments.

Reynaud meanwhile was telephoning Weygand at Briare; he was staggered by what he heard. Unknown to Reynaud, Churchill was visiting Briare that very day to discuss the military situation. As Weygand's rasping voice announced the news, de Gaulle – his phone call finished – entered the room. He, too, was horrified, and remembered being certain that 'the C.-in-C., through military liaison channels, had begged him [Churchill] to come urgently to Briare'. He could hear Weygand's unpleasant voice over the telephone, snapping, 'Mr Churchill must be directly informed about the real situation at the front.'

De Gaulle exploded to Reynaud, 'Are you really going to allow General Weygand to invite the British Prime Minister on his own authority? Don't you see that General Weygand is not concerned with a plan of operations, but is pursuing a policy that is not yours? Are you going to leave General Weygand in command?' In fact de Gaulle was mistaken, since Churchill was flying to France of his own accord.

The two men were still in the Prefecture in Orléans. 'You are right,' replied Reynaud. 'This situation must stop.'

Reynaud and de Gaulle had earlier discussed the possibility of replacing Weygand as Commander-in-Chief with General Charles Huntziger and now, as Reynaud summoned their car, he said to de Gaulle, 'Let's go at once to see Huntziger.' By the time the car drew up at the steps of the Prefecture, Reynaud had changed his mind. 'It's better that you should go alone to see Huntziger,' he decided. 'I shall prepare for the interviews with Churchill; we will meet again at Briare.' So the two men split up. Reynaud set off for Briare, sixty miles east of Orléans, de Gaulle for the village of Arcis-sur-Aube where Huntziger, in command of the centre group of armies, had his headquarters.

He reached Arcis later in the morning and, though at this very moment Guderian's Panzers were smashing these armies on the Champagne front, de Gaulle was 'struck by Huntziger's coolness'. After a little preliminary verbal skirmishing de Gaulle came to the point.

'The battle of France is lost,' he said, 'but the Government means to continue the war from Africa with all the resources it can get across. The present Generalissimo is not the man to be able to carry it out. Would you be the man?'

Without hesitation Huntziger said, 'Yes.'

'Well,' a delighted de Gaulle shook hands on it, 'you will be receiving the Government's instructions.'*

Early on Tuesday morning the Countess de Gelabert and Jimmy Ashworth, with thousands of others, left Paris, 'jerking along in bottom gear a few yards at a time'. Leaving his beloved Paris was to Jimmy Ashworth like 'burying someone. I was so busy with the practical arrangements that I didn't have time to think of what was happening.' Paris itself was calm but empty, shops closed, shutters drawn, with here and there oases of incongruity, as at the corner of the rue St Antoine where the old ladies still tended their flower stalls. Near Versailles they passed a party of British soldiers shaving out of tin mugs. 'They waved cheerfully, they looked so pink and healthy, they can't have realised what was going on.'

Ashworth decided to drive via Chartres. It was a nightmare journey, packed with incidents that still haunt the Countess – the *curé* trundling along with a very old lady in a wheelbarrow; the sudden incongruous spectacle of a Paris à Nuit charabanc – the sort that tours nightclubs – filled with excited nuns. Just before Épernon they were held up for nearly an hour, and watched as half a dozen men rushed a nearby farmhouse and shouted, 'The Germans are coming. Run for it!' The farmer and his wife set off perched on their tractor – then the six men calmly took over the house.

Jimmy Ashworth walked ahead to discover the cause of the delay and came back with astonishing news. 'It's not a car, it's a dust-cart,' he explained, and when Madame de Gelabert asked what on earth a dust-cart was doing on the roads at this time Ashworth told her, 'It's come from Rambouillet – and it's filled with files and documents. It's even got an old duplicating machine on top.'

Everywhere the countryside was littered with the signature of the refugees – broken bottles, filthy paper, torn umbrellas,

---

* De Gaulle is quite explicit in his memoirs that Huntziger agreed; Huntziger, however, denied this to Weygand in north Africa in September 1941. By then, of course, Huntziger was in the opposite camp to de Gaulle and may have found it expedient to be careful.

punctured tyres, smashed suitcases, straw from mattresses that had burst open.

When they set off again – the original plan to reach Tours in twenty-four hours long since abandoned – they came across a stretch of road where zealous defenders had erected anti-tank traps of huge stone boulders, which meant that the cars choking the roads were squeezed into single file as they passed through the narrow apertures. 'Damned stupid,' growled Jimmy Ashworth, pointing to the fields of ripening wheat on either side. 'Tanks don't need roads – they can go straight through the fields.'

Outside every village they found abandoned cars – and sometimes abandoned people as well. And at some isolated farmhouses they saw burly farmers standing outside their gates, crying almost cheerfully, 'Come on – out with your money! Ten sous a glass of water, two francs to fill your bottle.' Near one village a haggard mother 'who looked as though she would faint at any moment' tried to force the door of the car and begged the Countess, 'Please, please, take my baby. Never mind about me.' Stony-hearted, Ashworth drove on. There was no room in the small car anyway. The back was filled with office papers.

At Épernon they came across a new and terrible echo of the exodus. In the square by the war memorial, the Hôtel de Ville notice-board was filled with Lost and Found advertisements; but these were for human beings:

Madame Lefarge, chez Hôtel de Ville, demande nouvelles de ses filles Marie-Louise et Hélène, 6 et 5 ans, perdue prêt d'ici le 9 juin.

Recherchons Edmond Landau, 5 ans, perdu dix kilomètres d'Épernon le 8 juin. Écrire Madame Landau, Poste Restante, Bordeaux.

Scores of pitiful signs, of agonising requests – one for 'Three children lost when our car broke down' – told their own story. Sometimes at the bend of a road, or at the top of a rise, one

could look back at the long, slow-moving procession, travelling along the white ribbon between fields of ripening grain.
It seemed a biblical scene, especially near the towns where
more people were on foot – the slowness of it, mothers hug-
ging at their children, on the verge of tears, the brittle
rebukes they used to try to mask their fear. It seemed as
though none could escape.

Ashworth reached one road junction just as a dozen German aircraft appeared overhead. He remembers not the fear,
but the contrast of the quiet countryside and the machine-
made menace above. Further on, he and the Countess trailed
behind a group of old, tired men huddled together in a
hearse.

There were similar scenes all over France. Near Nantes,
Corrine Luchaire, the film actress, who had an isolated farm
which she used at weekends, found every neighbouring
village shop shut and barricaded. She calmly settled down to
milk her own cows – then stood by the gates, offering free
milk to children who passed by.

At St-Benoit-sur-Loire, a Catholic priest begged Max
Jacob, the Jewish poet, to leave. 'They have evacuated the
hospital, the children, the old,' cried the priest. 'You must go.'

'I'm not a child, I'm not old,' retorted Jacob, 'I prefer to
stay. I would rather die in my home than be killed in a queue
of refugees.'

Élie Bois, on his way to join the Government in Tours,
found people of every kind in trucks, limousines, light cars,
coaches and carts 'emigrating no one knew whither'. Yet
mixed among the distraught refugees were teenagers who
slipped in and out on bicycles among the string of vehicles,
laughing as they went; for them it was almost a great adven-
ture.

In some hamlets or villages the line of refugees 'passed
between two hedges of curious onlookers, who stared as if
watching a parade'. But then the attitude of the peasants
was philosophical, as the writer Emmanuel d'Astier, who was
in the forces, discovered when trying to reach his unit;
driving through the countryside he found that the French

peasants 'merely wondered what effect the Germans would have on everyday life; war and peace were like hail and sunshine. Mobilisation, requisitioning and invasion were hardships which were to be judged in relation to labour, the sowing and the harvest.'

It took the Countess and Jimmy Ashworth nearly two hours to drive through Épernon, then Ashworth cut off the main road leading to Maintenon and Chartres and made for the small township of Houx. 'I know a farmer there,' said Ashworth. 'He might be able to help us.'

A couple of miles before Houx – and not long before nightfall – they found themselves almost alone on the winding country-lanes. There in front of them was an old-fashioned hand-operated petrol-pump and a man filling up a car. It was a desolate country scene, near a village, shuttered, empty, grey.

'Liquid gold!' cried Jimmy Ashworth.

The car in front moved on and Ashworth edged his Citroën into the right position and leant out of the window. As he did so, the man locked up the pump, pocketed the key and waved him away.

'Oh no,' groaned Ashworth. 'No petrol left?'

The man was surly. 'It looks like it, doesn't it?'

'Not just a couple of litres?'

'We're closed,' shouted the man.

Ashworth caught sight of a gauge indicating that some petrol at least was still in the tank.

'Hey, you *have* petrol,' he cried.

Without turning round the man almost snarled, 'What if I have? I've been pulling that pump handle all day. My arm's so tired I can't use it any more. If you want some petrol, come back tomorrow.'

With his massive bulk sunk in the depths of the car, Ashworth perhaps looked deceptively small; but not when he got out. As two other cars queued behind him, klaxoning for attention, Ashworth seemed, to the Countess, 'to uncoil and bound out of the car in one movement'. Ashworth charged at the man, grabbed his iron-grey hair with one ham-like fist and dragged him back.

'Give me that bloody key,' he said. 'I'll operate the pump. And don't worry – you'll get paid.' The scuffle was short-lived. The peasant muttered something which the Countess could not hear from inside the car, then started to operate the pump.

By mid-afternoon, they reached the farm that Ashworth knew, an old-fashioned, low building, set back from the road. The owners had fled. At least twenty people occupied the ground floor, and when Ashworth tried to enter – merely to seek news of his friends – he was met with a barrage of insults from people terrified of losing their living-space. In the stables a girl, her mother and her father were preparing to lie down on a pile of straw. The girl kept guard at the double doors with a pitchfork. Another family with two sickly, whimpering babies had brought a tent and was camping in the garden. The mother was cooking watery potato soup over a fire. On the roof of their car was a cage with a canary in it, presumably the children's most precious possession.

The Countess took one look at the children – and their miserable, sad-looking mother – and whispered to Ashworth, 'We've got to give the children something to eat.'

'If any of that gang in the kitchen think we have any food at all, they'll cut our throats,' Ashworth warned her, as they drove away.

From time to time there was the hum of approaching aircraft, first distant, then suddenly overhead. They could have been friendly planes, but no one was taking chances. Cars jerked to a halt, passengers dived for the nearest ditch and waited, cowering, until the aircraft vanished.

Strangely, fear was not the predominant emotion. 'I don't think I was really afraid,' the Countess remembered later. 'It was the feeling of impotence, of frustration, that we could do nothing, that made the journey so awful. I think that anger is more tiring than fear.'

After a gruelling day in the sun, they reached Chartres by evening – just fifty-five miles as the crow flies from Paris. The sprawling Place des Épars, flanked on one side by the Hôtel

Grand Monarque, was jammed with cars, and it took them half an hour to find a place to park the Citroën among shouting, irritable people. By luck there was a small café nearby; though the wrinkled old *patronne* was scarcely polite when Ashworth ordered two *fin à l'eau*, at least she consented to serve them. But when he asked for sandwiches she shrieked, 'I've been serving sandwiches all day. Why can't you people stay where you belong?'

Not until Ashworth employed his considerable knowledge of rough, tough *argot* – accompanied by a brandished note – did she finally shout an order back to the kitchen through the small open window behind the bar. Everyone was in a foul temper. The waiters looked exhausted. When one spilled a drink over a man sitting at a table, he snarled, 'Why do you have to get in my way?'

At the Grand Monarque, where Ashworth was known, they were more politely received. There was no food left in the hotel, and there was really no room to spare, said the harassed manager, but they could stay if they didn't mind mattresses and sharing a big room with twelve people. They accepted gratefully.

To stretch their legs they walked across the Place des Épars and up to the cathedral. On the way, miraculously, they discovered a small grocer's shop stacked with canned food. Ashworth bought all he could carry – enough for supper in the hotel, with supplies for the following day. The cathedral looked down on them, enchanted, spell-binding, serene.

As they set off back to the hotel, Jimmy Ashworth said, 'I wonder how long it'll be there.'

## 2. *The reason why*

In the crowded lobby of the Grand Monarque, a portable radio blared, 'Paris is ready to meet the German invader!' But the official spokesman sounded unsure of himself, with

uneasy references to French withdrawals in the north, 'to
consolidate our positions'.

What had happened? Why was the much-vaunted French
Army in pell-mell retreat? And why were eight million
refugees choking every French road leading south?

When Marguerite de Gelabert, eating sardines out of a tin,
asked Jimmy Ashworth these questions, he answered,
'Because for years the French have been too busy fighting
each other to bother with Germany.' There was some truth
in this, for the French Revolution sparked off hatred which
had lasted ever since. Indeed, since 1789 France had been
gripped in a struggle – varying in form and intensity –
between revolution and counter-revolution. 'We've had to
kick out half a dozen fifth columnists from the *Mail*,' Ashworth added. 'Some Communist, some Fascist; each one was
determined to wreck the other half of France.'

French fears that extremist politicians would ruin France
had obscured the dangers from without. The Countess de
Portes, admitting that Nazism was 'not perfect', passionately
believed it was preferable to Communism. Weygand was
terrified of French Communists who unswervingly followed
the Moscow party line – particularly now, after the Nazi–
Soviet pact, for didn't that, as Weygand had asked Reynaud,
make French Communists tacit allies of Germany, the enemy
of France? Fifth columnists – from left or right – lost no
opportunities to fan the extremist ideological flames that
threatened to destroy the fragile Third Republic.

The defeatists were now winning the battle to betray
France for another reason: the Germans had, in the years
before the war, better advocates than other countries. Otto
Abetz, Hitler's ambassador to France, was a frequent visitor
to the Countess de Portes as well as to other political leaders.
He did not find it difficult to persuade them that friendship
with Germany was preferable to friendship with the British.
(One is tempted to speculate whether history would have
been different if the brilliant Abetz had been sent to London
and the numskull Ribbentrop had spent the pre-war years as
ambassador to France.)

Between the wars both France and Britain were ruled by politicians of indifferent stature, lacking the supreme quality needed at the time – the courage to be unpopular when in power. Clemenceau would have whiffed the scent of danger, for his life was motivated by the belief that 'The German lust for power . . . has fixed as its policy the extermination of France.' But existing leaders never tried to form public opinion. They preferred to hold to their offices by encouraging people in an illusion.

When people looked around them many were attracted by the new régime of Hitler with his cult of physical fitness, of Mussolini whose Blackshirts gave an impression of efficiency. To many Hitler and Mussolini were preferable to Stalin in the east.

The traditional right wing of France – headed by the fanatically anti-semitic Action Française, which had been formed as far back as 1899 – was joined by Colonel de la Roque's Croix de Feu and the Solidarité Française. In 1934 they marched on the Chamber of Deputies, forcing the Government to resign after the police had opened fire.

The pro-Fascist Pierre Laval knew the dangers when, as Foreign Minister in 1935, he closed French ports to the British fleet blockading Italy after she invaded Ethiopia. It made a mockery of the League of Nations. And Pierre Flandin, who succeeded Laval a year later, knew the danger of allowing Hitler to march into the Rhineland. So did Stanley Baldwin, who was horrified at the prospect of taking up arms against Germany, and who dominated the vacillating Flandin. It was this that caused André Siegfried to remark, 'On March 7, 1936, we lost the next war.'*

Men like André Maurois were not alone in feeling that 'in 1940 France was so divided, political hatreds were so violent and the decline of public morality so far advanced that no obstacle was interposed to personal hatreds'. The Allied lack of military, diplomatic and industrial preparation might be the root cause of the disaster, but to Maurois 'the quarrels of

* In a private conversation quoted by the American historian Hamilton Fish Armstrong.

the Ministers and the lack of any leader capable of imposing unity on the nation deprives the armies of their last chance'.

The malaise had been accentuated by the *drôle de guerre*, as the French called the 'phony war'. Its effect on the morale of both the French and British armies was shattering. When one is living away from home in a squalid, dull routine it is hard to take seriously a war that does not appear to exist. It was brutally hard on one particular class of soldier – those whose fathers had been killed in the First World War and whose mothers had been living on a pittance ever since. Their weekly pay was barely enough to buy two packets of Gauloises, and in many cases there was no one to write to them, to send them comforts – a scarf, extra socks, a bottle of wine to cheer them through the coldest winter in living memory.

And then, as A. J. Liebling found, 'The appetite for disaster in some human beings is so strong that they feel let down when nothing terrible happens.' So unreal was the war that it resulted not only in apathy, but in a vague, undefined belief that it would all come out right in the end. It was the same in Britain. Only the previous Sunday de Gaulle had been in London, and remembered the parks full of strolling people, the queues outside the cinemas, and particularly the sight of 'burly, healthy doormen opening taxis outside hotels'. It was, as he wrote later, 'certainly obvious that the bulk of the population was oblivious to the gravity of events in France'.

'I wonder if the last war hadn't a certain *dynamisme* this one distinctly lacks,' Alexander Werth asked himself. 'We don't even hate the Huns properly as we did in the last war. The papers are genteel; and so is the B.B.C. with Herr Hitler this and Herr Hitler that.'

The French military machine had also been riddled with problems since 1923 when Raymond Poincaré was compelled to shorten the term of military service from three years to eighteen months (and five years later to one year). How could he do otherwise in a country lacking the boys who should have been sired by the million Frenchmen slaughtered in the First World War? It was hard to believe that the army of

France was no longer the great army that had stood fast against Germany. It was also hard to accept the prospect of Germans once again ravaging their country. And so the Maginot Line was born, with people only too glad to place unquestioning faith in 'the trusted heirs of the heroes of 1918'. The High Command was convinced that the war would be one of a 'fixed and continuous front' – a pattern that would of course save lives, for neither the soldiers in the Maginot Line nor the enemy in the Siegfried Line would be insane enough to attack each other's impregnable fortress.

So costly had been the Maginot Line, with its honeycomb of air-conditioned underground cities with food stocks large enough to last for a year or more, that few dared to suggest spending equally vast sums on a newer, mobile military machine that would have rendered the line obsolete. It was true that the line extended only from Belfort on the Swiss frontier to Sedan, leaving the area between the Belgian frontier and the sea open. No matter, said General Chauvineau of the French High Command in his book *Is an Invasion Still Possible?* Forgetting the doctrine of Clausewitz, that 'the heart of France lies between Brussels and Paris', Chauvineau set out to prove that a successful invasion of France was quite out of the question. Marshal Pétain stamped his seal of authority on the theory by writing a foreword to the book, while Gamelin told A. J. Liebling, 'There isn't enough heavy artillery in the world to get the French out of their concrete.'

No one thought to remind France that her own greatest strategist Napoleon had insisted, 'The tactics of waging war must be changed every ten years.'

In a block of military complacency as thick as the Maginot Line, only one man sought to move France into the present – the tall, arrogant Colonel recently become a General, Charles de Gaulle.

## 3. *The forgotten city*

In Paris, it was for the most part the brave who stayed
behind, thinking, or hoping, that they might be able to help
France. Yet at this moment of crisis the city produced no
leader around whom they could rally, nobody to whom they
could turn for strength, for guidance, for courage.

The radio blared warnings that people must prepare for
the rigours of a siege, for the terrors of street fighting. But
how? Where were the spades to dig trenches, the machine-
guns for a civilian militia, the makeshift hospitals for those
who would be wounded, the coffins for those about to die?

A few people conjured up revolutionaries dropping everything to man the barricades, or the issuing of weapons to
small knots of people in makeshift uniforms or identifying
arm-bands who would defend a given street corner to the
death. But this was never a possibility. It was one thing for
the radio to exhort, 'We will fight shoulder to shoulder.' But
what use was a shoulder without the butt of a rifle against it?

Some tried to rally their comrades – a dangerous business
in a city where many belonged either to the extreme left or
extreme right. When massed workers outside the Citroën
plant in the Quai de Javel demanded arms to fight the Germans, the meeting was quickly broken up by police swinging
their blue, lead-weighted capes, and ten men were arrested as
'Communists'.

The troops of General Héring's 'Paris Army' were as confused as the civilians. After much censored news, they could
now see with their own eyes dispirited soldiers, usually without arms, often drunk, milling around the suburbs, without
direction, not knowing where to go, hoping to get as far as
possible from the horrors they had already lived through.

In Menilimontant, the crowded and poor *arrondissement*
where Maurice Chevalier was born, a bunch of French *poilus*
– this time with arms – looted grocery stores, stocked up with
provisions, then forced their way into a seedy hotel as refuge,
and kept the police at bay for eight hours with rifle fire.

When a clerk named Maurice Phillipe carried his wife who was in labour to the General Hospital, she was refused admission because neither had identity cards. 'How do we know you are not a spy?' he was asked. Finally a nurse delivered Madame Phillipe's baby in the hospital's downstairs toilet. Despite the emergency, the dead hand of bureaucracy lingered on.

The new mother, Madame Phillipe, was far luckier than many others – for she had a man to help her. But many women and children did not have the faintest idea what to do, where to go. Authority appeared non-existent. The Government did not use the French radio to offer advice. The civilian population of France seemed to have been forgotten.

Rumours of spies terrified everyone in a city that believed itself to be on the verge of annihilation. Bertrand de Juvenal who as a young journalist had spent some time in Germany making many friends, received a copy of an obscure German magazine to which he subscribed and told Clare Boothe, 'On the cover was scribbled, "From an old German acquaintance who just wants you to know *he* is in Paris".' Cecily Mackworth, the British nurse, saw people panic when large pieces of a barrage balloon drifted down. They were convinced German paratroops were landing.

'It got to the stage,' Dynevor Rhys felt, 'when you hardly dared to say anything to anyone.' Jean Cocteau commented wryly, 'All you can see now on the roads of France are nuns winding on their puttees.'

In Berlin on this Tuesday, Goebbels told his staff, 'The effects are beginning to be felt in Paris.' He issued an order: 'The creation of panic is now the principal task of the propaganda machine. It would mean the crowning of many months' work if it proved possible to trigger off a revolution in Paris.'

Goebbels' hopes were a little ambitious. The 'panic' was visible only at the Paris railway stations, though by now all but two were closed. The occasional train still left the Gare de Lyon or the Gare d'Austerlitz. Outside the former, Gordon Waterfield of Reuter met a party of glum Britishers who had managed to escape from Italy just before Mussolini declared war. After reaching Paris they queued for twenty-four hours for tickets. Finally they reached the *guichet* and put down their money, only to be told they could not be issued tickets as they had no identity cards. An hour later Waterfield saw one of them with a broad grin on his face. He had discovered that in the far section of the station they could walk onto the platform without tickets.

'See you in Bordeaux,' he cried cheerfully.

Outside the besieged Gare d'Austerlitz, Jean Chamby was giving last-minute instructions to a French railway porter. Or so it seemed. The porter was slight of build, but at least the uniform fitted moderately well. Ginette Chamby had spent most of the night trying to pierce the thick rough cloth with a needle as she shortened the sleeves and legs.

Chamby could not take her into the station, but left the 'porter' – short hair tucked into her official cap – with a gendarme who helped her force a path to the barrier. Chamby ran round to the back of the station and once again climbed the gate leading to the goods yard. Deschamps, the assistant stationmaster, was as good as his word. He let Ginette change back into her own clothes in his office. Then he took her down the line, beyond the station, to an empty train that would leave later in the day. There was nothing more Chamby could do, after seeing his wife installed in a corner seat with a small suitcase and a bag of provisions, for the long journey to the south of France, which she reached safely.

Near the Bourse, Gordon Waterfield and his colleague Harold King spent the rest of the morning burning Reuter files. They were convinced that the end was a matter of days, perhaps hours, away and decided to have lunch at Maxim's while it was still possible.

The rue Royale was not exactly busy, but many of the shops were open and a fair sprinkling of people dotted the pavements. However, when King and Waterfield walked out of Maxim's after a good lunch the short, wide street linking the Madeleine and the Place de la Concorde had undergone a startling transformation. In two hours every shop had put up its shutters. The street was empty – except for two wounded soldiers on crutches, limping along the pavement.

Though many other journalists were leaving, Waterfield and King decided to remain in Paris for another twenty-four hours, for there was already a Reuter correspondent in Tours.

Alexander Werth spent his time stocking up with food – canned meat and fruit and *biscottes* – when a friend solemnly advised him to take a large stock of chewing gum.

'What on earth for?' asked Werth.

'It stops up machine-gun bullet-holes in the petrol tank, and also stops your teeth chattering.'

Werth visualised himself and his passengers on the route, 'sitting round the car, chewing the stuff as hard as we can go in order to mend the bullet-riddled tank'. As he prepared to leave, the concierge and her daughter wept bitterly. 'Not for my sake,' Werth realised, 'but because of the circumstances that make one leave Paris.'

Some stayed out of sheer lethargy. Gordon Waterfield went round in the afternoon to collect a pair of trousers that were being made for him by a Scottish tailor. When he asked the tailor when he was leaving, the tailor shrugged. 'I've got no car, and I can't be bothered to wait in the queues at the station. I'm staying.'

One elderly widow refused the offer of a lift to the south because she was convinced that even if she remained in Paris, she would never starve. She had 'something of value' which could always be turned into ready cash. Jeanne Lefèvre's wedding so many years ago had been graced with a speech by Anatole France, who had presented her with a copy in his own hand. She also had a bundle of letters from the famous author. Wherever she went, she clutched close to her a small briefcase filled with these precious documents. If the worst came to the worst 'they were worth a lot of money', though she hoped that she would never have to sell them.

Still not knowing of Weygand's decision to declare the capital an open city, General Pierre Hering was preparing for the fighting that lay ahead. Hering, an old soldier called back from the reserve list, had once been a member of the French Supreme War Council and Military Governor of Strasbourg; a soldier to the fingertips, he had a thorough dislike of politicians.

Early on Tuesday morning, he summoned the Prefects of the Seine and Paris to his headquarters and told them gravely, 'You are now under my command, and the capital will be defended to the last.'

He was delighted to be back in uniform, but, in Reynaud's words, he was 'a wise old bird' who perfectly well knew that the task entrusted to him was too big for one man. The 'Paris Army' was in truth a rag-bag affair consisting largely of units from the 7th and 10th armies, together with other troops who had never been under fire. In all they totalled around 10,000 officers and men. They were armed with 200 anti-tank guns, several hundred machine guns, and were already manning 400 blockhouses recently built on the eastern approaches to the capital and linked by several miles of anti-tank obstacles and ditches.

Hering also had 30 tanks. But he realised that even if the French 7th Army fell back to help – as it would have to do – this was still not enough to hold the German Panzers. However, profiting by the example of Warsaw, he did believe that once the German Army reached the city proper determined resistance in the scores of miles of narrow streets, with tall buildings offering cover for snipers, with courtyards out of which determined fighters could ambush the Germans, could do a great deal to neutralise the effectiveness of the armoured columns which had played such a vital role in Germany's surge across Europe.

Though this was no enviable task, Hering never flinched from the prospect. What did worry him was that, as well as commanding his motley, quickly assembled army, he was also responsible for maintaining law and order in Paris.

When the police chiefs had left, he sent for General de Lannurien, a senior aide, and told him firmly, 'I would like you to go at once to General Weygand at Briare. Tell him I can't devote myself to the organisation and command of an improvised army, which might have to pull out at any moment, and at the same time retain responsibility for the military government.'

As de Lannurien reached the door, Hering added, 'I will telephone General Weygand and warn him of your arrival. I'll try to explain something of the position to him.'

Within a few minutes the operator told him he could not get through to Briare. By then de Lannurien was on his way.

At the time de Lannurien was leaving Paris, and de Gaulle was talking to General Huntziger, Reynaud arrived in Briare, Weygand's new headquarters. Marshal Pétain was already there and after lunch he and the Prime Minister took a stroll through the grounds of the château, not so much to talk to each other – for they had little to say – but rather to leave Weygand free to study the latest war news.

Reynaud was already having misgivings about the white-haired Marshal who walked beside him – still stiff-backed at eighty-four, though his eyes were milky and his hearing bad. Pétain had been ambassador in Madrid when Reynaud appointed him Vice-President of the Council in May, largely to bolster morale. He had been a living legend since Verdun, and since he had put down, with great humanity, a series of army mutinies in 1917 that could have spelled defeat for France. The civilians saw him as their saviour; the *poilus* worshipped him, believing that, like Napoleon, he considered that 'my soldiers are my children'. Ever since November 1918, the mystical bond linking Pétain and the people of France was so profound that if Reynaud thought for a moment he had made an error of judgment in May, he would not dare to dismiss their hero.

Though Pétain was a patriot, he was also the son of a cautious, pessimistic peasant; he now openly advocated that France must capitulate. Indeed, lunching with the United States ambassador, Pétain had told him bitterly that he felt Britain 'would permit the French to fight without help until the last available drop of French blood should have been shed and that then, with quantities of troops on British soil and plenty of planes and a dominant fleet the British, after a very brief resistance, or even without resistance, would make a peace of compromise with Hitler, which might even involve a British government under a British Fascist leader'.

While Reynaud was determined to carry on the fight from north Africa if the Battle of France were lost, Pétain – with the viewpoint of a peasant – was making it clear that nothing would induce him to leave the soil of France.

Reynaud had tried gentle persuasion, but it is difficult to hold a rational discussion with a man so old. For, when the guns of August began to sound in 1914, Colonel Henri Phillipe Benoni Omer Pétain was fifty-eight, and delighted because he had just bought a house to which to retire after apparently reaching the end of an uneventful army career in which he had never heard a shot fired in anger.

That war offered Pétain a new life, but in the years that followed he became disillusioned by the moral disintegration he saw in the country he was convinced that he alone had saved from defeat. The mutinies left a scar which was translated into a nagging fear of Communist revolution. He came to see the most abominable aspect of French life as the moral decadence of its leaders. To him a man in high office should never, as Reynaud did, openly flaunt a mistress while his wife was living round the corner. When a friend asked him once why he did not return from Spain and seek political office, Pétain retorted, 'What should I do in Paris? I have no mistress.'

It is strange that old age plays such tricks. Who would have thought – did Reynaud even know? one wonders – that this sedate old man, a model of rectitude, had in his day been a compulsive womaniser? When Marshal Joffre in 1916 decided to entrust him with the defence of Verdun, an aide was sent to find Pétain – and discovered him snuggling between the sheets with a girl in the Hôtel Terminus at the Gare du Nord in Paris.

Over the years, another factor compounded the stubbornness of old age. Adulation had nurtured in Pétain a breathtaking vanity, so that by now, with the help of his acolytes, he had convinced himself that he was the man chosen by destiny to cleanse France of the moral decay he saw around him, perhaps by letting it suffer the pain of defeat.

Inside the château, Weygand studied the latest war news. Along the Channel coast, by the mouth of the Seine, part of the French 10th Army, whose retreat to the south had been cut off by Rommel's tanks, had its back to the sea. Grouped in the area also were the British 51st Division under General Fortune, and two French Alpine divisions that had been flung into the battle immediately after being evacuated from Namsos in Norway. More than 10,000 men were encircled.

Further south the Germans had crossed the Seine in force below Paris, and with virtually no opposition were moving swiftly along the River Marne, threatening Paris with an attack from two sides.

Weygand made his battle plans quickly. With Paris now an open city (though Paris did not know it yet) he issued orders that nothing was to be blown up, and that any retreating French troops must bypass the capital. He laid down two successive lines of withdrawal. Starting from the River Nonette – the limit of the defensive position around Paris – the first line ran through Écouen, Gonesse, Aulnay-sous-Bois; the second through Rambouillet Forest, Chevreuse, Juvisy.

Weygand had spread out his maps ready for Churchill's inspection when an orderly entered the dining-room to announce the arrival of General de Lannurien from Paris. Weygand looked up, astonished and irritated at the disturbance, and asked curtly why the General was not at his post.

De Lannurien was equally astonished until both men realised that Hering, in Paris, had not been able to telephone. Briefly de Lannurien gave his message; and Weygand reacted with commendable speed. He decided Hering would still command the grandiloquently named 'Paris Army', but would be allowed to withdraw and 'go wherever fate took it'. The responsibility for law and order in Paris would be delegated to General Dentz, who had already been transferred from the Alsace front, and would command the 'Paris area'; he would remain in the capital until the Germans entered the city, then hand it over.

De Lannurien could not contain his astonishment. He had left a city where the Army was preparing to defend it brick by brick, and now the nation's commander-in-chief was casually referring to Paris as already lost. He was almost in tears as Weygand told him that Paris was to be declared an open city. He was ordered to drive back to Paris urgently and give all the details to General Hering.

Alas, the poor people of Paris were to remain in ignorance for another twenty-four hours. What happened to de Lannurien on the journey back across the choked roads is not certain; how long it took him nobody knows; but the ancient telephone in Briare was still not working efficiently, and General Hering did not receive the news until the following day.

Only when de Lannurien had left did Weygand go outside into the grounds to join Reynaud and Pétain, and tell them what steps he had taken. According to Weygand, they both 'voiced neither objections nor approbations'.

Instead Reynaud once again broached the question of the 'Breton redoubt'. 'Wouldn't it be possible to muster our forces in the Brittany peninsula?' he asked, adding, 'Like a hand extended to England and America.'

To Weygand – already committed to peace at any price – these were 'airy notions'. Where would the troops come from to defend such a front? Who would supply them with food and guns? An hour was spent in confused argument. Finally Reynaud said, 'Anyway we must fight on. The British Government is not aware of our true situation.'

'It soon will be,' retorted Weygand.

De Gaulle had also arrived after his nightmare journey from General Huntziger's headquarters, and had found 'signs of disorder and panic everywhere . . . sections of units retreating southwards, mixed pell-mell with refugees'. At Méry, 134 kilometres from Paris, he had been held up for an hour by traffic. Almost the first person he saw when he reached Briare was Marshal Pétain, whom he had not met since 1938. He saluted stiffly.

'So you're a general now,' said Pétain. 'I don't congratulate you. What good are ranks in defeat?'

An outraged de Gaulle retorted, 'But you, Monsieur le Maréchal, received your first stars during the 1914 retreat. A few days later there was the Marne!'

'No comparison,' grunted Pétain and walked away.

## 4. Churchill at Briare

Early on Tuesday morning, while Churchill was still in bed poring over papers before setting off to meet the French leaders, a private secretary brought in a message from the Admiralty. The envelope was marked, 'For the Prime Minister's Eyes Only'. Churchill ripped open the top (carefully, for he insisted on all envelopes being re-used) and pulled out the sheet of paper he had been waiting for. It was an answer to the question above all others that haunted both Churchill and Roosevelt: the future of the French fleet.

On a single page, the memorandum set out the 'considerations which arise and the demands we should meet' to safeguard the French fleet if France capitulated. The answer was blunt: if necessary, 'We should aim at getting the fleet scuttled.'

Realising the pressure the Germans could bring to bear on France in the event of an armistice, Churchill had asked for the report, which was prepared by Sir Dudley Pound, the First Sea Lord, Lord Hankey and Sir Alexander Cadogan. They foresaw no problems if the French fought on from north Africa and took the fleet with them. There would, however, be serious problems if the French continued to fight from north Africa but sent the fleet to British waters, for then 'we should be in the intolerable position of watching the continued devastation of French towns from the air for which we should be regarded as responsible as long as we held the fleet'.

If the French sued for peace, the Germans would unquestionably continue to 'batter' the French until the Navy was handed over to them. Darlan could not be trusted to send the fleet to British or American waters. 'The humiliation of handing over a fleet was so great that a naval commander would do his utmost to avoid it.' Therefore, the report concluded, 'the best course would be for the fleet to be scuttled before a request is made for an armistice'.

The future of the fleet was of equal concern to Roosevelt, who had asked his Joint Planning Committee to analyse America's position should France fall. Even if Britain survived, the report said, the combined naval power of France, Italy and Germany in the Atlantic would be a third greater than that of Britain. And the United States could do nothing – even had Congress voted for war – for its one-ocean fleet was in the Pacific. The Japanese were threatening the Dutch East Indies, and were only prevented from invading (as was learned later) by the presence of the United States fleet at Pearl Harbor.

With these factors in mind, Churchill cabled the President suggesting that Britain and America should hold naval staff conversations 'in regard to fleet movements both in the Atlantic and the Pacific'. At the same time he thanked Roosevelt for the promise of aid 'in a dark but not unhopeful hour', though insisting that the greatest need at the moment was for the loan of as many old destroyers as the United States could spare, for convoy work in the Atlantic.

Churchill never lost sight of the need to 'encourage' Roosevelt, to emphasise again and again that Britain would never surrender, despite the hostile opinions held by Roosevelt's two key ambassadors in Europe. In Paris the anti-British Bullitt, whose voice carried considerable weight, was sadly misleading the President (and his beloved France) by persuading Washington that France would continue to fight, while telling Reynaud that he could expect greater aid than was possible. In Britain Joseph Kennedy was openly anti-

British, and while Churchill was begging Roosevelt for aid Kennedy was advising Cordell Hull not to send any. He warned his fellow Americans in a speech at Boston, 'There is no place in this fight for us,' and warned Roosevelt too against 'holding the bag in a war in which the allies expect to be beaten'. When he had the temerity to voice his opinions to King George VI, the King answered frigidly, 'As I see it, the U.S.A., France and the British Empire are the three really free peoples in the world, and two of these great democracies are fighting against all that we three countries hate and detest.' The King was polite. The British government circles, however, loathed Kennedy and coined a blunter phrase, 'I thought my daffodils were yellow until I met Joe Kennedy.'

Fearing that Kennedy might put the wrong interpretation to Roosevelt on the possible fall of France, Churchill before lunch drafted a cable to Lord Lothian, the British ambassador, asking him to stress again to Cordell Hull Britain's absolute determination to continue the fight should France surrender.

He need not have worried. 'Any friend of Great Britain like myself', Hull told Lothian later in the day, 'would expect her to fight to the last dollar, to the last man and to the last ship if necessary.' It had never entered his head, he assured Lothian, that Britain would surrender, much less turn over her fleet to Germany, even if she experienced 'unexpected temporary defeat due to sudden attack with new devices or weapons'.

About 2.30 p.m. Churchill left Hendon airfield outside London for Briare, flying in unbroken sunshine, his yellow-painted Flamingo escorted by twelve Spitfires. He took with him Anthony Eden, the War Minister, Generals Dill, Ismay and Spears, Brigadier Lund, together with Ismay's assistant Captain Berkeley, a superb translator.

The journey took two hours, for, as Churchill remembered, 'The German aircraft were now reaching far down into the Channel, and we had to make a still wider sweep.' The plane, however, was fitted with comfortable armchairs, and

Churchill spent the time brooding, while Eden and Dill discussed tables of figures, and Ismay went through 'an enormous number of folders' in his despatch case.

Occasionally Churchill asked a question, then relapsed again into deep thought, perhaps reflecting on the way 'the French tragedy had moved and slid downwards'. Churchill had few illusions about the plight of France. Short of a miracle, she would soon have to give up the struggle, and it was this problem that tormented him now. There was a fundamental difference between losing a battle and losing a war. If France lost a battle – if all metropolitan France were laid waste and in Nazi hands – a France still continuing the fight from abroad would mean a French Navy denied to Hitler. Therefore he would waste no time on recriminations, offer no false hopes for beating the Germans in France, but he would use all his powers of oratory, all his strength of will, all his very real and genuine love for France, to instil in the hearts of the faint-hearted the courage to fight on – no matter if ineffectually – for the honour and soul of France. Even if all of France fell, France 'must not go under, and its soul must live'.

Shortly before 5 p.m. the Flamingo landed at the small airfield outside Briare. It seemed to Spears 'flat and deserted . . . and quite a beastly place', while Eden felt 'almost ashamed' of the neat escort of Spitfires in comparison with Briare's scattered confusion of aircraft. Churchill, however, looked around beaming as though 'he had reached the one spot in the world he most wished to visit at that particular moment'. To Spears 'he conveyed the impression that the long journey had been well worth while since at last it was vouchsafed to him to walk about the aerodrome of Briare'. Churchill later remembered that moment when, as a colonel arrived in a car to greet them, 'I displayed the smiling countenance and confident air which are thought suitable when things are very bad.' But the Frenchman was unresponsive, and Spears felt that 'from his expression [he] might have been welcoming poor relations at a funeral reception'.

Even Churchill realised, as they drove off to the Château

du Muguet, where Weygand had established his headquarters, 'how very far things had fallen even since we were
in Paris a week before'.

It was an eight-mile drive, past the Hôtel de Ville in the
small town of Briare itself, then up a winding, narrow road,
past the village of Ouzouer with its pencil-thin grey church
steeple and an iron bridge over the canal, until the leading
car reached a pair of handsome wrought-iron gates decorated
with pots of plants on each stone pillar and a scroll with
spikes on either side.

A soldier pulled the heavy gates open and saluted. At first
Churchill could not see the château, which was hidden by a
clump of chestnuts, but as the car veered left along the drive
he saw the building at the end of some pasture land.

Spears took an instant dislike to the Château du Muguet
or, as he translated it mockingly (and literally), 'Lily of the
Valley Castle'. It not only had a 'ridiculous name', but was 'a
hideous house, the sort of building the *nouveau riche* French
bourgeoisie delight in, a villa expanded by successful business
in groceries or indifferent champagnes into a large monstros-
ity of red lobster-coloured brick, and stone the hue of unripe
Camembert'.

Spears was being a little unfair. While it could never com-
pare with the great châteaux of France, it had belonged to the
same family for five generations (being rebuilt after a fire in
1863) and had fifteen bedrooms which were no more nor less
comfortable than those on other large French provincial
estates. There were stables for twelve horses, and three aged
men pottered around the gardens in front of the Fontaine-
bleau-style double staircase leading up from the grounds. And
the view across the fields to the lodge at the gates was beautiful. Eden found it agreeable though small – it had only one
telephone near the toilet in a passageway at the back of the
house; to Eden it seemed 'ominous that this was the headquarters of the French army at war'.

Ominous it certainly was. General Beaufre, who had travelled
to Briare with Weygand, found it was almost impossible to

keep track of the German advances. As he remembers, 'Often the best way of finding out if a town had been taken was to ring up the Post Office, where the switchboard operator would say if the Germans had arrived or not.'

After the French had thoughtfully provided tea for the English guests, the conference opened at 7 p.m. Before the British arrived Reynaud had dismissed the possibility of holding the talks in the château's large salon – really the only word to describe its stiff formality – because of the lack of tables and the uncomfortable chairs. The study was too small, so, in the fading light, menaced by gathering clouds, the leaders trooped into the large, dark dining-room and sat down round a long, old table.

Churchill was next to Reynaud, facing Weygand, who placed himself next to Pétain. Ismay, with his back to the window, sat next to Spears and de Gaulle. Spears looked uneasily at 'the Frenchmen with set white faces, their eyes on the table', and with relief turned to de Gaulle, who radiated confidence and self-possession and whose recent action on the battlefield (where he had fought one of the few successful tank engagements) 'had given his sallow skin a healthy colour. His cheeks were almost pink.'

The British visitors were puzzled by an awkward pause before the conference opened. It was obvious that Reynaud was hesitating before performing a distasteful task. Finally, clearly ill at ease, he said he wished to raise a point that had nothing to do with the conference proper.

It appeared that a joint Anglo-French bombing raid on Genoa, Turin and Milan had been planned for that very evening. (In fact all the details had been arranged. British bombers flying from airfields at home would join other British bombers already based in Marseille together with French bombers and launch a concerted attack.)

Reynaud now said that 'to his great regret' he must ask if Churchill would agree to countermand the raid. His uneasiness stemmed from the fact that Churchill had repeatedly urged that the Allies should 'hit Italy hard' if she came into the war. But now French intelligence warned that if the raid took place the Italians planned massive reprisals on Lyons, which was unprotected, and Marseille, site of one of the largest oil and petrol depots in France.

The thought of reprisals had never worried Churchill (then or later), yet it was hard to refuse a request from such a hard-pressed ally. He sat with pursed lips, debating with himself, until Ismay, who had been studying his watch carefully, leaned across and whispered to Churchill, who suddenly beamed, and Spears felt that 'had he had a tail to wag it would have been wagging hard enough to break the back legs of his chair'.

Carefully laying his cigar along the edge of the table, Churchill leaned forward and said with obvious satisfaction, 'I am deeply sorry, but the operation cannot be stopped. The planes left England quarter of an hour ago.'

Spears saw Reynaud arch his eyebrows, though he said nothing. Weygand looked at Ismay 'with faint distaste', while Pétain's face was 'as expressionless as a slab of marble'.

After an awkward pause Reynaud formally welcomed Churchill, then turned to him and asked if he would care to address the meeting. Churchill did so. There were no recriminations, no excuses, no bitterness. As Churchill put it, they had come together to face up to reality without flinching, and to discuss how best to hold on in the face of such fearful pressure by Germany. Churchill felt that, once the Germans were stabilised in France, they would turn against England, and this was a prospect he welcomed for two reasons: it would bring relief to France, and give the Royal Air Force the chance to shoot the Luftwaffe out of the skies.

Yet Churchill could promise very little immediate help, perhaps between twenty and twenty-five divisions in 1941 if the French could hang on – which was manifestly impossible. Spears felt the 'suppressed irritation' of the French at 'the inadequacy of this trickle'.

What about the proposed Breton redoubt? asked Churchill, describing it in the colourful sentence, 'A kind of Torres Vedras line across the foot of the Brittany peninsula.' It would, he felt, give hundreds of thousands of French soldiers

the opportunity to escape to fight again. Before Reynaud
could answer, Weygand cut him short; it was the moment
he had been waiting for. As the dusk of the June evening
faded into night, with gathering clouds heralding a storm,
Weygand, with a touch of relish, outlined the hopelessness of
the French position. To Spears it seemed as though he was
more interested in proving that all was lost than in searching for ways to continue the war, while Eden thought
'he was certainly not the man to fight the last desperate
quarter'.

Churchill, flushed with emotion, leaned forward, hunched
against the table as Weygand rasped, 'I wish to place on
record that I consider those responsible embarked upon this
war very lightly, and without any conception of the power of
the German armaments.'

Weygand might have been defensively minded in his military operations, but just the opposite was true when he was
seated at the conference table. He was not only aggressive,
but almost abusive. When Churchill reminded Weygand
that a Canadian division with seventy-two heavy guns was
due to land in France that night, Weygand interrupted him
icily, 'That sort of aid is insignificant. Messieurs, we must
face up to the situation that confronts us.' His voice fell to a
whisper. 'If you consider it might help our cause, I am ready
to stand down.'

'There is no question of that,' Reynaud cried.

'General,' Churchill looked Weygand in the face, 'both of
us know through our experiences in the last war how situations which may seem desperate are followed by sudden
victorious recoveries.'

As if waiting for such an opening, Weygand retorted, 'No
doubt you refer to the rupture of the British front in 1918. I
would like to remind you that we immediately sent five divisions, then fifteen more; and we had ten others in reserve.
Today I have one regiment in reserve – and it will be used up
tomorrow in the first hour.'

Then Weygand turned to Reynaud, 'If we must anticipate
the complete occupation of metropolitan France, we must

ask the question how France will be able to carry on the war.'

The British felt the tenseness of this confrontation. To Spears, Weygand's parchment skin, tightly stretched on his Mongolian face, looked as if it would crack under the strain of his moving jaw.

In an effort to restore calm, Churchill said, 'If it is thought best for France in her agony that her army should capitulate, let there be no hesitation on our account, because whatever you may do we shall fight on for ever and ever and ever.'

Again he emphasised that time was the key to victory, that given time help would in the end reach France. No matter where the French Army fought, in France or overseas, it could hold or wear out a hundred German divisions.

'Even if that were so,' Weygand replied, 'they would still have another hundred to invade and conquer you. What would you do then?'

Churchill replied, 'My technical advisers are of the opinion that the best method of dealing with a German invasion of the British Isles is to drown as many as possible on the way over, and knock the others on the head as they crawl ashore.'

With a 'sad smile' Weygand said, 'At any rate I must admit you have a very good anti-tank obstacle.'

Churchill then suggested that General Georges, in command of the north-east front, should give his report. Churchill admired Alphonse Georges greatly. He was a soldier's soldier with a square face, dark, lively eyes, a firm mouth and strong chin beneath a pencil-thin moustache.

While waiting for Georges, Spears looked around. He felt that Weygand 'was drained dry like a squeezed lemon'. He could produce no ideas, no suggestions. Churchill sat hunched up, playing with the ring on his finger. De Gaulle chain-smoked, lighting one cigarette with the butt of another. Not a muscle of his face had moved while he listened to the Commander-in-Chief's recital.

Georges could offer little comfort. Out of forty-nine French divisions on 6 June – less than a week previously – only the equivalent of twenty-four remained, and most were in headlong retreat. The thrusting German front stretched for 290 miles, but only in the centre were the French holding – and there, only for the moment. East of Paris the Germans were in Château-Thierry on the Marne, in the west at Rouen on the Seine.

What Georges did not tell Churchill was that just after Reynaud's promise to fight 'in front of Paris and behind Paris' Weygand had given Georges personal instructions to start a general retreat on the following morning – this meant in a few hours. The new line would run through Caen – Tours – Clamecy – Dijon.

The French were understandably bitter about the lack of British armed support in France – a bitterness exacerbated by the successful British evacuation at Dunkirk – but now the topic turned to a far more sensitive area, one in which Britain could help, but refused: the despatch of British fighter aircraft to bases in France.

The French felt deeply that R.A.F. fighters operating from Britain were valueless because their flying time over the German lines was limited. But if R.A.F. fighters were based on French airfields they could fly straight into the attack.

When a few days previously de Gaulle had begged Churchill to send planes across the Channel, Churchill had not explained his real fear: that they would be destroyed on the ground, for the simple reason that the R.A.F. had not been designed for 'a war of rapid movement'. Its ground staff had not been trained to deal with a long, fighting withdrawal where plans had to be adjusted frequently, where there was little transport and inadequate airfields. It should be remembered that at this time no way had been devised of constructing temporary airstrips. Churchill's thinking was affected by the fact that R.A.F. plans for a possible war with Germany 'had been based on a strategic conception which was radically at fault'.*

So, though Churchill was 'haunted' by the paucity of Britain's war effort and 'the slaughter and suffering that has

* *History of the Second World War* (H.M.S.O, 1957), vol. ii.

fallen upon France and France alone', he was still adamant in the face of earnest pleas by Reynaud and angry demands by Weygand.

Turning to Reynaud, Churchill said, 'Twenty-five squadrons must be maintained at all costs for the defence of Britain and nothing will make us give them up. To give them up will destroy our chance of life.'

'History will say', Reynaud retorted bitterly, 'that the battle of France was lost for lack of planes.'

'And through lack of tanks,' added Churchill.

General Georges broke in, 'It is hardly likely that Britain will be attacked immediately, and in the meantime a massive intervention of British planes might change the situation.'

Weygand bridled, 'Every available British fighter plane should be sent over to play its part in the battle that will seal the fate of both nations.'

'That isn't true,' Churchill replied. 'Anything that is lost today can be retrieved tomorrow.'

'But now is the decisive point,' cried Weygand. 'Now is the decisive moment. It is therefore wrong to keep *any* squadrons back in England.'

'This is *not* the decisive point, and this is *not* the decisive moment,' Churchill roared. 'That moment will come when Hitler hurls his Luftwaffe against Britain. If we can keep command of the air, and if we can keep the seas open, as we certainly shall keep them open, we shall win it back for you.'

To Spears, Churchill 'looked very fierce and it was quite evident that nothing would make him surrender the last air defence of Britain ... there was obvious relief among the English'.

The chilling decision not to commit Britain's last fighter planes to help the French was of course a purely military one, taken in the hope (true, as it turned out) that Britain would not suffer the same fate as France. But the military decision inevitably became translated into a political issue between two nations who saw the war from utterly different viewpoints.

To the French, with the Germans overrunning their

country, with the French commanders bewildered by tactics and speed unfamiliar to them, there seemed to be little point in resisting when an ally with aircraft refused to help.

But the British had no thought of defeat. Protected by their moat of the English Channel, the evacuation from Dunkirk of 338,226 British and French troops – which in Churchill's words saved 'the spinal column' of the British Army – seemed to them almost a victory. The Germans might be masters of land warfare, but they had yet to prove they could match Britain in the air and at sea.

To Churchill it was imperative, therefore, for the last line of air defence to be kept intact. But de Gaulle rightly felt, as he wrote later, that this was the moment when 'strategic unity between London and Paris was practically broken. A reverse on the Continent had been enough to make Britain desire to absorb herself in her own defence. That meant the success of the Germanic plan ... to separate the French and British forces and, simultaneously, to divide France and England. It was only too easy to imagine what conclusions would be drawn by defeatists.'

Certainly the French were horrified. Eden, who was watching their faces, found Reynaud inscrutable, while Weygand concealed only with difficulty his obvious scepticism. Marshal Pétain was 'mockingly incredulous'. He hardly said a word, but to Eden his attitude was obviously, 'C'est de la blague.'

The formal meeting of the Supreme War Council ended at 9.30 p.m. but there was so much work to be done that it was decided to take a break of half an hour, then serve a light meal at the conference table. It had been a long day for Churchill, but before washing his hands he cornered General Georges. Was the situation as black as Weygand had painted? 'It is,' Georges admitted. 'The French Army's capacity for resistance is running out. Before long, the signing of an honourable armistice will be the only way out.'

As Churchill waited to return to the dining-room, he beckoned an aide, and asked him if he would seat General de Gaulle next to him.

The men walked to their places, Reynaud at the head of the table, Weygand – with Eden on his right – at the opposite end. Churchill took his place on Reynaud's right. At this moment, the tall, angular, uniformed figure of de Gaulle walked past Eden, and Weygand invited him, pleasantly enough, to sit down next to him. De Gaulle replied that he had been asked to sit next to Churchill. Eden thought de Gaulle replied rather curtly, and certainly Weygand flushed, though he made no comment as de Gaulle sat down on Churchill's right.

It was Churchill's first opportunity to get to know de Gaulle better, but even so protocol might have prevented a long conversation between the two men had not the meal been punctuated by a series of unfortunate incidents.

It consisted of indifferent soup, an excellent omelette, some light wine. It had hardly started when there was, as Churchill remembered, 'a jarring note'. Air Marshal A. S. Barratt, Commander of the British Air Force in France, telephoned Ismay with the startling news that the British bombers at Marseille were not taking off after all against Italian industrial targets, even though the bombers from Britain, which they were to join, had left their bases. The British adjourned for a few moments, then Churchill spoke to Reynaud, who agreed to give orders for the planes to leave Marseille immediately.

Somewhat mollified Churchill proceeded to eat the omelette and, in an attempt to ease the strained atmosphere, leaned over towards Pétain, who seemed half-asleep, and said, 'Think back! We went through difficult times in 1918, but we got over them. We shall get over these in the same way.'

Pétain seemed to wake up. 'In 1918 I gave you 40 divisions to save the British army. Where are the 40 British army divisions that we need to save ourselves today?' he asked icily.

Churchill went scarlet, turned his back on Pétain, and spoke only to de Gaulle for the rest of the meal. De Gaulle felt that 'our talk strengthened my confidence in his determination', while Churchill quickly sensed de Gaulle's 'massive strength'.

Dinner had hardly finished when Air Marshal Barratt was on the phone again. His news was blunt. The local commanders in Marseille refused to obey Reynaud's orders, and the raid by British planes from Marseille had been cancelled.

Had Churchill known of the extraordinary events taking place near Marseille, he might never have finished his dinner, for the British bombers on two French airfields near Marseille were loaded up, ready for take-off, and the pilots had been briefed, when the French liaison officer on each airfield suddenly received telegrams marked 'Urgent Attention'.

They came from General Vuillemin, and the message was simple: despite Reynaud's orders, the raid was to be cancelled. The British commanding officer was horrified. Ground crew, spare parts, maintenance units had been sent from Britain to France at a perilous cost. He begged the French liaison officer to ignore the message. He tried to reach Barratt, but the lines were in such confusion that he could not get through. So he decided to ignore the cancellation order, and gave orders on the radio telephone to the crew dispersal huts on the perimeter, 'Prepare for take-off!'

In the pale moonlight the planes trundled towards the end of the runways. At that moment the two airfields were transformed from ghost-like darkness into a frenzied activity. Arc lamps burst into light. Searchlights illuminated an incredible assortment of vehicles moving over the grass towards the runway. Military trucks and light armoured cars jostled with civilian cars and horse-drawn carts.

The French Air Force commander in Marseille had called on the local population to prevent the planes taking off. By now the British commanding officer had managed to contact headquarters and begged for permission to clear the runway by shooting off the obstruction. This was refused. The raid never took place.

With admirable restraint Churchill (perhaps because he was unaware of the full details) decided not to mention the matter to the hard-pressed French Premier. It was just as well, for as Churchill was sipping a well-earned brandy with his coffee Reynaud guided him to a corner and told him that Pétain had already prepared a paper on the subject of an armistice 'which it would be necessary for France to seek'.

Reynaud added, 'He has not handed the paper to me yet. He is still ashamed to do it.'

Churchill's reaction – unspoken but recorded later – was that if Pétain had already decided that an armistice was inevitable he 'ought also to have been ashamed to support even tacitly Weygand's demand for our last 25 squadrons of fighters when he had made up his mind that all was lost'.

As everyone prepared for bed, de Gaulle asked Reynaud if he could speak to him alone. The General had long believed it possible to fight on in a Breton redoubt, and now urged Reynaud again to see if they could assemble troops there, and ask Churchill to transport them, some to north Africa, some to Britain.

'Can it be done?' asked Reynaud.

'I will have a couple of hours' sleep and leave before dawn for Brittany to find out for myself,' de Gaulle offered.

Excited, but still doubtful, Reynaud asked, 'What about Weygand?'

De Gaulle replied, 'When a general has lost all fighting sense, he is replaced by someone else.'

The thoughtful hosts had discreetly placed a bottle of brandy by Churchill's bedside. General Beaufre noticed that 'it was found empty in the morning', after Churchill and his colleagues had talked over the events of this doleful evening.

Far to the north, Rommel, who had reached the sea west of Dieppe, also prepared for bed. He had spent the day at the beach.

# Wednesday, 12 June

## 1. *'The country will not forgive you'*

EARLY Wednesday morning, two young French officers in the dining-room at the Château du Muguet were quietly dunking their *croissants* in *café au lait* when their breakfast was interrupted by an apparition so astonishing that one of them upset his coffee over his neatly pressed trousers.

The double doors opened, and there, framed in the doorway, stood Churchill, dressed in a long, flowing, red silk kimono, a white belt encircling his ample stomach. His sparse hair stood on end and he was obviously in a temper.

'Uh ay ma ban?' he roared in his excruciating French.

One of the officers – startled by the sight of the Prime Minister in his night attire – jumped up and led him to an ancient bathroom. The water was barely warm, and Churchill was not mollified. He was still in a bad mood when Spears, rushing over from the military train where he had slept, reached Churchill's dressing-room. As Spears strapped his revolver to his belt, Churchill barked, 'Don't point that revolver at me!' Spears, who had been provided with an unexpectedly good English breakfast on the train, could not help wondering if Churchill's ill temper stemmed from *his* breakfast, the remains of which were on the bed – the usual French coffee-pot and rolls and butter balanced on a tiny metal tray. Churchill always enjoyed a good breakfast.

Not until the Prime Minister had sampled a breath of fresh air was he his normal self. Heavy rain had fallen during the night, but by dawn the storm had spent itself and the morning was sunny but cool. Churchill and Eden went for a short stroll and, as they returned, saw Reynaud. The three men stood together on the 'Fontainebleau' steps facing the park, talking, and at that moment Pétain tottered in their direction. Reynaud's remark was typical of the tragedy – and irony – of the political bitterness that split France.

'The old man looks buoyant this morning,' said the French Premier. 'There must be some bad news.'

The Wednesday morning meeting at Briare, which started at 8 a.m., was brief. The subjects ranged from British air support to the future of the French Navy, with Churchill remaining adamant that he could base no more fighter squadrons on French soil, though, as he pointed out, 11 squadrons, totalling from 50–60 fighters and 70–80 bombers, *were* operating from French bases.

He did not at first mention the cancelled British bombing mission from Marseille because he felt recriminations could do nothing but harm. But during the discussion on air policy the puffy-faced Air General Vuillemin 'bursting out of his jumper' suggested that it would be wiser to refrain from all bombing attacks on Italy, saying that they would only invite massive reprisals.

This was too much for Churchill who now told Reynaud how the R.A.F. bombing raid had been sabotaged by the French the previous night. The decision to bomb Italy, he said, had been made by common assent. France had been notified of the date 'well ahead of time'. Eden, who had not been told of the cancelled raid, looked straight at Vuillemin's protruding, glaucous eyes and said, 'It is regrettable that so much time has been wasted.'

Reynaud did the only thing possible. He apologised, after learning what had happened, with, as he put it, 'a sense of humiliation'. 'The French are completely in the wrong,' he said sincerely, 'and I can only express my deep regrets.'

Churchill made one last bid to persuade the French to defend Paris. 'Would not the mass of Paris and its suburbs', he asked, 'present an obstacle dividing and delaying the enemy as in 1914, or like Madrid? Would not a stand in Paris enable a counter-attack to be launched across the Lower Seine by French and British forces?'

Spears noticed that Weygand's jaws worked as if he were 'masticating a bolt'. The situation, he snapped, was totally different from 1914 (in this he was right). Then he added icily, 'It is not the intention to hold Paris.'

The 'it', Spears felt, was imperative. 'I had never heard even Clemenceau or Lloyd George use the neuter pronoun so purposefully as meaning the personal one. . . . It was so final even Churchill said nothing.'

'And what about the Breton redoubt?' Churchill asked.

Reynaud explained that de Gaulle, after only two hours' sleep, had left early for Rennes to make arrangements for the Government to move to Brittany. (Though he had to fight his way through streams of refugees, he had made good time, reaching Rennes at 10 a.m. He planned to reach Tours later in the day.)

At least that was good news. The Breton redoubt seemed to be 'on' – though Weygand did not give his official assent. As the meeting ended, Churchill returned again to the one issue that was always uppermost in his mind. He asked Reynaud, 'If the French army is forced to break off the struggle, what happens to the French fleet?' Reynaud gave an undertaking that it would never fall into the hands of the enemy, and Churchill then turned to Admiral François Darlan, the rubicund French naval chief.

'Darlan,' he said, 'you must never let them get the French fleet.'

'There is no question about that,' Darlan replied. 'It would be contrary to naval tradition and to honour.' Then he added, 'If the worst happens I am resolved to sail with the fleet to Canada rather than surrender it to the Germans.'

Certainly Churchill now realised the French were on the edge of collapse. In the hall of the château, just as he was on the point of leaving, he had a last talk with General Georges, who again insisted that the French Army could not continue the fight much longer.

Georges had the feeling that 'Mr Churchill did not dispute this point of view'. So did General Doumenc, who saw Churchill into the car taking him to Briare. Churchill said to him, 'Rest assured that whatever happens, England will never abandon France.'

At Briare airfield there was a problem. Lack of suitable petrol made it impossible for the Spitfire escort to accompany Churchill. He had to decide whether to wait or fly home in the Flamingo unescorted. The pilot assured Churchill there would be cloud most of the way, and Churchill felt that 'it was urgently necessary to get back home' as a cabinet meeting had been arranged for that evening. So they set off in the Flamingo, calling for an escort to meet them over the Channel. As Churchill's plane approached the French coast, the skies cleared. Eight thousand feet below on his right he could see Le Havre burning. And the escort had not yet arrived.

Without warning, the Flamingo dived steeply, then skimmed the waves a hundred feet above the sea, where planes are virtually invisible. The pilot had spotted two German aircraft firing at fishing boats. As Churchill remarked laconically, 'We were lucky they didn't look upwards.'

While Churchill, dodging German planes, was on his way back to London, General Spears was planning to drive to Tours and find the British ambassador, wherever he might be installed. Spears had no car, and while an officer was requisitioning one he saw Marshal Pétain in the hall of the château.

To Spears' surprise, the old man seemed in want of an audience. Usually Pétain was so reserved that at times the Britishers wondered if he were asleep, but now he buttonholed Spears and, leaning up against a wall, talked at length, giving the British general a rare insight into the workings of his mind. After discussing 'the hopeless odds the French were contending against', Pétain announced bluntly, 'An armistice is inevitable. While ministers hesitate and think of their reputation, soldiers are being killed and the land of France is being ruined. We must pay now – and pay dearly – for the anarchy we have indulged in for too long.'

It was the first time Pétain had spoken so openly in private to a Britisher since Reynaud had appointed him Vice-President, and to Spears, it was particularly painful to hear the old man speak this way. In the First World War he had been liaison officer when Pétain was grappling with the French mutineers. Spears himself had a French mother and had been brought up largely in France. He loved France as much as he loved Britain. He tried to argue that Pétain could not let France be 'absorbed into the German stomach and there quietly digested'. Did not Pétain realise that Britain, anyway, was determined to fight on? 'Surely, Marshal,' he said, 'you must fight on in Africa or elsewhere until we have developed our strength and we can make an offensive together.'

'Africa?' snorted Pétain. 'What's the use of sending recruits to Africa? There are no rifles there to arm them with.'

Perhaps a little tactlessly, Spears commented, 'You can't leave us to fight on alone.'

With 'an edge of subdued anger' Pétain retorted, 'You have left us to fight alone.' The old man thought for a few moments and then suggested that, as it was now clear that France could not continue the struggle, 'wisdom dictated that England should also seek peace' for – and he looked at Spears – 'You certainly can't carry on alone. You have no army. What could you achieve where the French Army has failed?'

Spears was not angry. In his own way he understood the old man, whose personal integrity was never in doubt. Instead he felt the real danger lay in Pétain's conviction of Britain's inevitable defeat. If only the French could be made to believe that Britain would fight on. 'Then', thought Spears, 'many of them would stand by us.' But of this, as Spears knew, there was no hope.

Reynaud, before leaving Briare, held a final discussion with Weygand; he put to him the dangers of breaking the solemn pact signed between Britain and France on 28 March. Originally a French proposal, the agreement, readily accepted by

Britain, forbade either party to embark on negotiations for an armistice without the consent of the ally.

Reynaud pointed out that if France did break her pledge, then England would have no obligations to France and 'we should be delivered, bound hand to foot, to Hitler'.

Weygand's reply so shocked Reynaud that he made a note of it immediately afterwards. 'The country will not forgive you if, in order to remain faithful to Britain, you reject any possibility of peace,' Weygand said.

## 2. *Chaos on the roads*

The politicians and generals now left Briare, making their separate ways round the loop of the River Loire to Tours – Reynaud to the Château de Chissay near Montrichard; Spears to try to locate the British ambassador; Weygand directly to the Château de Candé, temporary home of President Lebrun, where a cabinet meeting was scheduled to be held that evening. For everyone it was a nightmare journey, and even Weygand was moved enough by the plight of the refugees to remember that 'the sad spectacle made me shudder' on that afternoon drive. Spears was struck by their resignation and acceptance of the inevitable.

The flood of human beings had by now spread across the map of France, like rivers overflowing their banks each time the Germans came closer. The fear was so infectious that all caught it, and it spread to the most unlikely people.

Saint-Exupéry, the famous French pilot, described what he saw: 'I fly over the black road of interminable treacle that never stops running. . . . Where are they going? They don't know. They are marching towards a ghost terminus which already is no longer an oasis.'

Every kind of conveyance crammed the roads. Some men rode on horseback, keeping to the grass verges; others sat their aged relatives in hearses. One family had unearthed an ancient Second Empire fiacre. There was even one farm tractor pulling a trailer emblazoned with the American flag and a sign proclaiming in large letters, 'This trailer is the property of an American citizen.'

Near Nemours, Emmanuel d'Astier passed a convoy of nearly a hundred freshly painted green post-office trucks. He asked a driver where they were going, and the man answered simply, 'I don't know.' One tiny car d'Astier saw was loaded with a canoe. Following it was a small truck containing three squealing pigs, and behind that a station porter's electric trolley was towing an American car 'full of fat, ineffectual bourgeois' who had run out of petrol.

D'Astier was driving to Paris, going against the main stream of traffic, and at times had to get out of the car and brandish his revolver to force cars on to the right side of the road. He had given a lift to a strange passenger, a brothel-keeper called Bordier, who was anxious to reach Paris to take his silver out of a safe and collect money from fourteen slot-machines in the hall of his bordello. D'Astier, who had a wry sense of humour, wondered if Bordier came with him because he felt the Germans would not hesitate to steal silver but would respect the French uniform.

As d'Astier reached Paris, Joan Kay, a twenty-seven-year-old secretary, was on the point of leaving. Joan, a pretty, brown-haired young woman with blue eyes, and her sister Frances – both lovers of France and both bilingual – worked for the International Chamber of Commerce in Paris, but Frances had already left and taken a temporary job in the British con-sulate at St-Diem, in the Vosges mountains.

Now the small skeleton staff that remained was ordered to leave for Bordeaux and Toulouse, where a banker associate had offered an empty house he owned to members of the Chamber.

Joan left with a colleague, another pretty girl who owned an old but sleek racing car, in which she spent most of her free hours tearing along deserted French secondary roads – the roads tourists, and that now included refugees, hardly realised existed. 'I'm going to get to Bordeaux in two days,' she boasted.

Virginia Cowles, the American journalist, was also driving south from Paris, and found it 'difficult to believe that these were the citizens of Paris, citizens whose forefathers had fought for their freedom like tigers, and stormed the Bastille with their bare hands. Try to think of a hot sun and underneath it an unbroken stream of humanity . . . and you have a picture of the gigantic civilian exodus that presaged the German advance.'

At the same time Quentin Reynolds, another American reporter, was taking eight hours to cover fifty miles, and found that his fellow travellers 'had only one thought: move south. Move away from terror that swooped down from the skies. Move away from the serfdom that would be theirs under German rule.'

Some had already found their refuge. In Rocamadour, at the edge of the Dordogne country, forty boys were living and learning in a small hotel. They were members of the famous 'Petits Chanteurs', 'The Little Singers of Paris', a choir which had already visited America as well as most of Europe. Their leader, Father Maillet, had requisitioned the hotel and two motor coaches, so that the boys could sing to refugees or in nearby hospitals.

Joseph Pistorio, a thirteen-year-old singer,* remembers how the hotel's main salon had been turned into a rehearsal room, and the excitement of leaving home and suddenly living in what was tantamount to a boarding school. 'Sometimes we gave four concerts a day, and I can remember many audiences – particularly the refugees – in tears. But I think we helped people to forget their miseries as we worshipped God with a song.'

Rocamadour was off the beaten track, and orderly, but inevitably in many parts of France there was violence, and looting, particularly in the villages.

When the village schoolmaster at Boismorand turned his school into a hostel, the refugees burned all the books, the

* Now manager of a shoe factory at Vernon, Normandy.

blackboards, the desks and chairs – perhaps for firewood but conceivably out of pure vandalism. Outside Poitiers a gang forced their way into a wine merchant's cellars, drank all they could, then pulled the taps out of every barrel. In the village of Andonville, where 230 out of the population of 250 had fled, thieves ransacked the church, threw out the holy vessels, then smashed the altar.

That stalwart figure of law and order, the village police-man, was helpless against the tide of angry humanity unless, as one refugee put it, 'he was prepared to risk a knife in his back'. For the villages had undergone startling transforma-tions. In a matter of hours the population of Beaune-de-Rolande swelled from 1700 to 40,000. Nothing could make the unwelcome newcomers budge until the food supplies ran out. The mayor of Coudray scrupulously took down the licence numbers of private cars whose drivers forced their way into abandoned farms and threatened to report them 'when things get back to normal'. In the end someone threw a brick at him and shouted, 'We can deal with the police – if ever we find any.'

As tempers became more frayed, ugly incidents increased. At the town of Gien, not far from Briare, a honking proces-sion grew so angry when a car stalled that they overturned it into the ditch, where it burst into flames, burning three trapped children to death.

The graveyard at Gien had some strange inscriptions on makeshift tombstones, including one that read:

Grave 19: Unknown woman, aged about 40, 1 metre 65 centimetres tall, found floating in the River Loire, dressed in red, with black belt, and shiny black raincoat.

And then another, even more sinister:

Grave 84: Man of medium height, wearing black jacket and trousers, his legs and arms tightly trussed with rope.

Why was a man buried with his arms and legs bound? Was

he perhaps a German parachutist out of uniform? Not likely.
Was he an abandoned political prisoner, or the victim of a
personal grudge?

So chaotic were the roads, and so swift was the German
advance, that one English girl actually drove into the German
lines by mistake, was captured, and escaped the next day.

Margaret Juta was a volunteer ambulance-driver with the
American 'Château de Blois Ambulance Corps', and had
been told to report to a French 6th Army unit. Long before
she and two other ambulances reached it on the Marne, she
was stopped at a French surgical dressing-post, where a
doctor shouted, 'We're evacuating. Help us to carry the
wounded.' In nearby fields graves for 2000 had been dug.

The Germans were already threatening the area, and Miss
Juta helped to load wounded into her Ford ambulance, and
set off in convoy for a new hospital south of Senlis. That
hospital was also being evacuated. They set off again, a part
of a huge cavalcade of 'Red Cross vans, ambulances, "75"
guns, artillery, foot soldiers' and 'gradually it dawned on us
that we were in an army in full rout – retreat was too orderly
a word. Wagons, mules, great straining horses, three abreast,
struggled up the hill.' One moment the air was filled with
noise, then it was suddenly so silent she could hear the clear
note of a cuckoo in some nearby acacia woods. A few miles
further on, when the convoy stopped for a few moments,
Margaret Juta remembers walking into a church where
there was 'no sound but the music of a solitary airman, quite
alone, playing the organ'.

By dusk, heading south, the three American ambulances
had left the army behind and were driving along without
lights, when suddenly a red swinging lamp appeared in front
of them and, as they braked, a German voice shouted, 'Halt.'

To this day Margaret Juta has no idea where she was: 'I
saw a revolver pointing at my ear.' Three German soldiers
appeared with fixed bayonets. Another climbed into the front
seat and directed her to a field where they spent the night
under guard. As dawn broke, the guard jumped back into
the ambulance and they set off into German-held territory.

Desperately she tried to find out where she was, but all the signposts had been torn down. The convoy had reached a small town when a German motorcyclist roared in from the opposite direction, waving frantically, shouting orders she could not understand. The German in her ambulance jumped out, then shouted in English that the convoy was to return the way it had come. Obviously they were running into some local counter-attack.

The vehicles were turned around, and they then made for the edge of the town, where a German tank stood across the road. And there she saw a signpost. The main road led south to Nogent. 'All was confusion as the convoy went back on its tracks', and as they reached the cross-roads Margaret Juta branched off to the left, along a secondary road leading to Provins. Then she put her foot down, 'waiting breathlessly for someone to open fire'. No one did – perhaps because the ambulance was clearly marked with the neutral American flag. She drove right through what seemed to be a large Panzer unit, the tanks standing at regular intervals in the cornfields. A mechanised column approached her but, 'holding to the right-hand side of the road, we drove ahead as fast as the ambulances could go'.

Every German soldier in the area had apparently one objective – to reach a battle that was raging somewhere behind them. Gradually the roads and fields became emptier, the German uniforms disappeared. Then suddenly Margaret Juta saw a French helmet. A few minutes later she reached a French camp well south of Provins. It was still intact, still in French hands.

3.  *Poste Restante, Tours*

The bedlam that greeted France's most important politicians when they reached Tours was as bad as it was on the roads. Everyone who arrived was tired, yet had to spend hours trying to find people, since local newspapers were forbidden to publish the addresses of government departments in case German agents tipped off the Luftwaffe.

Even if one found a political friend, he was more likely to be fractious than accommodating, for many were being bullied by their mistresses; there were not enough first-class hotel rooms, so those ladies relegated to second-rate hotels felt the indignity a slur on their social position.

Poor Drexel Biddle, deputising for Bullitt, was trying to keep the State Department fully informed. A. J. Liebling felt that 'his despatches must have read like a play-by-play account of a man falling downstairs. Paul Reynaud . . . was beginning to succumb to self-pity. Hélène de Portes . . . wept continually and urged him to ask terms from the Germans, with whom she had dubious relations.'

Labelled by Goebbels 'the provisional, the *very* provisional capital of France', the beautiful old city of Tours seemed to be doing its best to live up to the German Propaganda Minister's denigration. When Ashworth arrived with Marguerite de Gelabert, he made straight for the Hôtel Métropole in the Place Jean-Jaurès – partly because it was near the station, but also 'because I know the manager, Roland Audemard, and if there are any rooms I'll get them'.

There were rooms, though most of the hotel had been requisitioned. But Monsieur Audemard, a tall, elderly Frenchman who sported a handsome white moustache, was doing his utmost to turn a blind eye to government demands. He explained to Ashworth: 'For every room the Government requisitions, I only get a voucher, a sort of promissory note. When will they ever be honoured? Do you think I'll ever see the money?'

'Never,' replied Ashworth. Understandably M. Audemard was happier receiving ready cash from old clients.

Ashworth's first call was at the Ministry of Information, which had been set up in a dingy grey building in the rue Gambetta, a small side street. It had once been a post office. Opposite was the equally depressing Bourse de Travail, and into these two buildings were crowded the French Ministry of Information, the censors, and – at the top of a flight of winding stairs – filthy rooms for the Press, furnished with a few ancient school-desks and 'a few packets of typing-paper'.

Other reporters were arriving. Alexander Werth drove in past an airfield that had been badly bombed, crossed the Loire bridge amidst 'a howling mob of traffic', crawled along the rue Nationale into the streets of the city, which were jammed not only with cars, buses and trucks, but also with the city's little blue tramcars, which should have been taken off the streets during the invasion of traffic.

Near the Ministry of Information Werth found a small open-air café in a square which boasted 'a 1918 war memorial – a naked lady with a helmet – and next to it a *pissotière*'. The square, he noticed, was packed with cars bearing Paris licence-plates. As he ordered a drink, he reflected, 'And so, here I am at Tours – La Touraine, garden of France, land of Rabelais, land of Descartes and all that.'

To Werth, there seemed to be only one way to pass the time: 'Crawling from one café to another, from one restaurant to another, was an all-day occupation at Tours,' he remembered later. The only place he could find to sleep was a hotel lounge (after borrowing a bathroom from a friend). A. J. Liebling slept in his car, after trying to find a spare bed in the local bordello, only to be told that all were occupied by Parisians, many of whom, as one of the ladies told him compassionately, 'are so tired that they are actually sleeping'.

Drue Tartière, the American actress working for Radio Mondiale, was luckier than Liebling, for she *did* sleep in a brothel. When the radio staff reached Tours the police requisitioned a group of brothels for them, after giving the girls two hours to vacate their rooms. There was no time to change bedclothes – nor, for that matter, many bedclothes to change – and when Drue Tartière reached her room after working several hours she found one rather prim girl called Nadine sitting stiffly in a corner of the room. 'She refused to sleep in one of these unchaste beds,' Drue Tartière remembered, 'but I was too tired to worry about who had used the beds last.' Not far away, a man who had just married spent the first night of his honeymoon on a bench on the pavement outside a café. He was a junior diplomat at the British embassy in Paris who had married after the other wives had been evacuated. His name was Donald Maclean.

Perhaps the most heartrending sight of all was the improvised arrangement for a kind of *poste restante*. Normally in France no one could collect a letter from the post office without producing identity papers. Now the staff at Tours cut through their own red tape. Outside the post office makeshift wires were strung along the railings like improvised clotheslines – complete with pegs which clipped thousands of letters to the wires in long lines. The letters came not only from France, but Belgium, Holland, even a few from Denmark. The names, the stamps varied, but each letter had one thing in common – the address: 'Poste Restante, Tours'. To thousands of hard-pressed, terrified men and women, fleeing in panic, it must have been the only address they could think of to give their friends in the last moments as they fled their homes.

Long queues moved slowly, studying the envelopes. For a few moments it reminded Marguerite de Gelabert of the Sunday-morning stamp-market behind the Champs Élysées. Every now and then a man or a woman quietly stepped forward, unfastened an envelope and took it away. The Countess noticed that people rarely tore open the cherished messages. They hugged them, stuffing them into pockets, seeming to want to read them in privacy – if there were such a thing as any privacy left in Tours.

Yet to many people the cataclysmic events taking place seemed remote. One man at least took the long view. When Liebling visited a bookshop in Tours, kept by an old man wearing a straw boater, and asked for a particular book, the bookseller said it might take up to a month to find it. Liebling politely wondered if events might not overtake the delay.

'The Germans will not succeed,' the old Frenchman reassured him, 'because they exaggerate. They lack a sense of measure. All the people that lacked a sense of measure perished, monsieur. Look at the Babylonians, the Romans of the late empire.'

Liebling left him happily – and carefully – dusting an early edition of Diderot.

Once the French ministers had found their billets and settled themselves in, they set off for the Château de Candé, head-quarters of President Lebrun, for a cabinet meeting at 7 p.m. In the great hall of the castle, built in the reign of Louis XI,* the evidence of disarray was visible. Through the windows the twenty-three ministers could see the endless procession of refugees passing by with their carts, prams or bicycles. Some even·stopped in the gardens to eat their evening meals. Others tramped past the windows to the woods beyond to spend the night hopefully hidden from aerial attack.

The effects of chaos spilled into the room itself, at this, the first cabinet meeting since the evening of 9 June in Paris. Gone was the stiff formality of the meetings in the Élysée Palace, where each minister had his specially labelled chair. Now, tired and dispirited, the ministers fell into the nearest chair or sofa. Only President Lebrun, Reynaud and Pétain, sitting at the head of the table, maintained some pretence of dignity.

None of the ministers – other than those who had been at Briare – realised how the military situation had worsened until Weygand, facing the President, spelled out the bad news with the remorseless relish he had displayed the pre-vious day. Detail by detail he refought the battle of Flanders, blaming the British for refusing to sustain the offensive he had planned in the last week of May. To cap the tales of earlier disaster, the first news of a major reverse this very day was trickling in. Rommel's Panzers, pushing up towards Dieppe, had encircled large French and British forces hoping to be evacuated from the small port of St-Valéry-en-Caux. The ships never arrived and the Allied garrison surrendered.

---

* In 1825 the château had been the scene of a 'Lady Chatterley' drama, when the owner was 'accidentally' shot dead by his wife's lover, a game-keeper on the estate.

By nightfall – at the very moment when the Cabinet was sitting – Rommel had taken 40,000 prisoners, twelve of them generals, including the entire British 51st Highland Division and its commanding officer, Major-General Fortune.

'If the battle continues,' said Weygand, 'our forces will be split up, disintegrate and fall into disarray. I will continue the resistance if the Cabinet orders me to do so, but from now on I am obliged to say clearly that a cessation of hostilities is compulsory. The war is definitely lost.'

The cabinet ministers were staggered. As one of them said, 'It was too terrible to believe.' Reynaud tried to rally them.

He had, he announced, asked Churchill through the French embassy in London to return on the following day for another meeting of the Supreme Council. Churchill had agreed. One minister asked if there were any reason why the British Prime Minister should not attend a French cabinet meeting after the Supreme Council conference. There seemed no objection, but the subject was sidetracked as some ministers cried 'French soldiers are being murdered,' or 'We must stop fighting.'

'Wait for Churchill,' pleaded Reynaud. Could they not understand, he exclaimed, that any thought of an armistice was dishonourable? And did they not realise what sort of a monster they were dealing with in Germany?

Looking Weygand in the eye, Reynaud said, 'You take Hitler for Wilhelm the First, the old gentleman who only took Alsace-Lorraine. But Hitler is a Genghis Khan.'

'If that is the case,' retorted Weygand, 'the French government has done its duty and should not be responsible for continuing the war. You say you want to hold out to the end? Well – this *is* the end.'

Reynaud could stand the defeatist talk no longer. 'Gentlemen,' he burst out, 'we are going to withdraw into the Breton redoubt if necessary. When all defence has become impossible, we shall be forced to embark on a cruiser. We shall embark under bombing, and if some of us are killed so much the better. At least this would prove that we left the soil of our country only when it was impossible for us to do otherwise.'

Weygand, on his feet immediately, said, 'The Breton redoubt exists only in the mind of the prime minister. There are no troops to defend it. It is a bad joke.'

Reynaud argued for fighting on, Pétain nodding half-asleep. By the end of the meeting, Reynaud had a majority of the Cabinet on his side. They did not know *how* or *where*, but at least they had agreed to fight – if necessary in the Breton redoubt.

Certainly that was Reynaud's intention when, at 11 p.m., he drove back under a full moon from Candé to the Château de Chissay, where he expected de Gaulle to greet him with details of the plans he had made at Quimper.

Indeed, Reynaud had even decided on a little scheme that he felt would delight his mistress, for he called in de Margerie, his *chef de cabinet*, and told him, 'There will be a lot of work needed on the Breton redoubt. I'm going to give it to a remarkable engineer, Monsieur Rebuffel.'

M. Rebuffel happened to be Hélène de Portes' father.


4.  *Paris – open city*

In Paris the eighty-one-year-old Cardinal Alfred Baudrillart, Director of the Catholic Institute of Paris, prepared to set off on his weekly visit to the Académie Française. Every Wednesday since the days of another cardinal – none other than Richelieu – the Académie had met and, though Monsignor Baudrillart was very feeble, he saw no reason for changing old habits merely because the French capital was ringed by German tanks.

His chauffeur had gone. At his age he could not drive himself, and there was no alternative transport available. The old man hobbled painfully to the Académie building, where an equally aged caretaker opened the door to allow him in. None of his colleagues arrived, but it made no difference. For two hours the aged man sat alone under the building's gilded dome, working methodically on the Académie's greatest unfinished work, the definitive dictionary of the French language.

Many people – resigned now to the worst – seem to have emulated the Cardinal, to have put into practice that most famous of all wartime slogans, 'Business as usual'. Panic had largely given way to a stoic fatalism. All knew – or thought they knew – that it could not last long but, if they could not die fighting, at least they would die working.

There were no buses but the occasional train still rumbled in the Métro. The gas supplies were fading – it was impossible to cook at times – and the electric light flickered fitfully. Many big stores were now shuttered, though on the Left Bank enough shops remained open to accommodate the reduced population. On the Boulevard St Germain an enterprising man was besieged with customers when he offered hundreds of warm winter reefer jackets at 'sale prices'. He was operating from a stall, and as soon as his barrow was empty two small boys appeared with replacements. It transpired that they were his sons, and he had bought the entire surplus stock (which nobody wanted in the hot weather) when one of the big stores on the Grands Boulevards closed.

The Ritz Hotel put up its shutters, the Crillon was barred and bolted, and Demaree Bess, a distinguished American correspondent, nearly found himself without a roof over his head when the owner of his hotel announced that he was leaving. Bess was staying at the Élysée Park Hotel at the Rond-Point des Champs Élysées, and the owner begged him to flee. Bess refused. Eventually Bess persuaded the owner to turn the hotel over to him and his friends – and stayed on.

During the night many people had noticed a peculiar acrid smell, and when Gordon Waterfield woke up at dawn he could not see out of the windows of his flat. A heavy evil-smelling fog obliterated everything. Hurriedly he dressed and walked to his office. As he crossed the Seine, the smoke was so dense he could not see from one bank of the river to the other; nor could he see across the Place de la Concorde.

He was not alone in feeling that fires had been started all

over Paris by incendiary bombs. Yet such a possibility was hard to accept – because there was no panic, no sirens, no clang of fire bells. Indeed the strange fog accentuated the silence that had become so much a part of people's lives in Paris, and because there was no traffic – and, as far as he could see, no people – it seemed as though Paris was a ghost city. Waterfield conjured up a picture of France's beautiful capital reduced to ashes 'with only the chimneys standing, like graves, to show where houses once had been'.

Some thought French troops had deliberately started the smoke pall so that trains could leave without being bombed, or to prevent refugees on the roads from being machine-gunned. Others believed the Germans had laid a smoke screen across the Seine. The truth was that the French had set fire to huge oil supplies at the Basse Seine outside the city.

By eleven o'clock the wind had blown the smoke away and the sun was shining through.*

Though few trains were running, the stations were still besieged by huge crowds, as Cecily Mackworth, the British nurse, found at the Gare Montparnasse, where for three days and nights the crowd had sat outside the station, refusing to budge, after rumours that a train would leave shortly. The 'hot and stinking' crowd blocked the surrounding streets; one woman gave birth to a child on the pavement.

A gendarme spotted Miss Mackworth's uniform and forced his way towards her. He had taken off his helmet, and Cecily Mackworth remembers 'his face was dripping with sweat and his uniform torn'. The policeman begged her to do something for the sick people, including many refugees, who had reached Paris from Belgium and Holland.

'These people aren't so much sick as starving,' she replied. 'If we don't get milk for the children a lot of them are going to die.'

---

* One of the rare cases of an intelligent scorched-earth policy. One American oil-producer was refused permission by the police to burn a quarter of a million barrels of oil at Nantes, and when a German officer discovered it he held his hands piously towards heaven and cried, 'God is with Germany!'

'But we haven't got any milk,' replied the policeman.

'There's still condensed milk in the grocers' shops,' she said, pointing to those that had been locked and shuttered when their owners departed. 'If you let me break into the stores, I'll make drinks for the children at least.'

The policeman looked startled and cried, 'I can't let you do that. It's private property.' Cecily Mackworth took a deep breath and told him that the Red Cross had power to requisition anything necessary. She suspected that he didn't believe her, but he hesitantly agreed. She chose two tough-looking men from the crowd and they forced their way into the nearest shop. She distributed the food to those nearest her, keeping the canned milk for the children. When the shop cupboards were bare, they ransacked the next one.

The roads from Paris were still crowded with cars. Among those who left on Wednesday were Waterfield and King, who had been ordered to leave for Tours. After buying some food and cognac, they packed the two-seater Ford with two typewriters, office files, luggage. Waterfield had bought a large metal drum and filled it with petrol, and this they strapped on the roof. The other office car followed with staff, and a pretty young reporter from the Agence France Presse called Joan Slocombe.

They planned to leave by the Porte d'Orléans, but the police stopped them as a new age-group of men had just been called up and were assembling there. Waterfield considered it 'unlikely they were being mobilised at this eleventh hour'. There was perhaps another reason: the youngsters, who were mainly students, would thus be placed under army discipline and not be tempted to resist the Germans.

Waterfield and King found another way out – and covered just five miles in three hours, for by now most of the cars on the road were so ancient that at least half of them had no self-starters.

One man and one woman, who left separately, soon returned – though for different reasons. British-born Mrs Ninetta Jucker, who lived near the Champs de Mars behind the Eiffel Tower, had had her first baby in March, and it never entered her head to leave Paris until a friend said, 'So you and the baby are staying behind with the Fritz?'

She packed supplies of milk and other baby food in the family Morris, said 'a dumb goodbye' to her husband Marco and set off. A few hours later, her car 'suddenly refused to obey the steering' and shot off the road into a ditch. Nobody in the car was seriously hurt – a friend shielded the baby – but the car was a write-off.

'That settles it,' declared Mrs Jucker, 'I'm going back to Paris.'

And she did. She hitched a lift, reached Paris that same evening and spent the rest of the war in France.

Around the same time Dynevor Rhys decided to leave Paris. He bought a few fresh provisions, including a *baguette* so crisp and warm, he remembers, that he broke off a piece and ate it as he walked back to the rue du Cherche-Midi to collect his rucksack.

Lacking all news, Dynevor Rhys was convinced Paris would soon become a battlefield and that his neutrality would be forgotten when the city was fighting street by street, house by house. His decision to go was reinforced when a dismayed American embassy official told him, 'Every other American is miles away by now.'

Dynevor Rhys had no car. He had sold his Chevrolet in part-exchange for a new Citroën which now looked as though it would never be delivered. So he set off on foot to meet Iris Schweppe, his studio assistant, at Vaucresson, where she lived. From there they started walking to Versailles. 'We didn't make any further plans,' Rhys remembers – which was just as well, for their expedition was short-lived. By the time they reached the outskirts of Versailles, Iris Schweppe was hobbling. 'Usually I never walked more than ten minutes from the Gare St Lazare to the office,' she remembers, 'and within a couple of hours my feet became so blistered I could hardly go any further.'

They rested against a milestone by the side of the road and peeled the grapefruit which Dynevor had put in his rucksack. All around them fleeing cars honked angrily. A little further down the road about fifty cars, top-heavy with luggage, had been pushed into the ditch and abandoned. They were wondering what to do next when a French soldier came towards them, walking rapidly in the direction of Paris. Screaming and waving his arms about, he seemed almost demented. Iris Schweppe thought he was drunk – and indeed he had had a few drinks, but not for consolation.

'Haven't you heard?' he shouted as he approached them. 'Paris has been declared an open city.'

At first they could hardly believe the man. How was it possible that such a momentous decision had been taken without anyone's knowledge?

'I've just heard it on the radio,' the man insisted; and soon others – who had also been listening in – confirmed the news.

'That's good enough for me,' said Iris Schweppe. 'I'm off home.'

'So am I,' echoed Dynevor.

What *had* happened? Roger Langeron, the Prefect of the Paris Police, made a note of the details in his diary. For several days he had known that Paris might not be defended, yet he had no choice but to prepare his force of 25,000 gendarmes for the worst. All attempts to learn any news had been frustrated; he had even telephoned Georges Mandel, Minister of the Interior, with whom he had worked as a colleague under Clemenceau for two years until 1909 – with no result.

He was in his office, 'wondering once again about the question of the defence of Paris', when General Hering telephoned. Weygand had at last managed to get through from Briare with the decision he had kept to himself so unaccountably.

Langeron at once informed his subordinates, then drove to the United States embassy. There he found Bill Bullitt ready to play his part. Bullitt, who was hardly lacking in self-confidence, had cabled Roosevelt earlier in the day with the reassuring news that 'The fact that I am staying here is a strong element in preventing a fatal panic.'

Bullitt was, in fact, preparing for his moment of destiny – a face to face meeting with the Germans. All foreign diplomats had left Paris and, being the only ambassador in the French capital, he was bound to play an important role. General Dentz, the commander of the 'Paris area', was a personal friend of Bullitt's, as was Langeron. Neither of these two stalwart and patriotic Frenchmen relished the prospect of handing over an intact Paris to the victorious Germans. Bullitt was only too eager to oblige.

One can only conjecture who – if anyone – originally asked Bullitt to act as 'host' to the German invaders. Bullitt insisted that he was asked by Reynaud, but seems to have overlooked an earlier cable to the President telling him that Reynaud had begged him to accompany the Government to Tours. Whoever made the original suggestion, there can be no doubt that Bullitt was strangely elated. One cannot help feeling, when reading his despatches to Roosevelt, that he was overwhelmed by the excitement of the unfolding drama in which he would be the central figure.

'Owing to danger of fires and mobs,' he cabled Roosevelt, 'they [the French] have decided to leave the police and the firemen of the city at their posts until the Germans shall have occupied the city fully. They have stated to me that at a given moment they will ask me in writing, as representative of the diplomatic corps in Paris, to act as guardian of the civil authority of this community during the transition from French government to German military occupation, and to treat with the general commanding the German forces for the orderly occupation of the city. I propose therefore, at the appropriate moment, to have broadcast a radio message stating that at a given time an automobile of the American embassy in Paris properly marked will move slowly along the road to Chantilly to the German line.'

It may sound like a work of fiction but, not satisfied with the real-life drama in which he was 'the hero', Bullitt was now enthralled by the idea of yet another secret code, and suggested this to the President. Once again his cable bypassed Cordell Hull and was marked 'Personal and secret for the President'. Bullitt was haunted by a phobia that Paris would be destroyed by Communists, and time after time his cables to the President were filled with woeful prognostications. Now he warned Roosevelt of the 'possible destruction of our official radio station' at the United States embassy and suggested that commercial radio stations broadcasting short-wave programmes from America to Europe should also broadcast messages for Bullitt at the end of their normal broadcasts. To make sure the isolated embassy knew which messages were for them, the announcer, suggested Bullitt, should broadcast, 'The following is from Pearl Smith to her father.' He added, 'The employment of any girl's name will signify that the message is intended for Paris.'

Bullitt no doubt honestly believed, as he explained to Roosevelt, that by staying 'It will mean something always to the French to remember that we do not leave though others do.' Perhaps it was with this thought in mind that he ended his cable on the dramatic note: 'J'y suis. J'y reste.'

## 5. *London, New York, Tokyo*

While Reynaud was struggling to bolster the more timid members of his cabinet in Touraine, Churchill was reporting on the Briare meetings to the British Cabinet in Downing Street.

On the flight home Churchill had warned Eden that he did not believe France could hold out much longer, and there seemed no point in mincing matters when he addressed the Cabinet. Sombrely he told them, 'A chapter of the war is now closing.'

He informed them frankly that Weygand was averse to continuing the struggle; that Pétain supported him. 'There can be no doubt', he added, 'that Pétain is a dangerous man at this juncture. He was always a defeatist, even in the last war.' France, he said, was nearing the end of organised resistance and 'we must now concentrate our main efforts on the defence of our island'.

Eden felt the same, but he also believed that every day, every hour gained was of immense value and strengthened the possibility – however faint – of persuading the French to realise the vital difference between an armistice and peace. He reminded Churchill that 'the former is military, the latter political. Holland has not made peace, nor Norway.'

Eden believed there was only one man who could help – Roosevelt. He told Churchill, 'If Roosevelt could go a stage further and break off relations with Germany, even without declaring war, if such an action be possible, he would perhaps give our hard-pressed French friends just that spice of encouragement they need. I do not know whether it is possible for you to telegraph personally to Roosevelt in this sense. But your relations with him are so good, and he is so heart and soul with us, that maybe the risk could be taken.'

Churchill, in a message to Roosevelt, posed the question, 'What will happen when and if the French front breaks, Paris is taken, and General Weygand reports formally that France can no longer continue? ... The aged Marshal Pétain, who was none too good in April and during July 1918, is, I fear, ready to lend his name and prestige to a treaty of peace for France. Reynaud, on the other hand, is for fighting on, and he has a young General de Gaulle, who believes much can be done.'

Telling the President that he felt many Frenchmen would want to continue fighting, he begged him to 'strengthen Reynaud the utmost you can, and try to tip the balance in favour of the best and longest possible French resistance'.

Churchill's – and Eden's – belief in the American president's support for the Allies was echoed, with concern, by one small but highly significant section of people living in America: members of the German spy network. For them the victories of the Panzers in the west had to be set against the slowly

mounting anger displayed by many Americans, not least by
the President, and on Wednesday evening Hans Thomsen,
the German chargé d'affaires in Washington, cabled Goebbels that he urgently needed between $60,000 and $80,000 to
take full-page advertisements in major American newspapers.
They would say simply, 'Keep America out of the war.' He
needed another $3000 to dine and wine fifty Congress mem-
bers interested in an isolationist policy, together with additional funds so that he could indirectly pay the fares of
isolationists to make sure they would attend the forthcoming
Democratic Convention.

Thomsen was also master-minding several ostensibly
American societies or groups, which were crude covers for
German propaganda. He personally directed the American
Fellowship Forum, the violently anti-British Flanders Hall
Publishing Company, and the Wertermann Library in New
York, all of which specialised in distributing subtle Nazi propaganda. He was making little headway, however. To justify
the demand for extra cash, Thomsen explained by cable to
Berlin, 'President Roosevelt has created an anti-German
atmosphere which can hardly be surpassed and is even beginning to penetrate into Republican circles. . . . Intervention
hysteria in influential political circles is accordingly on the
increase.' To combat this, Thomsen suggested a new strategy:
counter-measures against pro-Allied propaganda. This would
consist of attractive, easy-to-read books by famous writers,
published with the help of an established literary agent
called William C. Lengel, who was known to Thomsen. Suit-
ably camouflaged, Lengel would arrange for publication of
books by, among others, Theodore Dreiser and Kathleen
Norris. None of these authors would have the faintest inkling
why the publishers were offering him such handsome
advances.

Goebbels agreed. On Wednesday he too issued strict
orders that no criticism of Roosevelt should appear in the
German press. He himself banned publication in Germany of
a violently anti-Roosevelt speech by Lindbergh, and also
articles from the isolationist *Baltimore Sun*.

Even on the German radio, which beamed eleven hours a day directly to the United States, Goebbels concentrated on giving distorted news of the attack on France or anti-British tirades, rather than warnings to the United States. Several pro-Nazi Americans lived in Berlin and broadcast regularly to the United States. Iowa-born Fred Kaltenbach, who was in charge of this German propaganda, gave talks to 'the folks back home' dwelling on the comfortable conditions inside Germany, the weaknesses of French policy, but nothing contentious to Americans. The same orders were issued to his colleagues who had either been born in America or lived there many years – men like Professor Edward Ward, once of Hunter College, New York, and Gertrude Hahn of Philadelphia.

If the Germans were worried because the United States was becoming *too* involved, the Japanese were furious that the United States did not commit herself more to the war in Europe. The German ambassador to Tokyo, General Eugen Ott, cabled on the Wednesday: 'The present government clique had secretly hoped that as a result of Germany's action [in Europe] America would enter the war and would thus be forced to relax her pressure on Japan.'

German victories were cheered in the streets of Tokyo. There was public rejoicing at the discomfiture of the Allies. British and French books were burned in public. But Roosevelt's 'aloof' attitude did in fact force the Japanese Government to make a drastic change of plan. On Wednesday the Japanese Navy was ready and waiting to sail south, with the express purpose of invading the Dutch East Indies. At the last moment the expedition was cancelled because, as Ott cabled Berlin, 'America ... had even increased the pressure on Japan by leaving her fleet at Pearl Harbor.'

Partly because America was *not* in the European war, and therefore a 'menace' to Japan, the Japanese Government was soon forced to give way to the 'expansionists'. The new government included a man who would change the destiny of Japan: Hideki Tojo, Minister of War.

### 6. *Tours: Madame de Portes vetoes the Breton redoubt*

It took Reynaud an hour to drive back to Chissay from the cabinet meeting, and almost all the members of the Cabinet had to travel some distance to reach their destinations. Yves Bouthilier, the Minister of Finance, remembers how 'Dusk had slowly overtaken the Loire valley. In the pale June darkness each returned to his lodgings. By some singular quirk of organisation the members of the Government had been allotted separate accommodation all over the countryside, from one end of the province to the other. On leaving the meeting, each minister vanished into some vast château or manor-house, there to conceal his alarm.'

Not until Reynaud reached the Château de Chissay at midnight did he recall that he had had no dinner. Famished, he ordered some sandwiches to be sent to his makeshift office. He had hardly begun to munch them when the telephone rang. It was the first of half a dozen calls in almost as many minutes – each caller begging him to reconsider his decision to move the Government to Brittany. 'Protests came over the telephone incessantly,' remembers Élie Bois, who was in and out of the château that night. Reynaud refused to listen to their various plans. He was unaware that the callers, when they realised that he would not budge, immediately telephoned Madame de Portes.

The sandwiches were half-finished when de Gaulle – back from Rennes – strode into the room. He was delighted with the progress he had made in Brittany, and told Reynaud he was convinced that large troop formations could hold out there until British merchant vessels arrived to transport them to north Africa under the protection of French naval units. He suggested flying to London as soon as possible to discuss the shipping problems with the British. Enthusiastically Reynaud agreed. 'Quimper was Brittany. It meant the port of Brest with possible communications to England, America and north Africa.'

De Gaulle was under no illusions that the tattered French

Army could hold out in Brittany for long, but he did feel that if the *government* could retire to Quimper 'it would', in his words, 'be bound to put to sea sooner or later. Once on board ship, the ministers would in all probability make for Africa, either directly or stopping off in England. At all events, Quimper was a move towards forceful decisions.'

Already de Gaulle had worked out a plan in some detail. It was decided, as he said later, that '500,000 men, a great many officers, a considerable amount of war material, our entire navy and merchant marine, and a large part of our aviation would be transported before the end of the month with the help of British ships from France to north Africa'.[*]

With the defeatists falling over each other in their eagerness to surrender, this plan was breathtaking in conception. Both men were convinced that Britain would show much more alacrity in making shipping available than in producing fighter planes.

It had been a long day for Reynaud, an even longer one for de Gaulle, and both were tired; but they were prevented from going to bed by an extraordinary interruption. The two men were still talking when the door of Reynaud's office was flung open and the Countess de Portes stormed in.

She was furious with de Gaulle. Élie Bois, who knew them both well, gave an account of this midnight confrontation, in the course of which she shouted words to this effect: 'What is this ridiculous joke about going to Quimper? Are you anxious to make a fool of yourself? I certainly don't propose to go and sleep in Breton four-poster beds. If you want to go to Quimper, go by yourself.'

This female 'defeatist watchdog', whose 'tyranny was a measure of the demoralisation which had set in', certainly gave some such ultimatum to her lover. If Reynaud was rendered speechless – as he usually was when Madame de Portes launched a tirade – de Gaulle was not. Resolutely he defended the move as the only hope of saving, not only part of France, but also the soul of France. She refused even to answer him.

[*] De Gaulle gave these details in a speech on 12 May 1943.

Lurking in the hall was the defeatist Paul Baudouin, for long a favourite of the Countess, who had forced Reynaud to include him in his cabinet. Skilfully he argued a partial truth: the movement of German troops was unmistakably towards Brittany.

'Wouldn't it be worse than risky to take the Government there?' he asked.

De Gaulle did not agree; Reynaud seemed torn; Madame de Portes interrupted every other minute. Craftily Baudouin added, 'Brittany would have been an excellent choice if precautions had been taken to organise solid lines of defence in front of it, but now. . . .' He left the sentence unfinished.

At this juncture, according to Élie Bois, 'during the heated, confused and grotesque argument, General de Gaulle had the foreboding that a fearful mistake was being made'.

Reynaud, under the remorseless battering of his mistress – following a four-hour battering at the cabinet meeting – finally gave in. He telephoned Georges Mandel, the Minister of the Interior, at the Prefecture, and told him to cancel all arrangements. The plan was aborted that might have saved half a million men from Nazi slavery, that might have given France the will to fight on – even when all metropolitan France were lost.

There is no doubt about who was the abortionist. It was not the pitiful Prime Minister, bullied into submission. It was the Countess de Portes.

# Thursday, 13 June

## 1. *'Get that woman out of here'*

By chance – or was it good management? – the British embassy was comfortably installed in one of the most beautiful of all the castles in Touraine, the sprawling and splendid seventeenth-century Château de Champchevrier, owned by the family of the same name. Its stone front 'rested on a high, wide terrace reached by a fine flight of steps'. Beyond were vast stables, also dating from the seventeenth century, now patrolled discreetly by British military policemen with newly blanco'd belts and polished buttons. From the terrace a breathtaking view took in lawns and a wide grass avenue swathing its way between acres of woodland.

There were enough bedrooms not only for the entire embassy staff, but also for all the drivers, radio operators, cipher clerks, policemen. In the large dining-room the embassy officials took their meals at one table, the Champchevrier family at another some distance apart, invariably polite, but leaving the embassy officials strictly alone and never dreaming to presume on the good nature of the ambassador for the odd snippet of news for which they must have been yearning.

Sir Ronald Campbell had been ambassador in Paris since shortly after the outbreak of war, though he had served in the French capital previously on his way up the diplomatic ladder. An Old Etonian, he was patient, tenacious, tactful – if a trifle aloof – and General Spears, who now came to report to him on the Briare talks, found him a man of great perception.

The embassy, despite its creature comforts, was as isolated as a South Seas island. The telephone did not function and the ambassador's field radio had broken down. Since the various members of the French Government were also in depressing isolation – many of them without telephones – Campbell decided to drive to Chissay and see Reynaud. Immediately after breakfast, the ambassador set off in one car, Spears in another, driving in rain which fell steadily all morning.

Reynaud's temporary home, the Château de Chissay, was very different from Champchevrier, though as beautiful in its own way. It stood on the edge of a village, flanked by the main road, with a narrow, steeply rising drive to the inner courtyard which the happy-go-lucky military drivers found difficult to negotiate when they met cars coming in the opposite direction.

On reaching the courtyard, Spears could hardly believe his eyes. There, in front of him, was none other than the Countess de Portes, wearing a dressing-gown over her bright red pyjamas. Standing imperiously on the steps of the main entrance, she was directing the traffic with all the authority of a policeman, shouting to the drivers where to park their cars. Spears' first reaction was that 'I had not seen red trousers on French legs since 1914'. He found the evocation depressing, for it confirmed an atmosphere of unreality he had been trying to ignore since his return to France.

He walked along an open gallery until he reached a small room, in happier times the den of the owner, but now the makeshift office of the loyal and hardworking Roland de Margerie. For some reason everything in that 'cobweb-haunted' room imprinted itself on Spears' memory – the pathetic antlers on the walls, a couple of French hunting-horns black with grime, an ancient fez grey with dust, two Victorian paperweights of bizarre shapes – and standing in the middle de Margerie, whose vigorous personality was slowly blowing the cobwebs away.

Spears and de Margerie were old friends, and both were eager to talk privately, but it was not easy. De Margerie himself kept disappearing. Someone – Reynaud perhaps – would send for him. A telephone bell at the far end of the gallery never seemed to stop ringing. True, there was another telephone in de Margerie's room – an extraordinary contraption fixed so high up on the wall that he had to stand on a chair to reach it – but it had no link with the phone that rang so insistently outside. De Margerie, with Reynaud's secretary – a woman called Leca – was receiving or trying to pass on messages to a dozen or more châteaux, each with only one ancient telephone.

To make matters worse, they were time and again subjected to extraordinary interruptions when, just as they were discussing a problem, 'an ancient man with a white moustache peeped in, then, bewildered and scared, withdrew, only to return, drawn back to his lair by instinct, his previous visit perhaps forgotten'. This was the unfortunate owner, Monsieur Costa de Beauregard.

He was not the only one who interrupted. By now the Countess de Portes had dressed, and on at least four occasions, while Spears was studying reports that de Margerie had given him, Madame de Portes herself appeared in the old man's room 'whispering mysteriously'. She never spoke to Spears, though 'her glances swept across' in his direction 'like the strokes of a scythe'. Spears – somewhat naturally – took a dislike to her, and remembered her as an unattractive woman, 'certainly not pretty and quite as certainly untidy, and her voice even in an undertone made one think of a corncrake'.

She was still in evidence when Spears left de Margerie to see Reynaud and Mandel. Reynaud was installed in a magnificent panelled room dating from the Renaissance, with a large Gothic desk facing the windows, and behind him a monumental stone fireplace. The three men studied a large map of France that was spread over the floor in the centre of the room. Suddenly Reynaud was called out to take a phone call. Almost immediately Madame de Portes walked in.

**The French Leaders.** Paul Baudouin, a member of the French Cabinet, holds a brief impromptu conference with the Prime Minister, Paul Reynaud. General Weygand, who bitterly hated Reynaud, and Marshal Pétain are trying to get a glimpse of the paper.

**Above,** Winston Churchill photographed on one of his trips to France during the last days of the fighting. **Below,** Major-General Edward Spears, the liaison officer to the French Government, and General Charles de Gaulle. It was Spears who was instrumental in de Gaulle's dramatic escape to England in a British plane.

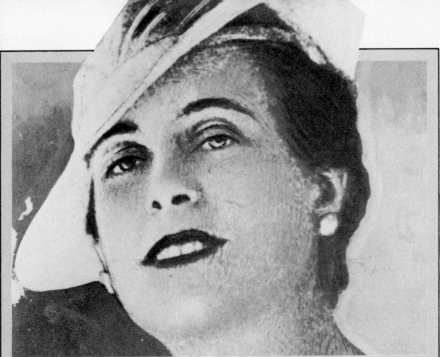

The violently anti-British Countess de Portes played an extraordinary role in the fall of France. Daughter of a Marseilles engineer, she became Reynaud's openly acknowledged mistress, and wielded immense power. **Below,** the notorious pro-German politician, Pierre Laval, wearing, as usual, his white tie ; he became one of the architects of the Vichy government.

As German troops made their triumphant entry into
Paris, many French people, like the weeping man
above, openly expressed their grief. Many had been
evacuated, like the French children, **below,** wearing
identification tags as they wait for transport.

Over large areas of France, German planes
mercilessly dive-bombed or machine-gunned
refugees on the roads ; often the only cover was a ditch
or a tree. When a German unit entered a town, it
employed a broadcasting truck **(below)** to issue
instructions from the German High Command.

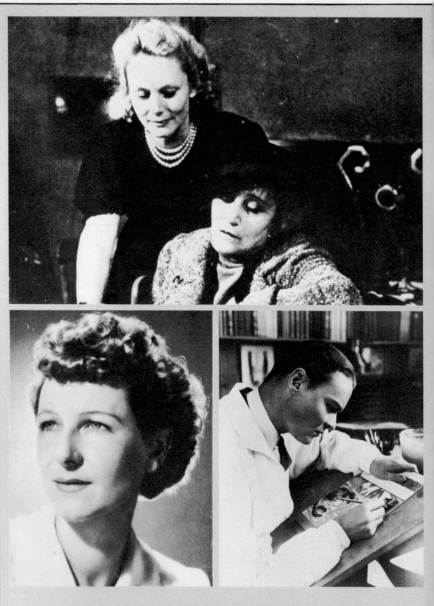

**Top,** the American actress, Drue Tartière who happened to be beside Pétain when he made his surrender broadcast. Here she is broadcasting with Colette, the French writer. Iris Schweppe **(bottom left)** was living with her mother outside Paris when the Germans marched in ; Miss Schweppe, who had German parents but a British passport, worked for Dynevor Rhys **(bottom right)**, a brilliant American photographer, with whom she tried to leave Paris.

Joan Kay **(top left)** is pictured in the grounds of the British consulate at Besançon in 1940 with the bicycle on which she escaped. The Italian-born Countess de Gelabert **(top right)** was warned by her French officer husband, before Italy declared war, to return home. She escaped by car. An English girl, Zena Marshall, spent days in a train after being bombed out of her school in Belgium. She is pictured below just before catching the train, and as she is today. She became a film star.

# POPULATIONS
## abandonnées,

# *faites confiance*
# AU SOLDAT ALLEMAND!

Within hours of the German occupation of Paris, the walls of the capital were plastered with huge propaganda posters. This one read: "Abandoned people, put your trust in the German soldier!"

Spears remembers that 'she wore the only expression I have ever seen on her face, hostile and aggressive'. She looked for Reynaud. Her eyes searched under the desk as if the Prime Minister might have been hiding there. She said nothing, but when she stepped back into the corridor, Mandel sighed and said, 'Her influence has been sinister this day. Reynaud is very subject to her influence.'

Spears was not the only one to suffer such interruptions. When Campbell had a long and private discussion with Reynaud, Madame de Portes 'popped her head round the door several times', and Spears learned that as soon as any British diplomat left Reynaud she invariably dashed in to ask what had been discussed, assailing him with a reproachful, 'What is the sense of going on?'

Compared with what happened next, this was nothing. The Foreign Office had asked the ambassador to be sure to study an urgent cable from the French embassy in London to Reynaud. The French embassy had not sent a copy to the British, perhaps to save time or because they were not sure where the British embassy was located.

De Margerie sent Leca to find it – in vain. The cable had vanished. It was not only highly important, but also highly confidential, yet there was no trace of it. De Margerie joined in the search – at first to no avail.

After some time, he had an idea. 'Wait a moment. I think I know where it might be,' he said to Spears.

His hunch was right, and a few moments later he gave the missing cable to the British general. It was crumpled up into a ball, and de Margerie was covered with embarrassment. Innocently, Spears asked, 'Where was it?'

'Chut,' replied de Margerie. 'It was in Madame de Portes' bed.'

Spears' 'mind boggled at the thought that this was the heart of France', but tragically that is just what this madhouse was – the focal point, symbolic or otherwise, of forty million people with a right to expect help. This was the nerve centre of the country, trying in vain to send out its impulses on one ancient telephone. The beaten armies of France,

bewildered refugees, the dismayed Parisians looked to the
Château de Chissay for wise counsel, saying consolingly to
their neighbours, 'Don't worry – the Government knows what
it's doing.'

Churchill arrived at the small airfield at Tours at 1 p.m. He
was accompanied by Lord Halifax, the Foreign Secretary, Sir
Alexander Cadogan, Permanent Under-Secretary for Foreign
Affairs, Lord Beaverbrook and General Ismay. Rain spattered
down. Thunderclouds threatened a heavy storm over the airport, which had been heavily bombed during the night, but
Churchill's Flamingo, with its escort of Spitfires, landed safely
among the craters. Churchill was extremely angry to discover
there was no one at the airfield to meet him and that no one
seemed to expect them. Reynaud in fact had been detained
at the Château de Chissay but had sent Baudouin to greet
the Prime Minister. Baudouin's car, however, had broken
down. It was an inauspicious beginning to Churchill's last
visit to France for four years, and 'immediately one sensed
the increasing degeneration of affairs'.

However, Churchill managed to commandeer a Citroën
from the station commander. With some of the party perch-
ing on others' knees, they drove past sodden fields to the
Prefecture at Tours, which Churchill understood to be
government headquarters. 'No one of consequence was
there,' Churchill remembered, and by now it was two o'clock
and he was famished. 'I insisted upon luncheon.'

The driver of the car was a stranger to the area. He knew
none of the local restaurants, so after some discussion
Churchill and one or two others got into the car and edged
their way forward from the neat white Prefecture, with its
ivy-clad walls, along the narrow rue Buffon, filled with
refugees.

The end of the rue Buffon opened out into a large square
in front of Tours station. It was jammed with milling, frustrated crowds, but finally Churchill spotted a sign on the right
proclaiming the 'Grand Hotel'. It was not only closed, but
the *patron* at first refused to serve them. He was exhausted,

he growled, adding, 'We are absolutely stripped. There's nothing to eat in the place.' Then he recognised Churchill. Immediately he opened the door of the glass portico leading to the restaurant and whispered that he might be able to find something to eat.

The party sat down in the empty restaurant, where they ate a 'very poor lunch'. As they were finishing, Baudouin appeared, profuse in his apologies, and then Churchill made the five-minute walk back to the Prefecture. He strode firmly past the main gate, across a gravel courtyard, through cloisters (the Prefecture had once been a convent) and into a back room facing a small and rather dreary garden. There he found Mandel on the point of starting a snack lunch. The first thing Churchill – obviously still very hungry – noted was 'an attractive chicken on the tray before him'.

The room in which Mandel was lunching was normally used by the Secretary-General of the Prefect of Police. Churchill sat down opposite Mandel, whom he liked immensely, finding him full of 'energy and defiance personified, a ray of sunshine'. With the warm, pale brown leather chairs, the Empire furniture, the bookshelves and the comforting red carpet, Churchill found only one thing lacking – an ashtray. He laid his cigar on the expensive desk* and sat down in a heavy brown leather armchair facing the desk, with the marble fireplace behind it, his back to the bookshelves. He talked to Mandel, who ate his chicken with his fingers, until Reynaud – who looked 'depressed' – arrived with General Spears and the British ambassador.

The first thing Churchill did was to ask Spears about Baudouin.

'He's doing his damnedest to persuade Reynaud to throw up the sponge. He's working on behalf of Pétain and Weygand.'

Spears remembered, 'Churchill growled that he had gathered as much, and that Baudouin had ruined an already inadequate meal by seasoning it with an outpouring of oily defeatism.'

* The cigar burn on the desk is still a treasured memento in the same room.

So much time had been wasted that it was decided to hold the meeting at the Prefecture instead of making the journey to the Château de Candé. Mandel picked up his luncheon tray and carried it out of the room. Reynaud took his place behind the desk. It was now 3.30 p.m., and the meeting of the Supreme War Council started.

Outside it was drizzling.

The composition of the nine people, crowded into the inconveniently small study facing the garden, was extraordinary: seven Britishers and two Frenchmen. Even more extraordinary was that the two Frenchmen – Reynaud and Baudouin – came from opposing camps, one hoping to carry on the fight, the other plotting for a dishonourable peace. In fact Reynaud had deliberately not invited the defeatist Weygand, though Weygand had been asked to wait in an anteroom in case the delegates wished to call on his military expertise.

Baudouin kept his eyes on Reynaud, even when Churchill was speaking. He made copious notes, obviously for Pétain and Weygand.

Spears was horrified at the change in Reynaud. On the previous day at Briare he had been in good humour, full of fight, but now, 'whatever the reason, he had radically changed ... his colour, his manner, his whole attitude, was different'. He found it difficult to control his nervous tic.

At Briare Churchill had exuded goodwill and sympathy. Now it was 'more like a business meeting'. Churchill, though sympathetic, looked stern and concentrated, watching Reynaud more carefully as though anxious to detect any subtle shades of meaning in his words.

Reynaud spoke first, giving a résumé of Weygand's latest report, which outlined the desperate situation of the French Army, leading Weygand to conclude again that 'it was necessary to ask for an armistice forthwith'. Reynaud pointed out that the majority of the Cabinet did not support the view, 'but', he added, 'if Paris is taken, and it is difficult to see how this will not happen, the question will inevitably be raised again'.

There was only one hope, he declared – and that was immediate aid from the United States. Reynaud was opposed to an armistice, but some of the cabinet ministers – he did not name them – had instructed him to ask what would be Britain's attitude if France had to sue for peace. They were saying, Reynaud added, 'Why carry on when the certain result will be the occupation of the whole of France?' The attitude of the Pétainists was that the Government could leave to fight from north Africa but the people of France could not. 'The Nazis would corrupt them and France would cease to exist.'

In view of this appalling prospect, would Britain release France from the solemn pledge not to engage in a separate peace? Could Britain understand that France 'had nothing left'?

The British delegation was stunned. At Briare, Churchill had admitted the possibility of a *military* capitulation, but suing for peace was a very different matter. Reynaud had spoken so earnestly, his attitude was so different from that of the previous day, that it was difficult for them to decide whether he was merely explaining the point of view of the Pétainists, or whether he was coming round to their point of view.

For a long time Churchill said nothing, looked at no one. Spears, watching him, felt that 'he appeared to be at his fiercest'. What was worrying Churchill, of course, was not so much that France might sue for an armistice – he expected this to happen shortly – but that Reynaud had given no hint of continuing the fight from overseas.

If Churchill looked stern to Spears, Halifax 'had never taken his eyes off Reynaud. His good hand, clasping his artificial one, was under his chin and ... his expression seemed slightly tinged with scepticism.' Beaverbrook 'did not hide his feelings' as he leaned forward in his chair, flushed, thinning hair untidy.

Finally Churchill spoke. Britain realised only too well the agony endured by France, and England was in no doubt that her turn would come. 'The British people have not yet felt the German lash, but they do not underestimate its force. This in no way deters them. Far from being cowed, they are looking forward to thrashing Hitler. They have but one thought, to win the war and destroy Hitlerism.' Churchill continued, 'No risk, however formidable, will hinder us, we will fight, and that is why we must ask our friends to fight on too. We ask you to fight on as long as possible ... down to the sea, then, if need be, in north Africa.'

Churchill, speaking with deep emotion, asked Reynaud, 'Does that answer your question?'

Reynaud hesitated, then with a slight sarcastic edge to his voice he replied, 'My question was not what England would do.' His question had been that if a French government, which would not include himself, told the British Government that it could fight no longer 'would Great Britain agree that, France having nothing further to contribute to the common cause, she would release her from the agreement and allow her to conclude a separate peace'.

Reynaud now put Spears in mind of a ventriloquist's dummy, 'voicing the views of whom? Pétain? Weygand? Could it be Madame de Portes?'

'Under no circumstances', replied Churchill, 'will Great Britain waste time in reproaches and recriminations. But that is a very different matter from becoming a consenting party to a peace made in contravention of the agreement so recently concluded.'

The conference – edgy, to say the least – was not made any easier by occasional faint sounds of a woman's voice shouting that percolated into the conference room from the ante-room and courtyard. The Countess de Portes had followed Reynaud from Chissay and kept asking to see Baudouin. On the two occasions when Baudouin popped out of the room to speak to her, she insisted that he 'tell Paul we must give up, we must make an end of it. There must be an armistice.' When she demanded to see Baudouin a third time, an angry *huissier* hissed at Baudouin, 'Get that woman out of here. If you don't I'll do it myself.'

Madame de Portes was not the only one to be angry. An

impatient Weygand finally lost his temper, and those in the conference room could hear him shouting, 'They sit with their arses on their chairs, and don't give a damn that all this time the French Army is being massacred.'

Churchill suggested a recess and, in his inimitable French, growled, 'Dans le jardin.' The seven Britishers trooped out through the french windows and into the rectangular plot of the 'official garden'. In the centre of the badly mown lawn was a small pond with a willow tree drooping over it, and laurel bushes edged a gravel path which ran round the four sides of the lawn. The gravel was muddy, steaming after the drizzle. The leaves dripped. It was difficult for more than two men to walk abreast without brushing against the branches, thus getting wet. Everyone seemed stunned by what Reynaud had said. All felt that Churchill was right to refuse to countenance a separate peace.

There was, however, one item of business to be disposed of before the serious talking started. Solemnly the seven Britishers lined up by the side of the path, Churchill nearest the french windows, and relieved themselves. It was, as de Margerie remembers, 'quite a sight'.

After forty-five minutes of walking round the garden, the dynamic Beaverbrook summed up the problem crisply. 'We are doing no good here,' he said. 'Let's get along home.'

Meanwhile Reynaud and Baudouin went into the next room to tell Herriot and Jeanneney, the two vice-presidents,* what had happened. Mandel was also there. Both vice-presidents were horrified. The tears streamed down Herriot's face as he cried, 'I can't accept that M. Reynaud should have allowed it to be understood that one day France will sue for a separate armistice.' Mandel was so angry that he tried to go into the garden, crying, 'I must see Churchill at once. It is unthinkable that matters be left as they stand.'

Meanwhile de Gaulle had arrived. He, too, was furious – because he had not been invited to attend the conference. He had heard about Churchill's visit by chance and rushed

---

* Édouard Herriot was leader of the Chamber of Deputies, Pierre Jeanneney was leader of the Senate.

over, 'fully alive to the alarming possibilities of this unexpected meeting' which Reynaud had not mentioned to him
even though the two had talked earlier in the day.

De Gaulle asked Reynaud point blank, 'Is it possible that
you are thinking that France will ask for an armistice?'

'Certainly not,' retorted Reynaud. 'But we must give the
British a shock, to get more help out of them.'

The Britishers trooped in from the garden. As Churchill
spoke, de Gaulle got the feeling that he was by now recon-
ciled to a French defeat, but was bargaining the release of
the French from their agreement against the future of the
French fleet. Churchill, he noted, talked at first in an even,
sad voice; but suddenly, 'moving on to the question of the
fleet, he became very precise and very firm'.

Churchill was equally firm on one other point: German
Air Force prisoners of war. By now more than 400 had been
shot down, mostly by British fighters, and were being held in
French prisoner-of-war pens. Since it took much longer to
train a pilot than to build a plane, Churchill was concerned
at the prospect of their being liberated by the advancing
Germans, and asked that they should be sent immediately to
Britain for safe custody.

Reynaud agreed. 'What is necessary will be done immediately,' he promised, and issued the orders later that day.

Reynaud's manner had dramatically changed. His voice,
Spears noted, 'was more natural, easier, more confident'.
Churchill's earlier suspicions that Reynaud was wavering
began to subside. So did those of Spears, who had been
aghast at Reynaud's temerity in suggesting a separate peace,
but who now felt that 'I must have been right in thinking he
was putting the case of the defeatists to get Churchill's reaction. Having found him completely firm he is building on it.'

Churchill had one last point to make. It was urgently
necessary that Reynaud should launch one last appeal to
Roosevelt. Britain would send a similar appeal on France's
behalf. 'If he advises a continuation of the struggle,' said
Churchill, 'he will doubtless back this advice with new
commitments and that may be very important.'

As the meeting was ending around 5 p.m., Reynaud turned to Churchill and said that, despite the black news, he still had complete confidence in victory. 'If we were to lose confidence in this,' he added, 'I should lose all reason for living.'

As the delegates dispersed, Élie Bois asked Reynaud if it were true that France was contemplating an armistice.

'Surrender? Never!' cried Reynaud scornfully.

Churchill also met Herriot and Jeanneney. Herriot remembered being ushered into the room in the Prefecture where Churchill was sitting, his back to the garden, the desk in front of him, 'with tears in his eyes'. 'I entreated him with all my power not to abandon unhappy France.' Churchill was impressed by the manner in which both these French patriots spoke with emotion about fighting on to the death.

As he was about to leave, Churchill heard a voice cry, 'Monsieur Churchill! Monsieur Churchill! I wish to speak with you.'

Churchill, 'hat rammed on head', cigar stuck in his mouth, pretended he had heard nothing as he made for his Citroën.

Again the voice demanded, 'Monsieur Churchill! My country is bleeding to death. I have a story to tell. You must hear my side of it. You must.'

It was Madame de Portes.

The outer courtyard of the Prefecture was crowded with journalists demanding an interview with Churchill, but this was no time to meet the Press. He did, however, see one person he knew – Madame Geneviève Tabouis, the distinguished French columnist, for whom he had a great admiration. Madame Tabouis was remarkably well informed. For one thing she and Hélène de Portes – then a schoolgirl called Hélène Rebuffel – had both attended the Convent de l'Assomption in the rue de Lubeck in Paris and had kept in touch ever since.

Madame Tabouis' column was appearing weekly in England at the time, and Churchill told Reynaud, 'Get her out if you can. We need her.'*

* Reynaud did. Madame Tabouis, who was still writing her column when the author lunched with her in 1975, escaped from Bordeaux.

Though Churchill refused to talk to the Press, Baudouin unfortunately did – with disastrous results, for he deliberately played on Churchill's love of speaking French whenever possible. Several times while Reynaud had been speaking during the meeting, Churchill, without waiting for a translation, had nodded and grunted, 'Je comprends' – meaning, of course, that he understood, there was no need to translate. But in certain contexts 'je comprends' can convey the sense of 'I agree', and no sooner had the conference ended than de Gaulle grabbed General Spears in a corner of the Prefecture just as Churchill was leaving for the airfield. Baudouin, he said, was telling journalists that 'Churchill had shown comprehension of the French situation and would understand if France concluded an armistice or a separate peace'.

Was it possible, de Gaulle asked, that Churchill would say a thing like that? Spears replied that Baudouin was lying. What Churchill had said was, 'Je comprends', meaning only 'I understand what you say', rather than 'I understand what you must do' which could have indicated tacit agreement.

'Well,' said de Gaulle, 'Baudouin is putting it about that France is now released from her engagement to England. It is unfortunate.'

Churchill was already on his way to the airport. Spears cried, 'I'll see if I can catch the Prime Minister before he leaves,' and jumped into his car and 'pelted after the English party'.

The motors of the aircraft were already revving up by the time Spears reached the runway, which was scarred with bomb craters against a background of smashed, twisted hangars. Over the noise of the engines he shouted his news to Churchill, whose reaction was typical.

'*Comprendre* means "understand" in French, doesn't it?' Churchill beamed at Spears. 'Well, when for once I use exactly the right word in their own language, it is going rather far to assume that I intended it to mean something quite different. Tell them my French is not so bad as that.'

Later in the day, the French Cabinet, meeting in the spacious drawing-room on the ground floor of the Château de Candé, opened on a sour note. To begin with, it was drizzling, and the dripping trees in the grounds 'cast a veil of melancholy over the horizon'. Then the meeting had originally been called for 3 p.m., and later postponed to 5 p.m., but several of the ministers had not been notified. In any event, even those who arrived at five still had to wait for an hour until Reynaud arrived with Georges Mandel. Finally – where was Churchill? It had been agreed that Reynaud would produce him, and everyone had been looking forward to meeting the British war leader who they understood had been invited to give his views. Certainly that had been Reynaud's promise at the previous day's meeting. Had Churchill snubbed the politicians?

Reynaud, with more than a touch of embarrassment, offered the lamest excuses. He explained that he had no control over Mr Churchill's movements, and that 'Churchill had been in a hurry to get back to England'.

This was nothing more than a patent fib, for, as Churchill remembered later, he would have been 'very willing' to attend the cabinet meeting, 'no matter how late we had to fly home', but 'we were never invited; nor did we know there was to be a French cabinet meeting'.

The most charitable view one can take of Reynaud's excuse is that under the stress and strain, and with the delay in meeting Churchill, he had forgotten to ask him. The less charitable interpretation (for which there is some evidence) is that Madame de Portes and Baudouin, who met several times during the morning, were afraid that Churchill's oratory, his fire, his determination might stiffen resistance among the waverers, and so they persuaded Reynaud that it would be unwise to allow Churchill to gain too much insight into French internal affairs. Certainly Reynaud carefully skated over the questions in his memoirs.

Churchill missed nothing, though his presence might have lent a sense of dignity to the shameful travesty of a cabinet meeting which followed, with Reynaud insisting that he was going to send a final appeal to Roosevelt, and Weygand snapping back, 'That is a mere gesture. Battles are won with men, not gestures.'

It was at this moment that Reynaud made the unfortunate remark that the military did not want to fight. Weygand jumped to his feet, crying furiously, 'It is painful to see a government apparently quite unresponsive to the efforts of an army that is being torn to shreds by shelling and bombing that it cannot return.'

'Anyway,' said Weygand, announcing his first specific act of disobedience, 'should the Government quietly decide to take cover in Africa, I would refuse to leave the soil of France.'

This was not just defiance. It gave the Pétainists clear proof that they could count on the Army. It also gave the cowards and waverers the excuse they were lacking, for, as the Minister of State, Yves Ybarnégaray, cried as he decided to change sides, 'The military leaders have spoken.'

The ineffectual President Lebrun tried to calm the quarrelling ministers. Then came a dramatic interruption. An officer entered the ornate sitting-room and whispered to Weygand. The parchment-like face crinkled with excitement, the eyes blazed hatred, as he rose and cried that a Communist government had been set up in Paris and Maurice Thorez, its leader, was being installed at the Élysée Palace. The news seemed to infuse him with a perverse sense of pleasure.

Immediately the meeting erupted in bedlam. Weygand shouted above the din that he had the information from the French Ministry of Marine – a reliable source – and that he had warned them this would happen all along. Like General Trochu, who capitulated hastily to the Prussians in 1871 because of a left-wing threat, Weygand was more terrified of the Communists than of the Germans. 'Remember Russia in 1917,' he cried. 'Some French army divisions must be kept intact to maintain order.' Like millions stumbling blindly on the road to defeat, Weygand was haunted by only one vision: the memory of the Popular Front.

President Lebrun demanded silence. The news was grave. Would ministers please keep calm. One man *was* calm – the stalwart and loyal Georges Mandel, who had been sitting so quietly throughout the turmoil that Baudouin thought him a pillar of contempt.

'M. Le President need have no fears,' Mandel announced quietly. 'Thorez will not sleep in your bed tonight.'

'Prove it!' shouted several members.

'It just happens', said Mandel, 'that I was talking to the prefect of police just before the meeting, and he told me nothing of this.'

Mandel was, of course, Minister of the Interior, but even so Weygand shouted at him, 'Do you doubt my word?'

Mandel, looking at the General with contempt, said he would telephone Paris. The meeting was adjourned while Mandel sought confirmation – or a denial.

Mandel telephoned directly to Roger Langeron, the Paris prefect, who noted the entire conversation in his diary.

'Anything new?' Mandel asked him.

Langeron replied that everything was as normal as could be expected.

Mandel persisted, 'No incidents?'

'None,' replied Langeron, puzzled. 'Why?'

'We've been told there have been several incidents in Paris. Would you like to have a few minutes to check? Then you could phone me back.'

'If you like,' replied Langeron, 'but there's really no need. I'm in complete control of the situation. There are no incidents of any sort.'

'Well,' said Mandel, 'I'll tell you why I asked. Someone important told us a few minutes ago that the communists are in control of Paris and that Thorez is in the Élysée Palace.'

Langeron was stupefied. 'Who told you that?' he exclaimed. 'He's the victim of a hoax. You can tell him that, though Paris is in anguish, Paris is calm.'

'Thanks,' said Mandel. 'That's good enough for me.'

Hanging up the telephone, Mandel returned to the conference room, looked Weygand in the eye and said contemptuously, 'People should check their information before they communicate it to the government.'

Weygand, beside himself with excitement, and perhaps because he hated Mandel in particular, suddenly jumped up and stalked towards the door, shouting, 'I'm leaving! A minister is laughing at me.'

Lebrun, trying again to keep some dignity and order, cried, 'Really! No one has laughed. Everyone is saddened by your report. Pray continue.'

Weygand, stamping out of the room, made no effort to keep his voice lowered when he bumped into Max Brusset, Mandel's *chef de cabinet*. 'They're mad,' those inside the conference room heard him shout. 'They have understood nothing. It will be necessary to arrest them.'

Pétain, his eyesight now so weak that he had to move from the conference table towards the window to gain the advantage of a little extra light to read a prepared statement, declared that the only possible course was to sue for an armistice. There could be no question of a prolonged military resistance, nor could there be any question of setting up the Government in north Africa. In his quavering voice he declared, 'It is impossible for the government to emigrate, to desert, to abandon the territory of France. The duty of the government, regardless of what happens, is to remain in the country.'

And then he revealed what was perhaps the key to his character.

'We must look forward to France's redemption much more from the soul than from a reconquest of our territory by allied guns at some unforeseeable future date,' he said. 'We should accept the suffering that will be imposed on the nation and its sons. France's renaissance will be the fruit of this suffering.'

This was really the moment when Pétain took over the 'leadership' of the defeatists from Weygand. One may wonder why Reynaud did not at this juncture decide to dismiss both men, or at least Weygand. He himself felt later, 'Weygand's attitude to the council of ministers would have completely justified the Government in relieving him of his command.' De Gaulle had several times urged Reynaud to dismiss both Pétain and Weygand, and Mandel had supported him. But Reynaud had weighed this drastic action against the fact that they were perhaps the only two men in France who were genuinely venerated as being above politics. After the initial mistake of appointing them, he dared not dismiss them.

It was getting late. The waning afternoon sun in the château grounds had given way to dusk, then darkness, as the unseemly clash continued. There was one other decision still to be taken – should the Government move to Bordeaux? That decision was made easier for the ministers by the Germans.

Without warning, the windows started to shiver, the frames to rattle, as a series of explosions made the old château shudder. War was suddenly transformed into reality. The German Air Force was bombing Tours.

It took only a few moments to decide to drive to Bordeaux the following morning, for, as President Lebrun remembers, 'It was like a summons bidding us to be on our way.'

Late that night, a disillusioned de Gaulle, with much bitterness of heart, sat down to write a letter of resignation.

Everything had gone wrong for the man blooded in his first big political appointment. Reynaud, he felt, had let him down. He had gone back on his word that he would replace Weygand with Huntziger after their decision at Orléans; his promised letter of appointment never materialised – no doubt because the Countess de Portes hated Huntziger as much as she hated de Gaulle. Indeed, de Gaulle had told his aide, Lieutenant de Courcel, earlier in the evening, 'I think I am wasting my time. She's going to convince Reynaud to give in.' This was after he had seen the Prime Minister's office turned into a 'petticoat mockery' when Madame de Portes overruled their plan – *his* plan – to move the Government to Brittany. And finally, at the morning meeting with Churchill, de Gaulle had been appalled that Reynaud could even discuss the possibility of a surrender with the British Prime Minister. There seemed only one honourable course left open to him. His uppermost thought was that 'my presence in the cabinet is going to become an impossibility'. Carefully he penned the letter, then sealed it himself, planning to send it later to the Château de Chissay.

In this tangled story of ifs and buts, it is strange to reflect that had de Gaulle's letter reached Reynaud – and certainly had Madame de Portes read it – de Gaulle might have sunk into oblivion. With the Government in disarray, the chances of de Gaulle – with no official status, no ministerial portfolio – ever reaching England would have been much slimmer than the likelihood of his immediate arrest by Weygand, who had already told some of his cronies that de Gaulle should be behind bars.

But for once the normally taciturn general was depressed enough to want to share his fears and doubts, and he told one of his aides of his intentions. The role of junior officer does not include arguing with a superior who is also a cabinet minister known for his stubbornness, but this aide, after listening, was seized with a brilliant idea. Secretly he telephoned Georges Mandel at the Prefecture.

Mandel telephoned de Gaulle and, without mentioning the letter, on the pretext of discussing last-minute arrangements for going to Bordeaux, asked the General if he could spare him a few minutes. Unsuspectingly, de Gaulle went straight to Mandel's office.

We have only the briefest version of what transpired at this historic meeting between a general then virtually unknown, and a great Jewish patriot who was later to be murdered by the Vichy government.* But we do know, from de Gaulle, that Mandel came straight to the point, speaking 'in a tone of gravity and resolution'.

Patiently Mandel went through the various points that had so disgusted de Gaulle. Of course de Gaulle was right, he said, to believe that the only way to save the honour of France was by continuing the struggle from north Africa. But, he insisted, it was because of this that de Gaulle must not be foolish. He was needed desperately and he must stay.

* On Laval's orders on 7 July 1944.

'Who knows', said Mandel, 'whether we shall not finally get the government to go to Algiers? In any case, we are only at the beginning of a world war. You will have great duties to fill, General.' Then, looking straight at the downcast de Gaulle, Mandel added one profound thought, 'And you will have the advantage of being an untarnished man.'

Perhaps it was this last sentence that gave de Gaulle the necessary resolution. For he admitted later that 'on this argument, perhaps, depended, physically speaking, what I was able to do later on'.

It was very late, and there were many preparations to make before the dawn start to Bordeaux. Suddenly the man who would one day lead France stood up, towering over the seated figure of Mandel.

A man of few words, he held out his hand and said simply, 'I'll tear up the letter right away.'

2. *'The hole in the ground'*

The Cabinet had been convened for 10.15 p.m. After a quick dinner Churchill made his way to the nerve centre of the war, the forty-feet-square underground cabinet-room, with its red girders supporting the ceiling. It was the heart of a huge complex of bomb-proof rooms covering six acres 150 feet below Great George Street, where 500 people worked in what they affectionately called 'the hole in the ground'.

Some ministers had gathered in the nearby waiting-room, which was also used as an officers' mess. It did not boast a bar, but bottles of whisky and brandy stood on a table, with a sink for washing glasses hidden behind a curtain.

Churchill sat down on a comfortable old brown wooden chair that he had specially asked for, the only wooden chair permitted in the room because of fire hazard. The ministers made for their metal chairs, each one with a place card in front on the baize-covered table. Churchill's place at the head of the table was marked by an old carved dagger someone had sent him, and of which he said jokingly, 'I'm keeping it here until Hitler is brought before me.' Behind Churchill's chair was a fire bucket – always placed on the same spot, with the care of a spittoon in a Western bar, so he could, with unerring aim, throw his cigar butts into it.

Quietly, Churchill presented his report on the visit to France. Not until the discussion ended did he introduce a note of his own, when he described the moment Madame de Portes tried to buttonhole him. He told the Cabinet in his most sonorous voice, glasses slipping down his nose, 'Paul Reynaud returned to Tours with the Countess de Portes.' Then with a puckish touch he added, 'She had comfort to give him that was not mine to offer.'

The Cabinet was still sitting when Kennedy arrived at Downing Street with a copy of President Roosevelt's belated reply to Reynaud's appeal of 10 June. In it Roosevelt went to great lengths to tell Reynaud how impressed he was by his declaration that France would continue to fight, even if it meant withdrawing to north Africa, and stressed that 'it is most important to remember that the French and British fleets continue mastery of the Atlantic and other oceans, also to remember that vital materials from the outside world are necessary to maintain all armies'.

These 'vital materials', Roosevelt promised, would go to France. 'This government is doing everything in its power to make available to the allied governments the material they so urgently require, and our efforts to do still more are being redoubled.'

Churchill was jubilant. With a flourish he read the cable to the cabinet ministers and declared, 'If Roosevelt will consent to have this published, it pretty well commits America to war.' The message, as he read it, contained two specific points – the promise of material aid, and the call to go on fighting from north Africa – which were 'tantamount to belligerence'. But the need for publication was urgent.

Turning to Kennedy, he asked him to telephone Roosevelt and explain this point of view. Alas, unknown to Churchill,

Roosevelt, when sending the message to Reynaud via the American embassy in Tours, had warned ambassador Biddle, 'When this message is delivered [to Reynaud] it must be made entirely clear that the message is personal and private and not for publication.' (In fact conditions were so chaotic in France that Reynaud did not receive the message until twelve hours after Churchill.)

Consequently, Roosevelt was flabbergasted when Kennedy came on the telephone between 6 and 7 p.m. Washington time with Churchill's request for immediate publication. Such a possibility had never entered his mind. Kennedy, whose faith in an Allied victory was virtually non-existent, had little difficulty in discouraging any change of mind on his President's part by telling him (as he later confirmed by cable), 'The danger of publication of your note to Reynaud as I see it is that Churchill sees in your note an absolute commitment of the United States to the Allies, that if France fights on the United States will be in war to help them if things go bad at some later date.'

Roosevelt's reaction was an immediate cable to Kennedy: 'My message to Reynaud not to be published under any circumstances . . . it does not commit this government to the slightest military activities in support of the Allies. This plan was carefully avoided in drafting the message to Reynaud . . . if there is any possibility of a misunderstanding, please insist that Churchill at once convey this statement to the appropriate French officials.'

With hindsight it is of course easy to understand how Churchill, clutching at straws after the wretched meeting at Tours, read more into Roosevelt's cable than it promised. He was so excited by it that, even before receiving Roosevelt's embargo on publication, he dashed off a cable to Reynaud – who had not yet received the original and must have been as mystified as Roosevelt had been. In part, it said:

If France on this message of President Roosevelt's continues in the field and in the war, we feel that the United States is committed beyond recall to take the only remaining step, namely, becoming a belligerent in form as she already has constituted herself in fact. I do beg you and your colleagues, whose resolution we so much admired today, not to miss this sovereign opportunity of bringing about the world-wide oceanic and economic coalition which must be fatal to Nazi domination. We see before us a definite plan of campaign, and the light you spoke of shines at the end of the tunnel.

At the same time Churchill sent a personal cable to Roosevelt thanking him for his 'magnificent message' but warning him that the French were 'very nearly gone' and that hope could only be sustained 'by American intervention up to the extreme limit open to you'.

Long after these messages had been despatched Kennedy brought Churchill the President's refusal to allow his message to Reynaud to be published. Though Roosevelt's decision was the only possible one, Churchill was bitterly disappointed – so disappointed and so angry, in fact, that, when the anti-British Kennedy asked him if he would explain the position to Reynaud, Churchill refused pointblank. Churchill always treated Kennedy with the scrupulous politeness due to a person one thoroughly dislikes, but on this occasion he warned the American ambassador bluntly of the 'disastrous effect' on French morale if the French felt that 'the President is now holding back'.

The entire cabinet was equally dismayed. General Leslie Hollis, Military Secretary to the War Cabinet, who spent the rest of the night in the 'hole', remembers leaving the next morning and thinking, 'with a shock, that hardly anyone in the crowds of people out in the sunshine – the clerks, the typists in their summer frocks, the shoppers – realised what fearful danger faced Britain'.

### 3.  *Paris – the last day of freedom*

In Paris it was the last day of freedom. To Dynevor Rhys, who had lived there so long, the realisation that at last the unthinkable was about to happen was almost too strong to digest. 'I couldn't take it in,' he remembers. 'I knew that as an American I really didn't have anything to fear, to worry about – and yet the thought of Germans marching up the Champs Élysées – it seemed impossible.'

Langeron made the rounds of his central police stations early in the morning. His faithful police, he felt, had suddenly taken on a new kind of quiet strength, as though the realisation that they alone stood between the Germans and the people of Paris had given them an added stature. A warm-hearted patriot of the old school, Langeron waited with a fatalistic resignation for 'the moment when we will be separated from the rest of the world'.

In the United States embassy, Bullitt was also waiting – for the moment when he would have to treat with the Germans. If Langeron's prefecture was a kind of semi-neutral territory, where duty would lie in helping both sides to save lives, the handsome white American embassy building was invested with an even stranger quality, that of an oasis, the only spot in all Paris where war in a sense did not encroach. Of course the war had fundamentally changed the functions of the embassy staff, yet even so they were not at war and, as one Frenchman put it, 'through no fault of their own, they were as safe from violence as the Romans in their ringside seats at the Colosseum'.

When Henri Malherbe of the *Daily Mail* (who had returned from Tours) walked along the deserted rue Boissy d'Anglas, turned right at the Concorde into the Avenue Gabriel and looked up at the Stars and Stripes, he remembers thinking, though without a trace of envy, 'I suppose that when the Germans occupy Paris the Americans in that building will still get their normal food and cigarettes, clothes and drinks.'

The city was eerily quiet, hushed with the same gravity as a house where the family is waiting for a loved one to die. Emmanuel d'Astier, who reached the capital at dawn (with his passenger Bordier, the pimp), was struck more than anything else by 'the strange silence of the city'. He missed the rumble of the Métro beneath his feet. There were no buses or taxis. Even in the occasional café that still remained open, people talked in whispers. He drove straight to Les Invalides, where he had been told to report. An officer told him, 'We are expecting them at any moment.'

All his friends had left. Even their concierges, those courtyard spies, had departed. Near the Opéra he dropped Bordier, after arranging to meet him later. Then he went to his home. The house was empty, but on the stairway he heard a woman sobbing. It was Lambertine, the maid, who clung to him weeping, 'I've been left behind, I've been left behind.' D'Astier promised to take her with him when he left to rejoin his unit. He looked around 'for some talisman to take'. Books had always been his passion and he stuffed six in his pockets, then set off with Lambertine to meet Bordier, who was waiting for him at a café miraculously open in the rue Richer. Bordier had found a half-sized stencilled news-sheet; 'it looked like the newspaper of a besieged city'.

One of the last to leave Paris was Pierre Lazareff, the dynamic editor of *Paris-Soir*. As a Jew he knew he would be doomed if he remained, but he took one last look round the empty offices. In the hall he saw Joseph Schliess, the liftman, who was supposed to have left two days previously.

'What on earth are you doing here, *mon vieux*?' Lazareff asked. 'Come on. Get ready to leave.' Schliess had been a model employee for several years, and Lazareff, who knew virtually all his workers by name, was concerned about his future. 'We're leaving right away,' he urged him. 'I'm sure we can find room in one of the office cars.'

Schliess shook his head. 'I think I'll stay in Paris. I've got lots of friends here,' he said stoutly.

'Don't be a fool,' Lazareff remembers telling him. 'You're

from Alsace. You might be in trouble if you fall into the hands of the Germans.'

Schliess was adamant, 'I just don't want to leave Paris,' he replied. 'Don't worry about me.'

There was no time to argue, so Lazareff wished him luck, shook hands and jumped into the waiting car.

Lazareff was lucky; he took a route not yet patrolled by the Germans. Others did not fare so well. When Mrs Etta Shiber, the New York widow, and her friend Madame Beaurepos heard that the Germans would probably be in Paris the next day, they decided to flee. 'I didn't come to Paris to live under the Germans, Kitty,' said Mrs Shiber. 'Let's try to get out before they get here.'

Within an hour they had packed a trunk each, brought Madame Beaurepos' car – luckily with a full tank – out of the garage and set off south. But they had left it too late. That night they ran into an advance party of German motorcycle troops who had bypassed the capital. Since one of the women was American there was no question of arresting them, but the Germans firmly ordered them to turn their car round and return to Paris.

Neither had eaten for twelve hours, so they stopped the car at a small inn where the *patron* gave them a cup of sugarless tea each and a small piece of salami. It was an extraordinary chance that took them to this inn – they could have stopped hopefully at any one of a dozen places – for, while they were drinking, the *patron* heard them talk English and blurted out that he urgently needed help. He could speak no English, and he was hiding a British flyer in the back of the building. The man could speak no French.

'I can't make him understand me,' he said. 'I don't want to ask him to leave, but there are Germans all around hunting for Englishmen, and I am likely to get into trouble if he stays.'

He was a twenty-year-old R.A.F. pilot called William Gray who had been shot down near Dunkirk. Helped by French peasants, he had worked his way south through the German lines. Mrs Shiber described him as 'tall, with reddish-blond hair, smiling as calmly as though he were surrounded by friends, miles from any danger'. He wore a leather flying-jerkin over his grey-blue uniform and was astounded to learn that the Germans were already in the area.

Through Madame Beaurepos, he begged the *patron* to give him some civilian clothes. The Frenchman was horrified. 'Never,' he said. 'I am a good Frenchman, I hate the Germans and respect the English, but if this man is caught in civilian clothes he'd be considered a spy. They'll shoot him at once.'

It was true. Gray made up his mind to run for it. But the two middle-aged ladies hit on a plan. Jettisoning their trunks, they hid Gray in the car luggage compartment, which opened from the inside behind the back seats. A few minutes later they set off.

By dusk the German Panzers had surrounded the capital on three sides. Crews of motorised units were cooking their supper near Pantin and Aubervilliers – as near to the heart of Paris as Wimbledon is to the heart of London. In the north, they were equally close at Sarcelles. In the west, they had broken through the French lines between Évreux and Pacy-sur-Eure, while to the south the road was wide open for the armour of General Guderian. General Hering's Paris Army had withdrawn southwards, leaving notices on the walls of the capital:

> General Hering, having been called away to command an army, is placing the military government in the hands of General Dentz. Paris is declared an open city. Every step has been taken to ensure in all circumstances the safety and provisioning of the inhabitants.

Dentz, of course, had no army. The 'safety' of the inhabitants was in the hands of the police and fire brigade.

The Germans acted quickly. Shortly after 2 a.m. (on Friday, 14 June) Langeron's police radio picked up a message demanding the immediate surrender of the capital. The German High Command announced that it would despatch an envoy under a flag of truce to the Porte St-Denis to discuss the surrender.

There was little time to waste but, even so, General Dentz did not relish the prospect of going there himself and told General Georges at Army headquarters that as commander of an open city 'he did not feel qualified to parley with the Germans and would not do so unless so ordered'. General Georges backed him up.

Before Dentz could decide what to do there was a hitch. At Noisy-le-Sec, a Paris suburb near Pantin, a German was shot dead. The Germans immediately demanded that the French police catch the 'murderer', and told Dentz that negotiations would now be held at Sarcelles, further to the west, at 5 a.m. 'If your negotiators do not arrive, the attack on Paris will be launched,' the message ended.

Dentz had no choice but to co-operate. 'The incident modified my attitude,' he remembered later. 'Continued silence on my part could have resulted in a catastrophe for Paris. I therefore responded to the German message and told them I was sending an envoy.'

He selected a Major Devouges for 'this unhappy task'. When the Major, accompanied by a young officer, Lieutenant Holtzer, reached the Mairie at Sarcelles, a German captain was awaiting them. They got into a car and drove to Écouen, a couple of miles away, where Major Hans Brink of the German High Command started to dictate terms for the German entry into Paris.

'All resistance must stop by 9 a.m. on a front from St Germain, through Versailles,' said Brink.

Devouges remonstrated. 'But I don't have the sort of power to make arrangements like that.' (In fact neither the French nor German officer knew that French forces had already retreated well behind that line.)

'Then you'd better communicate the terms to the French High Command,' said Brink, who outlined several other points, such as curfew hours, orders not to blow up bridges and so on.

All this took time. Even as the French and German envoys were discussing surrender arrangements isolated Germans entered the capital. Around 5 a.m. a solitary German motorcyclist drove across the Place Voltaire and at 5.20 three German cars drew up outside the St-Denis prison, to be followed ten minutes later by motorcyclists, who reached the Porte de La Villette and then drove along the rue de Flandre towards the Gare du Nord.

Finally the French officers reached agreement, and were driven back to Sarcelles, where the instrument of surrender was signed by 6 a.m., delivering up 'the capital to Lt-Col. Dr Hans Spiedel'.*

Throughout the night Dentz had been in constant touch with Bullitt, who had managed to get a radio message to General von Studnitz, the German Officer Commanding, explaining that he was the only foreign diplomat left in Paris and suggesting that the German general should delay his 'triumphal' entry into Paris until after daybreak. This von Studnitz agreed to do – willingly, no doubt, for there was little point in staging a display of military conquest in the small hours of the morning.

All these decisions took place while Paris slept – or tried to, for not everyone was happy at the almost casual manner in which Paris was being surrendered. Thousands of Frenchmen felt like Captain de Normandie, who was still fighting at the Front but managed to get a message to his parliamentary representative Senator Bardoux: 'I implore you, tell the civilians, the Parisians, your women, to let us fight to the end. Paris will be taken, perhaps destroyed *quartier* by *quartier*, but we must never give it up, never. We cannot do this, for the sake of our country, our traditions, our honour.' 'Pertinax', the famous French columnist, felt that 'psychologically the almost casual abandonment of Paris struck the most grievous blow of all to French morale', while many echoed the belief of Gordon Waterfield that Paris could have emulated the heroism of Madrid, which had stood out for months against Italian and German bombing, because 'it was in her

* Spiedel came to know Paris extremely well, both as friend and foe. Four years later, as a lieutenant-general, he was defending Paris against the Allied forces, and in 1951 returned to the French capital to negotiate the rearmament of the New Germany. Then in 1957 he was back again – ironically as the first German commander of the Allied Land Forces in Europe.

[French] revolutionary tradition [but] they had not been treated as intelligent human beings'.

It was too late now. Once again a historic decision had been taken of which the people most concerned knew nothing, and by midnight Paris was a city of the dead.

When Robert Murphy of the American embassy and Commander Roscoe Hillenkoetter, the naval attaché, went for a stroll in the sultry, oppressive night, they found not a café open, not a light showing except for the occasional distant flash of gunfire. As the two men returned to the embassy at the corner of the Place de la Concorde, they were met by a small group of agitated people, led by one man who must have known that his life would be forfeit if he remained in Paris – the Grand Rabbin, the leader of the Paris Jewish community. Until this moment, he had decided to remain, but now, at the gates of the American embassy, he begged Murphy to find seats for himself and his wife in one of the embassy cars.

Murphy told him the last cars had already left and that, anyway, the Germans now ringed the city and would allow nobody out. The Grand Rabbin could not believe it – and was so desperate that Murphy did summon one of the few remaining embassy cars to take him to the outskirts of Paris in the hope that he could leave. At the gates of the capital the Germans promptly turned him back.

It was past midnight now, and Murphy took one last look at the city he loved before turning in. Up the Champs Élysées, which he regarded as 'the world's worst traffic hazard', the only living creatures in sight were three abandoned dogs beneath the French flags which still hung at each corner of the great concourse. He had never experienced such an 'eerie atmosphere'. Only the previous day the capital had been filled with milling crowds of refugees, and now suddenly, on this last day of freedom, 'the Paris from which they fled was almost empty'.

# Friday, 14 June

### 1. *The Germans march into Paris*

LIKE a grotesque, endless assembly belt, the procession of lead-coloured vehicles, with their fresh, blond, silent robots sitting stiffly four abreast, poured through the empty streets of Paris on this, its blackest day.

In the shuttered city all but those on duty could close their eyes to history in the making, but no shutters could blot out the sound that was the one symbol above all others of victory – the machines of the new-style conquerors: the spurting, sudden noise of a motorcycle and sidecar racing ahead, the sinister purr of rubber tyres on infantry trucks, the ominous rattle of caterpillar tracks on cobbled streets.

Because the hum of a dynamic city starting the day's work – the sudden squeal of a braking taxi, a boy late for school clattering down wooden stairs, the shouts of friends meeting – because these were missing, the noise of the invaders took on a heightened, unreal quality that people remembered long after other first impressions had faded.

By 8 a.m. a solid phalanx of Germans had already entered the city along the main boulevards north and east of Notre-Dame, the bizarre traffic regulated immaculately by German military police with bright red discs attached to short handles rather like those used to flag in planes at airports.

Here and there knots of people stood and watched in what one man described as 'the silence of death'. The women wept, the men were grim; all were stupefied by the freshness, the youth, the discipline of the German troops, the trim spick and span armour, so smart it was almost as though there had been no war, that this was just another military parade.

With scant knowledge of what was happening in the rest of France, some people hardly knew what to do, how to behave. Had they lost the war, or had they only lost a battle? Their confusion was increased by the sight of thousands of French policemen, in neatly pressed uniforms, still with their white batons, lining the streets.

German war correspondent Leo Leixner, who reached Paris with the first troops, was probably right when he cabled his Berlin newspaper later in the day, 'We met very few civilians, and they seemed resigned to the inevitable. Resignation is more in evidence than consternation. . . . Above all, there is great relief that the war is over.' It was not over, of course, but the licence was perhaps understandable to the Germans on this triumphant day, while the sense of relief was equally understandable to the people of Paris, unaware as yet that for thousands the real killing was still to come.

From his office in Les Invalides, General Dentz watched the long German column approach the Pont Alexandre and cross it, every boot and button polished, every bayonet glinting in the sun. They goose-stepped their way up the Esplanade and advanced towards him as though prepared, if necessary, to march straight into the building, as unyielding as a crowd scene in a film spectacular, until – and again he was reminded of a film – the formations wheeled right and left at the very last second. As though every movement had been rehearsed (as, indeed, perhaps it had been), four officers stepped stiffly forward and Dentz could hear them barking orders. Sentries, by prearranged drill, moved to their posts, guarding every entrance. A party under a young officer marched to Napoleon's tomb and, ignoring the sandbags, searched among the battle flags arrayed round the tomb. Methodically and in silence they took away every German flag they could find – each a symbol of a German defeat in the 1914 war.

At almost exactly the same time, Langeron in his office was

interrupted by a policeman who warned him that four German cars were crossing the Seine and approaching the Île de la Cité. A few minutes later a German colonel was shown in. He saluted 'very correctly, even with a touch of deference', Langeron thought, as he asked the police chief in excellent French if he would go to the Hôtel Crillon at 11 a.m. to meet General von Studnitz.

General von Studnitz, the man chosen to command the second German forces to occupy Paris within seventy years, had decided to make his headquarters at the Hôtel Crillon, on the Place de la Concorde, separated from the United States embassy only by the narrow rue Boissy d'Anglas. He expected the Prince of Wales suite on the first floor to be ready to receive him by 9.45 a.m.

When a German colonel arrived at the hotel at 8.30, however, he found it barred and bolted. The irate officer looked around until he found a policeman – who happened to be the luckless Commissaire René Hainnaut – handed him a swastika flag and told him, 'Open that hotel. It will be our headquarters. Take down the French flag and replace it with this German flag.'

The hotel was not only empty – even the steel shutters on the windows were closed. 'We tried to get in and then we tried to get a locksmith,' Hainnaut remembered later, 'but we couldn't find one and time was passing.'

The German colonel returned in a fury. 'If that hotel is not open in fifteen minutes and the French flag is not down, we will shoot it down – and shoot you too,' he said. Fortunately Hainnaut found a locksmith in time but, as he also remembered, 'Comme j'ai transpiré.'

At precisely 10 a.m. General von Studnitz, with strict attention to protocol, prepared to visit the American ambassador, who would hand over to him the city of Paris on behalf of the French. Though the distance from the front door of the Crillon to the front gates of the embassy was little more than fifty yards, von Studnitz was determined to squeeze the last ounce of drama from this historic moment. His boots polished like glass, his spurs clinking, his chest a spectrum of medals, his monocle firmly screwed into his right eye, he climbed into a large, black Mercedes outside the Crillon. An escort of leather-jacketed motorcycle outriders revved up their motors, and the impressive cavalcade covered the distance, crunching to a halt in the embassy courtyard.

Bullitt himself has never revealed his feelings about the moment von Studnitz arrived, though many American students of the war have made their feelings painfully clear. As Theodore Draper put it, 'The surrender of Paris without a blow was the final step in the moral capitulation of the French command. It was made all the more costly by the prominent role which ... Bullitt chose to play in it. ... Bullitt's role in the capitulation was not merely negative. The United States was the supreme hope of the French people and Reynaud's last card. Bullitt could not hand over Paris to the enemy as a meaningless gesture. Whatever he may have thought, he could not control the thoughts of the French people.'

Von Studnitz and Bullitt had met before – the last occasion being at a dinner party in Warsaw – and the confrontation now was politely formal and lasted exactly ten minutes.

Outside German troops were being ordered 'Eyes right!' as they marched up the Champs Élysées, where General Bock, Commander of Army Group B, had hurried into the capital to take a formal salute. This chore over, he then drove like any tourist to see Napoleon's tomb, followed by, as he noted in his diary, 'A very fine breakfast at the Ritz.'

Langeron's visit to von Studnitz at 11 a.m. was equally businesslike. When the two men faced each other at the Crillon, von Studnitz – 'monocled, with a small moustache and the rather *démodé* air of a cavalry officer' – asked Langeron only one question: 'Can you guarantee to maintain order?'

'If you let me run the police my way, yes,' replied Langeron.

Almost without hesitation, von Studnitz declared briskly,

'If order is maintained, if I can count on security for my troops, you won't hear any more from me. Good day.'

So far all diplomatic meetings had been formally conducted. But once the city was under control von Studnitz seemed inclined to relax, as three American diplomats discovered when they paid their return call – a necessary protocol – to the Crillon on behalf of the American ambassador.

Bullitt deputed Robert Murphy, Commander Hillenkoetter, the naval attaché, and Colonel Fuller, the military attaché, to represent him, and as the three men stood outside the embassy gates a military convoy roared up the narrow street separating them from the Crillon. A German lieutenant asked in excellent English, 'You're Americans, aren't you?' They nodded, at which the German told them he had spent several years in the United States. He then asked them an absurd question: 'Can you tell us where we can find a decent hotel?' The three Americans burst out laughing. 'The entire city is yours,' said Murphy. 'There are hundreds of empty hotels. Take your pick.'

As the convoy moved on, the three men entered the lobby of the Crillon, and paced up and down for a few minutes until an orderly informed them that the General was awaiting them in the Prince of Wales suite.

Standing in front of the door was a German colonel, and as soon as he saw the Americans he cried, 'Murphy! What are you doing here?'

Murphy looked at him in astonishment. His face was vaguely familiar.

'I am Colonel Webber,' said the German. 'We met when you were vice-consul in Munich.' That was fifteen years ago, and now the Colonel was von Studnitz's aide and 'welcomed us as if we were all old friends'. He immediately took the Americans into the suite, where they found von Studnitz sitting before an ornate French period desk, 'a dapper monocled caricature of an old-time Prussian officer, who prided himself on his immaculate manners'.

The Americans had expected the meeting to last only a

few formal moments, but von Studnitz received them 'most graciously and affably'. Though it was not yet noon, he ordered vintage champagne from the Crillon's cellars, telling them, 'It is the very best the Crillon can provide.' Moreover, he answered all the questions put to him by the Americans, whose picture of the war's progress, gathered from Berlin and Allied radios, was necessarily confused and sketchy, even admitting with a wry smile that he had once been an attaché, so he quite understood that it was the duty of attachés to gather intelligence for their government. 'But I am quite willing to talk to you frankly,' he added. 'We have nothing to hide.'

Mopping-up operations in France would, he told them, take maybe ten days more, after which preparations would start for the invasion of Britain. When Hillenkoetter asked how the Germans proposed to cross the Channel, von Studnitz somewhat airily said that all plans were ready and the war would be over in six weeks.

For good measure on this first morning of German euphoria, von Studnitz assured the embassy officers that all American property would be protected. 'You can count on the best co-operation as far as the German military is concerned,' he said.

The three Americans were on the point of leaving when von Studnitz asked the two military aides if they would be kind enough to 'assist' him in a review of the crack German Green Heart Division, which he had once commanded. A ceremonial march past in the Place de la Concorde was timed to take place shortly. 'There being no easy way to decline, Fuller and I accepted,' Hillenkoetter remembered later.

But when the time came they hastily changed their minds. General von Studnitz, affable as ever, politely asked the Americans to stand next to him on the rostrum and watch the review, but suddenly Hillenkoetter saw a movie cameraman, then a press photographer, and 'both Colonel Fuller and I could see how that would look in the newsreels, photos etc. – two American officers taking a review with a German general'.

Politely but firmly the two Americans begged to be excused. They did not feel worthy to share the General's honour, they said. It was his division and his must be the glory 'and it would be a shame to deprive him of even a share of the glory'. The General accepted the hint and the two Americans melted unobtrusively into the crowd of civilians.

While the niceties of diplomacy were being observed, three men who had elected to remain in Paris despite the exhortations of their friends to flee now faced their moments of destiny.

To Dr Thierry de Martel, brain surgeon, director of the American Hospital, a friend of Bullitt's – who alone among his friends had advised him to remain in Paris – life under German occupation would be impossible, as he had hinted to André Maurois.

In his neat, careful script, de Martel now composed a telegram. It was in English, and he was careful to choose a messenger who spoke only French to despatch it – or, if that proved impossible, to deliver it by hand.

Then, as methodical as ever, de Martel went to his glass-fronted instrument cupboard, took out a hypodermic needle, charged it carefully, and gave himself a lethal injection of strychnine.

The cable was addressed to Bullitt, and read, 'I promised you not to leave Paris. I did not say if I would remain in Paris alive or dead. To remain in Paris would be a *cheque barré* for our adversaries. If I remain here dead it is a cheque without any provisos. Adieu. Martel.'

At the other end of the city, in the deserted offices of the Paris *Daily Mail*, Charles Vallotton, who had sworn to remain because 'I have one last job to do', heard the German trucks clattering along the Grands Boulevards, a few yards from the rue du Sentier. Determined that the *Daily Mail* offices would never be used by the Germans, he took a swig of red wine, then deliberately started to deface all the lead type in the composing-room, cutting or scraping the soft metal where possible, then throwing the type indiscriminately into sacks so that no team of printers could ever sort it out, or hope to use the only newspaper office in Paris which could print in the English language. Then he went home.

One other newspaper worker had stubbornly refused to leave. But, though Joseph Schliess, the liftman at *Paris-Soir*, had spurned Lazareff's offer of a last-minute lift, he did vanish during the night before the Germans arrived.

Not for long. When he returned to Paris he carried in his pocket a bulky list of addresses of the newspaper's linotype operators, foundrymen, machine-room engineers, in fact all the key personnel needed to produce a newspaper.

It had been prudent foresight, for Lieutenant Joseph Schliess of the German Army, member of a wealthy German publishing family, one-time model liftman, had been planted as a spy years previously in readiness for this very moment. Almost immediately he started to plan a Nazi version of *Paris-Soir* for the following day.

As Schliess telephoned the staff of *Paris-Soir*, another car flaunting a swastika drew up at a requisitioned building in the Champs Élysées. Out stepped Captain Maier and Lieutenant Weber of the German Army. Weber had for years been chief of the Paris bureau of D.N.B., the German news agency, a traditional cover for a spy; but when Thomas Kernan, the American director of *Vogue*, went to see if he could restart his magazine, and was confronted by a smiling Maier, it was like meeting an old friend. For months the freelance photographer Maier had been pestering *Vogue* to accept his photographs. Everyone on the editorial staff knew him – and indeed many felt sorry for the ambitious young photographer who kept on struggling, despite his lack of success.

Everywhere the thoroughness of the German fifth column was evident. In a dozen restaurants favoured by politicians, waiters who had eavesdropped for years now welcomed the first Germans for the old friends they were. In Heugot's, a bistro just behind the Place du Palais Bourbon, a startling transformation took place when a nun who for months had made regular collections among the political clients patronising the bistro appeared as a man – and a German. As Cocteau pointed out, there were 'nuns' everywhere, since penetrating the disguise was a delicate matter.

Not only were the members of the fifth column active. Following hard on the heels of the storm troopers came experts ready to take over every section of Paris life. One group of uniformed engineers drove to the main telephone exchange in the rue de Louvre, while trained announcers and operators, also in uniform, seized the main radio station in the rue de Grenelle. Before midday Radio Paris was broadcasting programmes in German and music by Wagner.

At the same time small detachments of troops selected for their policy of 'correctness' escorted French fire brigade officers along the main boulevards, where they were ordered to haul down the French tricolour and replace it with the swastika. Soon four blood-red German flags dominated the Concorde – two over the Ministry of the Marine, the other two over the Hôtel Crillon. Others floated over the Chamber of Deputies, the Senate, even over the Arc de Triomphe, with the tomb of the unknown warrior and the eternal flame beneath.

The first flag to fly over the Eiffel Tower was too large. It had taken some effort to hoist it, for the lift had been sabotaged and the Germans had to walk up its 1671 steps – to the annoyance of Ninetta Jucker, whose windows were only 200 yards from the Tower and who was at first puzzled by the curious grating noise of heavy boots on metal. The first swastika was so large that Madame Jucker could hear it 'flapping like sails' and then the sudden noise of ripping as the wind tore it. Half an hour later, more German soldiers climbed the tower again to replace it with a smaller flag.

Nothing would ever wipe from Langeron's memory 'the long, immense, interminable columns' of German troops pouring in hour after hour from the direction of St-Denis and Montrouge. Soon he could see Germans with loudspeakers patrolling the streets in small cars warning people, 'No demonstrations are permitted while our troops march in. The

Paris police will function normally. Any hostile act will be punishable by death.'

Occasionally an officer barked an order and a section of a column would be detached to deal with a special problem. In the Boulevard de Clichy troops tore down a cinema hoarding showing a picture of a cringing, terrified Hitler, advertising a war film. All French war-bond posters carrying the cry, 'We shall win because we are the stronger!' were immediately removed.

Every detail of the occupation had been worked out meticulously. On the heels of the storm troopers came a posse of men with ladders who covered advertising signs and brick walls with a rash of three-colour posters showing a handsome, smiling German holding a tattered French urchin on one arm while doling out biscuits to another who clung to his knee.

As people trickled out into the streets, German cars distributed leaflets telling them the war had been brought about by their 'traitorous politicians' and advising them, 'Frenchmen! Think of your poor children, think of your lonely wives. You must demand that your government stops the fight.'

From time to time the theme was taken up on a more personal note, as when a small crowd gathered to watch a group of Germans raise the swastika near the Hôtel de Ville.

One officer cried to them in excellent French, 'You are free now. You can go where you like. We wish you no harm.' Then, turning to a woman, he said, 'Madame, you want your husband back, don't you?'

When she nodded, he exclaimed, 'Of course you do! And my wife wants me back home too. We will sign the peace with France – and, as for the English, don't worry, we will settle that affair in a couple of weeks.'

Leo Leixner described how this convoy stopped so that an officer could buy some bananas, while 'timid mothers hid their children behind their skirts' – until the kind officer went back into the shop, bought chocolates and shared them out among the children.

Before lunch the Germans had posted troops at the corner of every avenue leading into the Étoile, together with machine-gun batteries and four motorised guns. Once these were in place, column after column of troops marched past the grave of the unknown soldier, saluting smartly as they did so. Martial music blared and drums pounded from five bands – one at each corner.

As soon as the troops had passed everything changed, for now the new tourists arrived – off-duty German soldiers carrying cameras instead of rifles. Soon the soldiers were photographing each other in their thousands before the Arc de Triomphe.

The Eiffel Tower was even more popular because the big open space of the Champs de Mars, on which it stood, quickly became an extraordinary market-place, thanks to French Algerians who started to cash in on this new brand of customer. When Ninetta Jucker looked out of her windows, the Germans were arriving by the coachload, and the Algerians, who had already ransacked every shop still stocked with chocolate or nuts, were selling them to the Germans, so that 'in a few hours the city was a litter of orange peel, nut shells and waste paper'.

Before lunch, specially selected 'economic' officers were proceeding to their allotted posts, some to run the Citroën works or other large industrial plants. Nothing was too small to merit their attention. One officer drove to Senlis, which had a population of only 6000, and requisitioned the house of American artist Carl Erikson in the rue de la Treille. Before nightfall he was making plans to expand the local tile factory.

At every street corner new decrees were posted, warning the people of the dire consequences of any hostile act. Newspapers would remain suspended, all printing was forbidden, even funeral announcements. Economists unobtrusively took over the main banks, their first task being to seize the safe deposit boxes of all British subjects as legitimate spoils of war. In the Champs Élysées, the German propaganda department requisitioned No. 52, the white stone and marble building of the American National City Bank, for their headquarters.

For the hungry French – if any were hungry on this miser-

able morning – the troops were followed by trucks pulling
forty-gallon tureens of soup, offered with the compliments of
the German Winter Relief. Thomas Kernan of *Vogue* noticed
that several French people did sample the free offering and
felt that 'the commonsense of the Parisian told him that
drinking the conqueror's soup would not compromise his
honour'.

The victors even provided up-to-the-minute reading
matter – during the morning, when two light aircraft landed
on the Place de la Concorde with Friday's German newspapers.

The first Germans reached Vaucresson in the afternoon with
just enough warning of their approach for Madame Villiers,
the postmistress, and her daughter Marie-Hélène to scream
to Iris Schweppe, 'We are going to barricade ourselves in.
Come and join us if you like.' 'No, thanks,' said Miss
Schweppe as the small post-office shutters were closed with a
bang. Most of the village awaited the enemy with a mild
curiosity, the women in groups of three or four standing by
the edge of the road.

Half a dozen trucks, followed by motorcycles with side-
cars, rounded the corner of the main Paris–Versailles road
which bisected the village. The trucks were filled with troops,
each one with a snub-nosed rifle between his knees. They
screeched to a halt outside one shop – the local *tabac* – which
the soldiers all but stripped of cigarettes. But at least they put
money on the counter for every packet they bought.

Iris Schweppe remembers them on that first day as young,
keen, 'very correct', but what struck her most forcibly was
that several were fast asleep sitting up and only awakened as
the truck jerked to a halt. Some of the soldiers shouted, 'Don't
be afraid! The war's almost over!' An officer alighted from a
grey Mercedes at the Hôtel de Ville, saluted briskly, and left
a pink slip notifying the mayor that forty rooms would be
needed by noon the following day.

Every German action was precise and prepared for like a
well-rehearsed play. Without anyone noticing, traffic police,

with white metal half-moons marked 'Field Police', suddenly appeared at the dangerous crossroads outside the village.

Some of the soldiers gave away bars of chocolate in an effort to make friends, and the postmistress must have been peeping between the cracks in the shutters, for suddenly Marie-Hélène ran out for her share of the same international currency the Americans would use five years later. Madame Villiers chased her daughter, and Iris Schweppe saw her lift an arm as if to drag her back inside. Suddenly she stopped and, arm raised in mid-air, cried, 'Mon Dieu! They are just like other people.'

Both sides in Vaucresson had work to do before the day was out. Iris Schweppe and half a dozen friends went on a foraging raid, in the kitchen gardens of those residents who had bolted. They stripped the gardens of all the vegetables they could carry, knowing that in a matter of hours the villas would be requisitioned for German troops. Iris Schweppe's 'bag' included real treasure trove: two sacks of potatoes dug from the garden, two bags of flour and other cooking ingredients that had been left in the kitchen of an unlocked villa which nobody had dreamed of entering until the Germans arrived.

The Germans had a grisly task to perform. Scores of families had bolted in panic without a last thought for their pets. Not only were hungry dogs and cats prowling the streets, but some people had left their pets locked up in empty houses. The Germans shot every stray they found, and even Iris Schweppe had to admit, 'There was nothing else they could do.'

Towards evening the Germans relaxed. A field policeman and a sergeant stood guard outside La Mère Cathérine, allowing German troops to enter, six at a time, to buy a beer or a *fine à l'eau* – though the first articles to vanish from the zinc counter were the hard-boiled eggs stacked on a plate. Each batch of soldiers was allowed half an hour of 'fun'; then out they came, to be replaced by another group of very young men.

*

About the same time that Iris Schweppe was lugging her potatoes home, two other women were passing through Vaucresson on their way to Paris. Madame Beaurepos and Mrs Etta Shiber – plus their hidden English pilot – were stopped three times by German guards on their enforced journey back to Paris. But, as Etta Shiber remembered later, 'None bothered to search a car driven by two sedate-looking ladies and each time we drove on again, hearts thumping, but bursting with relief.' At Vaucresson there was a more elaborate control and a German soldier, after a casual look inside the car, told them in perfect French, 'Well, ladies, your wanderings on the French highways are over – if you can prove you live in Paris.'

They showed him their identity cards, with their Paris address, and were waved on.

Outside their flat in the rue Balny d'Avricourt they waited till the street was empty, then the two women went in first to make sure the lift was on the ground floor. Gray followed, and Madame Beaurepos pressed the sixth-floor button. To Mrs Shiber, 'the lift took long enough to reach the top of the Empire State building' before finally it stopped at the sixth floor. The three hurried inside and Mrs Shiber threw herself 'against the door and pushed the safety bolt in a state approaching panic, then I tottered towards a chair and sat down'.

Madame Beaurepos seemed to have stronger nerves. She actually 'laughed happily'. 'Who would believe us,' she said, 'if we told them we had smuggled an English flyer past hundreds of German guards into Paris and into our apartment?' Then she added practically, 'Now we must find a way for him to escape.'

As evening approached the early tensions relaxed. A few restaurants opened, though even the French chefs, used to customers with hearty appetites, were astounded by the regular requests for steaks weighing a kilo, or 'a twelve-egg omelette'. In the streets there was visible evidence of the truth of Goering's dictum 'Guns before butter'; on several occasions

Henri Malherbe saw Germans licking what he took at first to be bricks of ice cream. In fact they were slabs of butter.

By late afternoon, Ninetta Jucker found the Champs Élysées and other boulevards filled with people. Some women wept, some simply stared, others had 'given birth to a kind of nervous hilarity' as an expression of relief. For nothing, really, could dull the grief and anguish that swept the capital, the barely disguised scorn on the faces of the German officers, the hated jackboots pounding the streets and, above all, the blood-red swastikas making their own German sunset from the summit of every tall building.

At the far end of the Champs Élysées, André Gaudin watched with hatred the jostling Germans taking photographs of each other outside a national shrine he had sworn to guard. A disabled victim of the First World War, he was an official guardian of the eternal flame at the tomb of the unknown warrior, and his problem was whether or not to extinguish the flame, whether it was sacrilege to allow it to burn in front of the hordes of conquerors.

During the day Edmond Farrand, a member of the Committee of the Flame, arrived and Gaudin explained to him, 'I was told that if the Germans arrived I was to put the flame out, but nobody has been to see me until now. What shall I do?'

'Do nothing for the moment,' replied Farrand. 'I will return at twenty-five past six this evening. If you have not received any orders by then, we'll come to a decision.'

No orders arrived, so at 6.30 p.m. the two men decided to keep the flame burning. The two Frenchmen, each with tears in his eyes, saluted ceremoniously. And in a strange way their decision was communicated to the Germans milling around the Arc de Triomphe. Maybe someone explained, maybe those closest saw the tears in the Frenchmen's eyes. No one will ever know; but whatever the reason the horseplay suddenly ceased, and the Arc became a small oasis of silence.

As Gaudin and Farrand saluted the flame, one German general who happened to be there saluted too, then dropped to his knees, his hands clasped in prayer. Other Germans followed his example or stood to stiff attention like the two guardians of the flame.

Late that night Henry Malherbe turned on the radio and – like millions of French people – listened to the B.B.C. Instead of the usual news, he heard a strange voice, a woman's voice, speaking carefully, slowly, in schoolgirl French, sending a message of love and hope to the hearts of her sisters in France. She was the Queen.

'A few days ago I was visiting in our hospitals the French wounded from Dunkirk,' she said. 'To each of them I spoke in French and asked how they were getting on. All of them, even the most seriously wounded, answered cheerfully one short phrase, "Ça va". I believe wholeheartedly that after these bad days the time will come when our two peoples will, by their endurance and hard work, have made good our armaments deficiencies, and will also be able to say to each other "Maintenant, ça va".'

Malherbe listened as the 'Marseillaise' was followed by 'God Save the King'. 'I was not ashamed of the tears in my eyes,' he remembered later, 'and I went to bed that night a happier man.'


## 2.  Berlin in triumph

To those back home in Germany, the capture of Paris was a signal for wild rejoicing. On Hitler's orders church bells were rung and the swastika was ordered to be 'prominently displayed' for three days.

Despite the fervour of victory, the Berliners were as phlegmatic as ever, and not as elated as one might have expected. The weather in the German capital was warm and sunny, and when William Shirer, the American writer, went to Halensee for a swim he found it crowded, 'but I overheard no one discussing the news. Out of five hundred people, three bought extras when the newsboys rushed in, shouting the news.'

Perhaps the lack of enthusiasm masked in effect a vague feeling that, though Germany was now riding on the crest of a wave, retribution would follow if Hitler went too far. The Swedish journalist Sven Auren found in Berlin that 'the average German, outside the ranks of the Party, was overwhelmed by what the new leaders had succeeded in doing, yet was deeply frightened of the consequences it might bring with it'.

On the other hand, as Shirer pointed out, 'It would be very wrong to conclude that the taking of Paris has not stirred something very deep in the hearts of most Germans. It was always a wish-dream of millions.' It certainly was the fulfilment of a dream to Hitler, who issued a triumphant call, 'The second phase of the campaign is over with the capture of Paris. The third phase has begun. It is the pursuit and final destruction of the enemy.'

Though the German press was ecstatic at the great victory, it was in its way as restrained as the Berliners, warning readers that there was still a long, hard road ahead. It put the capture of the capital in its proper perspective – unlike the Italians, whose war effort so far consisted entirely of vainglorious boasts, but who now gloated as though the Italian Army was responsible for the victory. In huge headlines, the *Lavoro Fascista* sneered, 'C'est Paris! Capitalists, Jews, Masons and snobs all over the world are in mourning.' The *Tevere* offered the arrogant advice, 'Let the nation of carrion learn once and for all, in the torture of defeat, to respect the honour of other peoples. Let them remain on their knees for centuries.' Coming from Mussolini, who admitted entering the war as a vulture, the use of the word 'carrion' was hardly appropriate.

Both Hitler and Goebbels decided, in different ways, to use the fall of Paris for strategic propaganda. Goebbels decided that the time had come to 'destroy' Reynaud, and issued the order. 'There is to be no more factual argument about Reynaud; he is to be dismissed in the German press in the strongest possible terms as a Stock Exchange fiddler and a lump of misfortune. The minister also wishes the contrast to be underlined pictorially: a photograph showing Reynaud shabby and repulsive in bathing trunks is to be juxtaposed to a picture of a wounded *poilu* still showing the horror through which he has passed.'

Hitler decided to use the occasion to air his views on future relations with the United States, and chose as his instrument Karl von Wiegand of the Hearst Press. 'Those who say the Germans have designs on the American Continent are lying,' said Hitler. 'Germany is one of the few countries which hitherto has never made any attempt to meddle in America. Germany has never had any territorial or political designs on the American Continent.' His policy, Hitler stressed, was 'Europe for the Europeans and America for the Americans', and any suggestion that he would ever interfere in the affairs of America was 'childish and grotesque'.

Nor, he insisted, had he any designs on the British Empire. He would only destroy those bent on destroying Germany. For the rest, his 'remote aims' could be summed up in one word – peace. (Which prompted Roosevelt to comment, 'That brings up recollections.')

The interview with Wiegand ended on a slightly more sombre note, when Hitler was joined by Ribbentrop. After making it clear that the official interview had ended, Hitler told Wiegand in confidence that, though Germany was sure of victory, he felt that if America intervened 'the war might last much longer'.

Certainly Germany felt in no immediate danger from the United States. Hasso von Etzdorf, Hitler's personal representative at army headquarters, told General Stulpnägel, 'There is not the slightest sign of United States intervention'; and Hans Thomsen, the German chargé d'affaires in Washington, cabled Hitler on Friday, 'America is paralysed by the coming election campaign.' This was perfectly true. The election would continue to dominate the scene for some time.

While Hitler made extravagant promises and Italy gloated,

Britain, as the writer Mollie Panter-Downes felt, took refuge 'in the classic national formula for disaster: calmness, and an increasingly dogged determination to hold back for bitter months – or years if necessary – against a juggernaut which everyone now knows is out to annihilate the nation in weeks'.

As the British newspapers proclaimed 'Germans Enter Paris', there was no bitterness towards a suffering friend, no recriminations – spoken or implied – of the French Army. The same, however, could not be said of the politicians who had led two great powers to this pass. As Mollie Panter-Downes (a delightful lady who had leapt to fame by writing a bestseller, *The Shoreless Sea*, at the age of sixteen) wrote in her weekly letter to the *New Yorker*, 'All the criticism is reserved for the criminal complacency of former leaders on both sides of the Channel who refused to see that this war would be one of steam rollers, not of gentlemen's weapons.'

Though shocked by the fall of Paris, Britain was also pre-occupied with her own troubles – including pitiful lack of planning. The Germans had served notice of the dangers of refugee-choked roads, and if the wide, sweeping highways of France could not cope with fleeing millions what hope could Britain have when the Germans unleashed their bombs? Yet the Government was having difficulty in per-suading East End mothers to evacuate their children.

Blinded to realism, nobody could *quite* believe the worst would happen. One elderly lady told the newspapers, 'Well, if the Germans win, at any rate I've got my pension, and Hitler can't touch that.' When Connery Chappel, the dyna-mic assistant editor of the *Sunday Dispatch*, took lunch, as he did every Friday, at Simpson's in the Strand, his favourite waiter presented him with one of their precious silver tankards, observing, 'We shan't be needing these much longer. We've got to start fighting now.'

Precious months had been lost through stupidity and lethargy; Britain had to start working. *The Times*, describing London's crowded hotels, cinemas, amusement arcades, asked in its headline, 'Are We Really at War?'

When people did work, there were wicked anomalies.

Because of red tape, men who were urgently transferred to new industrial plants often left their families almost destitute – in one case, a woman and two children were left with the equivalent of less than a pound for the week it took to sort out the problem. Yet that same week, a wealthy family advertised for 'Butler-valet and cook (married couple) wanted for Surrey home. Ten servants kept.'

When she read of the fall of Paris, Lady Baldwin (who in view of her husband's negligence in the pre-war years might have been wiser to keep silent) suggested in *The Times* that churches should fly their flags to show that Britons were Christians fighting evil powers. Bertrand Russell wrote from America that he considered himself 'no longer a pacifist' and would have been proud to fight had he been younger.

Britain was also gripped by spy mania. From the moment Italy entered the war earlier in the week, many Italians had been interned, including (to the dismay of gourmets) the Quaglino brothers and Ferraro, the head waiter of the Berkeley – in addition, it must be said, to dozens of unsavoury characters in Soho who had been on the police books for years. Even Cyril Connolly was questioned while sitting innocently in the Mitre at Oxford because he 'seemed interested' in the conversation of a group of nearby officers. When it was discovered that his passport had been issued in Vienna, he was in dire trouble – until he was able to prove that he had been to Eton and Oxford.

If one question did dominate others in Britain, it was a question that had suddenly become more urgent because of the fall of Paris and the obvious dangers ahead. It was: will the Americans come in? Mollie Panter-Downes wrote on this Friday night, 'There is an increasingly trusting belief in American assistance – first with guns and planes, and eventually with men. People simply cannot believe that the great power whose chief representative spoke to them so nobly on Monday night* can continue to contemplate these horrors unmoved.'

---

* Roosevelt's 'dagger in the back' speech; see page 47.

## 3.   *The battlefield*

The battle of France was now virtually lost. As regiments of the 18th German Army paraded along the Champs Élysées, General Guderian entered St-Dizier, to find the French commander, Colonel Balck, taking the sun in a deckchair in the town's picturesque market-place. Rommel had captured Le Havre, and before pushing on to Cherbourg wrote to his wife on Friday, 'Went into Le Havre and inspected the town. It all went off without bloodshed.' General Halder was poised to storm Verdun, a fortress which now had little will to fight, but which had cost the Germans hundreds of thousands of dead in 1916. The sunless, sunken caverns of the Maginot Line, with its armies of 400,000 men, had been by-passed and isolated. Weygand himself admitted that the French armies had 'disintegrated into four widely separated groups and were now incapable of organised resistance'.

General Alan Brooke considered the only thing that mattered was to rescue all the British troops possible. He had succeeded Gort as commander of the new British Expeditionary Force, consisting of little more than four divisions, all in grave danger of being overwhelmed in the French débâcle.

At 8.30 a.m. on Friday, Brooke saw Weygand, finding him 'very wizened and tired', and was astounded when Weygand told him the Supreme War Council had decided to hold the much-discussed Breton redoubt. Brooke, who was under Weygand's command, understood that Weygand had ridiculed the idea of the redoubt to Churchill at Briare, but now took the line that since it was a government decision he had no option but to obey. Consequently, he suggested that Brooke should concentrate a newly landed Canadian division near Rennes, to cover Brittany. (In fact no official decision had been taken after Madame de Portes' veto.)

When Weygand saw the look of dismay in Brooke's eyes, he suggested they should both drive to the headquarters of General Georges 'to draw up an agreement for this manœuvre'.

They had no sooner set off by car than Brooke had a revealing insight into the state of Weygand's mind, for as they were 'trundling along' Weygand said, 'This is a terrible predicament I am in.'

Brooke was about to commiserate on his heavy responsibilities when Weygand blurted out, 'Yes, I had finished my military career, which had been most successful.'

Brooke was 'struck dumb ... it seemed impossible to me that the man destined to minister to France in her death agonies should be thinking of his military career'.

At General Georges' headquarters, Weygand explained that the Breton redoubt line would pass through Rennes, with both flanks on the sea, but beyond that both he and Georges seemed a little hazy. Brooke's first question was 'How long will the line be?' Weygand gave an evasive answer; in fact he did not know. Neither did Georges, so Brooke took out his pocket dividers and measured the proposed line on the map for himself. It was about a hundred miles long.

'It can't be as long,' protested Weygand, so Brooke measured it again. It *was* a hundred miles, and Brooke said that such a line would need at least fifteen divisions. Brooke could muster at most four divisions, the French perhaps three from the badly mauled 10th Army.

Knowing Weygand's antipathy to the whole idea of the Breton redoubt, Brooke urged him to try to convince Reynaud to countermand the order; but in the stubborn way in which some men persist in carrying out a foolhardy mission, if only to prove a superior wrong, Weygand replied that it must be considered as an order.

Brooke, of course, had no means of knowing whether Weygand was speaking the truth, but as soon as Weygand left he sent a message to Field-Marshal Dill, the Chief of the Imperial General Staff, who had been with Churchill at Briare. It read in part: 'Weygand ... told me of decision taken by governments yesterday to attempt to hold Brittany.'

All three officers, he stressed, were completely agreed as to the 'military impossibility' of holding such a line with the available troops.

Only then did Brooke start back on the 170-mile drive along congested roads, reaching his headquarters at Le Mans at 4 p.m. Almost immediately he got through to Dill in London and begged him to stop the flow of British troops to France. Dill assured him that this had been done, at which Brooke told Dill frankly, 'There is only one course open to us – to re-embark the expeditionary force as quickly as possible.'

As to the Breton redoubt, Dill was as mystified as Brooke had been. 'He had heard nothing about it.' Dill called Churchill, who said emphatically that there had been no formal agreement to defend Brittany, after which Dill telephoned Brooke again that 'the Brittany scheme is off, and that I was to proceed with the embarkation of troops not under orders of the French 10th Army'.

With the thought in his mind that the crack 51st Division had fallen to Rommel only two days previously, Brooke felt that his task now was to save British lives to fight another day. He immediately issued orders for those Canadian units that had landed to return to Brest – and England. The 52nd Division – less one brigade with the French 10th Army – should make for Cherbourg. British lines-of-communication troops – including 7000 at Le Mans, 65,000 at Nantes, 20,000 at Rennes – were to be dispersed to various ports.

After Brooke gave the orders it was each man for himself. Few knew whether they would find ships to carry them home, or whether the Germans would be in command of the port they were making for. Some received odd welcomes. Bombs were raining down as twenty-six-year-old Lieutenant Ivan Foxwell of the Royal Norfolks clambered desperately up the ladder netting of a freighter waiting to evacuate troops. Exhausted, he was pulled aboard in front of Colonel Grey Horton of the Scots Guards. The Colonel seemed uninterested in the dishevelled young officer – but, then, he was engaged in a heated argument about the wartime precautions needed to maintain the cricket pitch at Lords.*

Back home in London, Churchill was horrified at the prospect of 'letting the French down' – though Brooke did not know this until 8 p.m., just before dinner, when Dill called him again on 'a very bad line'. Brooke assumed that Dill was calling him from the War Office. He told Dill what he was doing.

Dill said, 'The Prime Minister doesn't want you to do that.'

'What the hell does he want?' asked a tired and exasperated Brooke.

'He wants to speak to you,' said Dill, who was not at the War Office, but at 10 Downing Street.

Churchill asked Brooke what he was doing with the 52nd Division. Brooke repeated that it was returning to Britain.

'It's not what I want,' replied Churchill. 'You have been sent to France to make the French feel that we are supporting them.'

Angrily Brooke retorted, 'It is impossible to make a corpse feel, and the French Army is to all intents and purposes dead.'

With Brooke determined not to sacrifice thousands more lives, the two men wrangled for half an hour on the telephone. Brooke was furious because of an increasing suspicion that Churchill 'considered I was suffering from cold feet', and admitted later, 'I was repeatedly on the verge of losing my temper.' But at last he won the day. With Brooke 'in an exhausted condition' Churchill finally grunted, 'All right, I agree with you.'

It was a great personal victory for Brooke, for as he remembered ruefully, 'The strength of his [Churchill's] power of persuasion had to be experienced to realise the strength that was required to counter it.' But a victory it was, for in all 136,000 British and 20,000 Polish troops were evacuated.

---

* Years later Foxwell met Horton in the lift at Claridges and reminded him of the incident, 'Ah, yes,' replied Horton, 'they damn well ruined that pitch, you know.'

## 4.  *Destinations unknown*

The fall of Paris sent shock waves reverberating across the entire country, though the French authorities were not always the first to know. At Besancon – barely a hundred miles from the neutral haven of Geneva – the police were first told by twenty-two-year-old Frances Kay of Twickenham, the younger sister of Joan Kay, who had been evacuated from the Chamber of Commerce in Paris. Frances worked at the consulate-general, heard the news on the B.B.C. and promptly telephoned Roger Hontebeyrie, the local Prefect of Police.

Within minutes he was back on the phone, telling her to bring round all the consulate passports to be stamped, a procedure that would make it easier to cross bridges held by French troops.

'Get out as quickly as you can,' Hontebeyrie told her. 'At five tomorrow morning we're going to blow up the bridges.' He was referring to the seven main bridges crossing the River Doubs, which curled in a loop round the old city, turning it almost into an island.

It was easier said than done. Frances Kay – a pretty girl with fair, wavy hair who spoke four languages fluently – had graduated to the consular service from the International Chamber of Commerce in Paris, and had been evacuated to Besançon, from St-Diem in the Vosges. The acting consul was Charles Ledger, and the offices were within 'the loop', a handsome building with a courtyard in the rue Charles Nodier, a few steps from the Prefecture. One wing served as offices, the other housed Mr and Mrs Ledger, with a separate flat for Madame Durot, the landlady.

Ledger had only a small Peugeot car, but the two Ledgers, their cook and Frances Kay could just squeeze in. They were told to drive to Lyons, but before setting off the code books had to be burned, and the unwritten law of the consular service had to be obeyed: the last official must not leave before the last British citizen was safe.

All the Britishers in Besançon had left except one old man who lived nearby, and Frances Kay quickly found him a seat in a government car. He had lost all his papers, but she told him, 'Don't worry. I can provide you with temporary documents. All you have to do is swear on the bible that all the particulars you give are correct.'

But when she looked for the office bible it was missing; it had already been sent to Lyons with the files. She lost no time in idle searching; he solemnly swore that he was telling the truth, the whole truth and nothing but the truth, with his hand reverently placed on an imposing leather-bound book – the fact that it was the *Concise Oxford Dictionary* was just too bad.

Once the old man was on his way, the small staff prepared to leave. Mrs Ledger strapped the luggage on the roof of the small Peugeot. It was now, as Frances Kay remembers, that 'in walked a starry-eyed couple in their early twenties, holding hands, gazing into each other's eyes and plainly in love'. Without preamble they announced they were on their honeymoon – and they had run out of cash.

After 'cursing them when I realised they just couldn't be abandoned', Frances tried to find spare seats in cars leaving the city. There were none. Finally, Frances, who had a bicycle, suggested to the young man, 'Look, your wife can have my seat in the car and I'll go by bike providing I can find another one for you.'

Doubtfully the groom agreed. But there were no bicycles left. At last Miss Kay found a garage with enough spare parts to assemble one, but when she returned to the consulate with her prize the groom said he could not be separated from his wife. There was nothing for it but to squeeze him into the consul's car. 'At that point I began to wish that one didn't have to be so frightfully well brought up about the whole thing, because it was obvious that I was going to be left behind to make my way as best I could on my bike.'

Aloud all she said was, 'You go, then, and I'll manage.' After arranging to meet at the consular offices in Lyons in

two days, the small, overloaded car lurched out of the courtyard at dusk – and Frances Kay 'celebrated' by popping
across to the Prefecture and having a farewell drink with her
friend, Monsieur Hontebeyrie. She only had to burn a few
books, then she could set off.

Until this moment she had never set eyes on the code
books, which were always kept in the safe, and she could
hardly believe her eyes when she was confronted by several
large, heavy volumes with almost indestructible covers.

She carried them down to the cellar. The consulate did not
boast a 'diplomatic furnace', so Frances Kay did the only
thing possible: she lit a fire in the ancient black iron stove
which served for the central heating in the winter. There
were no problems about lighting the fire, but the code books
just would not burn. 'The thick pages seemed to have been
made of fireproof material,' she remembers. Even when she
put the pages into the flames one at a time, it took hours to
destroy them.

It was now midnight, only five hours before the bridges
would be blown up. At this moment Madame Durot, the
landlady, stumbled down the cellar stairs, clutching a huge
bundle of multi-coloured cloth.

'If the Germans find this in my house, they'll shoot me,' she
wailed, and threw the consulate's Union Jack on the floor.
'You must burn it.'

At twenty-two, Frances Kay's first instinct was of horror.
'It could be a treasonable act to burn the British flag.' Her
second was fear – of being charged with the cost of burning
government property without authorisation; and this was a
very real fear, for during the past few weeks the consul-
general and Whitehall had been locked in a deadly battle
over the cost of one typewriter ribbon. Nevertheless she cut
up the flag and thrust it into the furnace piece by piece.

Only then did she start to pack a few belongings into her
bicycle's saddle-bag. She was looking doubtfully at a pile of
silk stockings that needed darning – 'in those days we didn't
have nylons' – when Madame Durot bustled in with some
coffee and cried, '*Ma pauvre*, this is no time to worry about

stockings. Just think of your legs and rest them while you can.'

She did – for an hour. Then at 4.30 a.m. she set off for Lyons, just half an hour before the bridges were due to be blown up.

While Frances Kay was preparing to pedal to Lyons, Zena Marshall, the British girl who escaped death when her school in Belgium was bombed, was trundling southwards in the packed refugee train that seemed to meander all over the countryside on its way to Bordeaux.

For days the train had been shunted from place to place, but always the same eleven people had shared the compartment, with Father Bezin, the benevolent Catholic priest, sitting opposite and the young blue-eyed boy next to her, both acting as her special protectors, taking her white Pekinese Gussy for a walk or offering to share their meagre rations with her when no food was available.

To Zena, the days and nights passed in a jumble of disconnected sequences. There was the night when she had the terrible nightmare, dreaming that the Germans stood her up against a wall and sprayed her with bullets that never killed her. She woke up screaming when the train screeched to a stop and the priest gathered her in his arms as the stutter of machine-gun fire from planes above told her the nightmare was based on reality.

There was the warm, summery afternoon when, for no apparent reason, the train stopped miles from anywhere. Everyone was ordered out and sat for hours soaking up the sun or walking in the fields, where the blond boy, whose name she discovered was Eric, made her a necklace of cornflowers. ('I was getting a bit of a schoolgirl crush on Eric,' she remembers.) While the trainload of people relaxed – for a brief spell as remote from reality as passengers marooned after a shipwreck – she saw Father Bezin on his knees, praying so devoutly that when the French police travelling on the train made one of their periodic identity checks they left him alone to his meditations.

'Why have we stopped?' she asked one policeman.

'Just a routine search of the train,' he assured her. 'We'll be starting any minute. You'll be in Bordeaux tomorrow, *ma petite anglaise.*' That was on Thursday.

Now, on Friday, the train stopped again in lonely countryside, but this time there were shouts, commotion, the sound of feet pounding along the corridor, even (she thought) the crack of rifle or pistol fire. Suddenly Zena was afraid – partly because her two protectors had left the compartment.

Suddenly she looked out of the window. Far away in the fields a figure was darting, followed by French soldiers firing at him as they ran. Then she saw the voluminous black skirt of Father Bezin and the lithe figure of Eric together with other civilians. They too, it seemed to her, had joined in the chase, but then they were all hidden by a clump of trees.

She heard the sound of more firing. Two policemen burst into her carriage, and when a woman began a tentative question one told her rudely to shut up. To her dismay, the train jolted and started. Zena ran into the corridor, grabbed the policeman by the arm and cried, 'We've got to wait for Father Bezin – and the other man. Please wait.'

'We can't,' the policeman patted her head. 'They'll be all right, but we've been ordered to move. We're only two hours out of Bordeaux.'

She could not believe the French could be so callous as to leave passengers behind, even when the woman opposite mumbled something about a German air attack. Blinded with tears she sat down. The others tried to console her, but she refused to be comforted. Cuddling Gussy in her arms, she cried herself to sleep. She barely noticed when the train occasionally jolted to a stop; in fact she hardly realised anything until two hours later when the train wheezed and puffed its way slowly into the station at journey's end.

Zena's carriage was one of the last in the long train. Carefully she took her 'birthday present' suitcase from the rack and put the lead on Gussy, before starting the long walk to the barrier at the other end of the grey platform. People milled and shouted, some perhaps hoping to find friends waiting for them, others wondering perhaps what their next move to freedom would be. Zena had money, letters to family friends in Bordeaux and, 'though I was a bit scared, I wasn't really afraid'. But she did miss her friends.

And then, as she reached the barrier, a wonderful thing happened. She saw them. 'That first moment, it seemed like a miracle,' she remembered later. 'I shouted to Eric and he looked up.' Both Eric and Father Bezin were standing in a group of men at the other side of the barrier.

Pushing through, all tears forgotten, she rushed up and cried, 'Eric! Isn't this wonderful?'

Not until she was within inches of the men did she see that they were handcuffed. The police seemed to be everywhere, whistles blowing, revolvers in hand.

'What's happened? There must be some mistake,' she remembers shouting.

Father Bezin said nothing, just looked at her. Eric spoke one short sentence: 'See you in London.'

Then, as Zena Marshall remembers vividly to this day, 'The man I thought was my friend, who had been so kind to me, did something too awful for words.'

As the police started to hustle the men away, Eric, the captured German parachutist, leant forward and spat full in the little girl's face.


5. *'You will be submerged in defeat'*

Early on Friday morning the bedraggled French Government prepared to leave its 'very provisional' capital of Tours for the equally provisional capital of Bordeaux. It is difficult to imagine a more disunited, disheartened, disenchanted body of men than the one entrusted with the destiny of a great nation tottering towards defeat.

Pétain despised Reynaud for the manner in which the

Premier flaunted his 'immoral' life. De Gaulle felt that, as he put it, 'old age is a shipwreck and the old age of Marshal Pétain was to identify itself with the shipwreck of France'. Weygand hated de Gaulle with such bitterness that in the previous month he had threatened him with arrest. General Spears detested Weygand so much that it must have been difficult for him to give Churchill unbiased advice. Even the ladies coloured the picture, for Madame de Portes was so jealous of the Marquise de Crussol, Daladier's mistress, that she had the previous month deliberately engineered Daladier's dismissal from the Cabinet, thus depriving Reynaud of the services of a politician whose experience might have helped in the crisis.

None of those in power had a total picture of what was happening. Reynaud was muddled, confused, misled. And, if Roosevelt was also uncertain of the future of France, the blame for both his and Reynaud's confusion must rest partly on the shoulders of the United States ambassador, Bullitt. Alistair Horne in his brilliant book, *To Lose a Battle*, summed it up as follows:

> ... the American Ambassador in Paris, William Bullitt, must be held greatly to blame. In an age when Ambassadors carried weight and were more than merely the post-office clerks they tend to be today, Bullitt appears to have sinned by misleading both his own country and France as to the true situation in the other. Washington was persuaded by Bullitt that France's fighting capacity was much greater than it was, while through him the French Government was led to expect far greater aid than could possibly have been forthcoming from the United States at that time.

Before leaving Tours, Reynaud had two things to do, one for France, the other of a more delicate and personal nature. Firstly he sent a last despairing message to Roosevelt. At 6 a.m., after an early breakfast, he took his thick black pencil and drafted the message, which read in part:

At the most tragic hour of its history France must choose.

Will she continue to sacrifice her youth in a hopeless struggle?

Will her government leave the national territory so as not to give itself up to the enemy and in order to be able to continue the struggle on the sea and in north Africa? Will the whole country then live abandoned, abating itself under the shadow of Nazi domination with all that that means for its body and its soul?

Or will France ask Hitler for conditions of an armistice?

We can choose the first way, that of resistance, only if a chance of victory appears in the distance and if a light shines at the end of the tunnel.

In the present situation, in spite of the weakening of the enemy's forces due to the sacrifice of the French Army, the defeat of England, our loyal ally, left to her own resources, appears possible if not probable.

From that time on France can continue the struggle only if American intervention reverses the situation by making Allied victory certain.

The only chance of saving the French nation, vanguard of democracies, and through her to save England, by whose side France could then remain, with her powerful navy, is to throw into the balance, this very day, the weight of American power.

It is the only chance also of keeping Hitler, after he has destroyed France and England, from attacking America, thus renewing the fight of the Horatii against the three Curiatii.

I know the declaration of war does not depend on you alone.

But I must tell you at this hour, as grave in our history as in yours, that if you cannot give France in the hours to come the certainty that the United States will come into the war within a very short time, the fate of the world will change. Then you will see France go under like a drowning man and disappear after having cast a last look towards the land of liberty from which she awaited salvation.

More than any other message, this one – compounded of distraught statements, unanswerable questions, even demands and threats – showed that Reynaud had almost given up hope.

When he had finished the draft Reynaud handed the message at 8.15 a.m. to Drexel Biddle, who was doing a splendid job as Bullitt's stand-in. 'Tony' Biddle was not only immensely rich, but was a man of great personal charm, good looks and gallantry, who felt a genuine compassion for his fellow men and wanted to be of service to them.

He rushed the cable off to Washington, though it reached the White House in jumbled fashion, for Biddle had to despatch it in four sections, and section four reached Washington two hours before the beginning of the message.

Biddle was so shocked at Reynaud's state of 'profound depression and anxiety' that he immediately added a cable of his own, telling Roosevelt: 'Immediate declaration of war by the United States is only hope for England and for France if she is to continue to fight in north Africa. The French Army is cut to pieces.' Speaking of the previous day's cabinet meeting, Biddle added, 'Reynaud obtained only with great difficulty the Government's consent to continue the struggle. It was clear to me that in the absence of some positive action by us within the next 48 hours the French Government will feel there is no course left but to surrender.'

Once the business of state had been disposed of, Reynaud again sent for Biddle. This time, the question put by the Premier of France to the acting ambassador had nothing to do with diplomacy.

'I wonder if as a favour', Reynaud asked Biddle, 'you could give the Countess de Portes a lift in your embassy car.' Somewhat hesitantly he explained that he was afraid that if she rode in a French car she might be recognised and even attacked.

Biddle agreed immediately for, as he remembered later, 'Without her he couldn't have carried on at all, so we took her.' It must have been a tiresome drive, for almost from the moment they set off Hélène de Portes launched into a tirade against de Gaulle and hardly stopped until they reached their destination.

The decision to go to Bordeaux was, in effect, a death blow to de Gaulle's hopes of continuing the fight, and as he prepared to leave he felt terrible guilt at running away. He had stayed near Tours with a family called Provost de Launay, an old-fashioned French family who owned the Château de Beauvais, and now he left with a heavy heart. 'I said my goodbyes to my hosts,' he remembered later, and as he drove off he could not help but reflect, '*They* would not leave. Surrounded by their people they would await in their home the battle of the retreat and then the arrival of the invader.'

The journey to Bordeaux was a nightmare. Not only were the roads more choked than ever, but to make matters worse rain started falling, causing Alexander Werth to comment bitterly, as he prepared to follow the Government, 'It just *would* rain for the refugees, when it didn't rain for Hitler's invasion.'

None who made that terrible journey would ever forget it. If there had been any spirit of *camaraderie* at the beginning of the week, it had long since evaporated. In its place was not only despair, but also a desperate and aggressive 'every man for himself' bitterness.

Near Poitiers, Marguerite de Gelabert saw a gang of roughs jump aboard an expensive chauffeur-driven car, beat up the driver, force the two women and three children out, then drive off, leaving them stranded. Worse than the actual scene was the awful realisation that nobody was prepared to do anything about it. The people in the queue of vehicles, or riding past on bicycles (a much quicker form of transport) deliberately refused to look. They did not dare to, for if they stopped someone would seize *their* transport.

Marguerite de Gelabert had parted company with Jimmy Ashworth, who had started back for Paris after he realised there was no point in trying to print the *Daily Mail* in Tours. He had found her a seat in the sports car of a young French air force officer cadet called Daney, who had been ordered to report to the training station at Mérignac, near Bordeaux – and who by an extraordinary chance knew Cadet Jean-Paul Joffre, grandson of her godfather Marshal Joffre; Jean-Paul was stationed at Bordeaux and was the one person she knew there who might help her. The journey took them eight hours; they were held up for two hours in a traffic jam, when a fire engine, loaded with fleeing firemen and their families, blocked the road.

It was very much a matter of chance. Freeman Matthews left Tours in an American embassy convoy after lunch, 'anticipating several nights on the road'. They loaded up with sleeping-bags, cooking-utensils, a supply of canned food. They were not needed. 'We took a back-road route and much to our surprise found little traffic and reached Bordeaux at eleven that night.'

There were other, more terrible, paradoxes. Cecily Mackworth, the British nurse whose unit had been evacuated from Paris and was now making her way to the Spanish frontier, came across two small children in a field who were on the point of death. Their mother, clutching her babies, begged for help. Miss Mackworth, who had forgotten that she was still wearing her Red Cross uniform, helped the mother carry the babies to a farmhouse half-hidden by trees, but even as they entered the kitchen she could see that every cupboard was bare. The kitchen had been stripped. The farmer's wife rocked in a chair, gazing dazedly into space, and answered automatically, as though repeating it for the hundredth time, 'We haven't got a crust left in the house.' People had stolen her last egg, she said, and the last drop of milk. Finally she did find two large potatoes, with which Cecily Mackworth made some hot broth for the babies.

A few miles further on she reached a village and found 'a stout and cheerful peasant woman selling the biggest, juiciest strawberries we ever saw, piled on their own leaves that served as plates. We bought all she had then looked round for somewhere to sit and eat them. One of the cafés was open and was serving coffee, although there was no milk or sugar.'

Alexander Werth had no trouble finding a square meal. Driving under a leaden sky near Poitiers, he stopped for a late breakfast, looking wonderingly as the *patron* placed on the table 'an enormous dish of butter and a gargantuan loaf of bread'. Drinking his coffee out of a huge cup, he spied something even more incredible – a fruiterer's and grocer's shop on the other side of the road, stacked with 'mountains of strawberries, cherries, peaches, tinned food, sausages, dozens of chickens'. He wondered how there could still be all this food after hundreds of thousands of refugees had been pouring through the town.

James Lansdale Hodson, a British war correspondent, was fascinated by some of the refugees he saw in a countryside wearing 'that deserted and brooding air that goes with invasion – a deathly quiet, a sudden coming upon dogs pitifully looking for vanished owners, a woman crying'. Some villages were deserted, in others men and women refused to budge, and they watched Hodson, 'half curiously, half timidly', as he drove through.

On the open road he passed a man of seventy pulling a cart, another old man wheeling a barrow of bedding; a third was 'stolidly gathering flowers as though no war existed'. He turned a corner and came on the incongruous sight of a French cavalry officer on horseback, drinking a glass of wine, and a French soldier with a *baguette* of bread stuck in his belt. Further on he met five lost British soldiers resting with a column of French troops, their trucks lined up on each side of the tree-lined road. The French soldiers had a gramophone which was grinding out 'You're the Cream in My Coffee', tinkling and echoing among the trees. 'Everything wore an air of beautiful casualness,' Hodson remembered.

That night Hodson drank champagne out of an enamel mug for supper, spent the night on the floor of a village school, and breakfasted on ham and 'bread so new it must surely be tomorrow's'.

Gordon Waterfield of Reuter also found that 'village life was proceeding as calmly and peacefully as it had done for hundreds of years. Wherever we went in the villages, the pulse was very firm, they did not have any intention of moving, whatever happened.'

Waterfield and his colleagues, including Harold King, were travelling in two cars, and the previous night they had slept in a secluded field. King remembers waking with the sun and 'feeling like the wrath of God' – until he saw one of their passengers, Virginia Cowles, the American writer, emerge from the other car, 'looking as neat as if she had just come out of the Ritz'.

Percy Philip of the *New York Times*, who had lived in France for twenty-four years, 'slept on the grass by the roadside, on cement floors, in the truck which I was driving with a typewriter for a pillow'. He typed his despatches in the oddest places, 'once in a mushroom grower's cave while a German bomber dropped his eggs on the road we had just left'.

For Joan Kay of the Chamber of Commerce in Paris, who made the trip with her colleague in an old racing car, only one unpleasant incident spoiled the journey. As they reached the bridge of St-Jean, which crosses the Gironde on the approach to Tours, the gendarmes saluted politely and asked to see their papers. Apart from her hand luggage, Joan had been entrusted with a rucksack filled with important documents belonging to the Chamber of Commerce, together with the office cash reserves in various currencies.

'I handed over the lot to the gendarmes,' she remembers. 'They looked at everything and handed it all back. Only later did I discover that the gendarmes had stolen the money.'

The girls spent the night sleeping on a café floor. In the morning Joan set about finding out how to get to Toulouse – and the free house she had been promised.

General Spears was also driving south, and noticed the extra congestion on the roads caused by troops. 'Nearly all the towns and villages I passed through were full of gaping, idle soldiers,' he remembered. 'They were not in formations, just individuals in uniform, hanging about.' He drove past several long French air force convoys, the aircraft on huge floats. In the accompanying cars 'sat ladies whose ample proportions and commanding looks proclaimed them to be wives of senior officers'.

Even President Lebrun, taking much the same route as Spears, was 'mystified' by the fact that 'the towns and villages are full of idle troops', and asked his colleague, 'What are they doing there, inert, when one needs them so badly elsewhere?'

Many of the troops wanted to fight, but did not know how to rejoin their units – if, indeed, their units still existed. To Hans Habe, the writer, who was retreating with the French Army, the strangest thing about his flight was that 'a nation was fleeing from an invisible foe'.

Those units who *did* know where to go often could not make their way through a countryside clogged with refugees. The French 7th Army, fighting between the Seine and the Loire, reported, 'Our movement has been rendered almost impossible by the afflux of refugees encumbering the roads with their cars and carts. The villages and crossroads are places of indescribable bottlenecks.'

Some troops who wanted to fight were simply stopped by the civilians, many of whom felt that since Paris was in German hands the war was over.

Late that night troops preparing to make a stand near Poitiers were stunned to see the mayor drive out in his car, brandishing a white flag as he prepared to surrender the town to the Germans. The local inhabitants backed him up, threatening to tear down the barricades. When the soldiers remonstrated, one man yelled, 'Why not? What's good enough for Paris is good enough for Poitiers.' At a small village on the River Indre the locals actually put out fuses that troops had already lit to blow up the only bridge in the area and slow down the Germans.

Towards evening the harassed members of the French Government crossed the Gironde and straggled into the great seaport of Bordeaux, twice previously the provisional capital of France – in 1871 when the Germans occupied Paris, and for a brief spell when it was threatened in 1914. It was still light as Yves Bouthilier crossed the river with the other cabinet ministers, finding that 'the invisible bonds that . . . turn a mass of human beings into a society were slackening already. We had reached the stage where the civilian population, feeling that it was no longer either governed or safeguarded, was seized by a strange vertigo; the stage where people, aghast at the spectacle of a state disintegrating, were ready to give way to despair.'

Already Bordeaux was overflowing with refugees unable to find shelter. For nights some had slept in their cars, others on park benches or on the floor of the big hotels. For, unless a Spanish or Portuguese visa miraculously appeared, there was nowhere else to go. For hundreds of thousands it was the end of the road.

Latent anti-semitism was spreading, fanned by the mayor, Adrien Marquet, a dentist by profession and a fervent admirer of Pierre Laval. When Léon Blum, the distinguished politician who had served France well, tried to find a room, he was thrown out of a shabby, third-rate hotel because he was 'a Jewish warmonger'. Laval, however, had no problems. Marquet simply ejected the ex-Queen of Portugal from the Splendide, the best hotel in Bordeaux, and handed over her suite to him. Madame de Portes, a useful ally, was given a double room with bath in the same hotel.

Marquet's principle in allotting rooms to government officials was simplicity itself: those in favour of continuing the fight against Nazism were sent to hotels near the main railway station, a frequent target for German bombers. Those in favour of capitulation were housed in the residential, safer sections of the city. Laval was not only given a 'safe' room, but was also provided with an office next to the mayor's parlour in the Hôtel de Ville so that he and Marquet could start intriguing against Reynaud.

Most people went meekly to the houses or hotel rooms allotted to them, but when Jeanneney was escorted to a magnificent building in the Cours Xavier-Arnozan, once the home of Queen Amélie of Portugal, he immediately decided against staying there. It had, he remembered, 'a long cold corridor,

stone steps to the first floor', a general impression of coldness
– and 'toilettes sordides'. He told the driver to take him to
the rue Castéja, where a cousin, Dr Georges Jeanneney, made
him much more comfortable.

Reynaud made his headquarters in the Quartier Général,
the headquarters of the Eighth Military Region in the rue
Vital-Carles, a short street leading from the main shopping-
street, the Cours de l'Intendance, to the Cathedral of St
André. A few doors away President Lebrun took up residence
in the home of the Prefect of Bordeaux. Mandel fixed up a
camp bed at the Prefecture itself, while Pétain stayed in a
friend's house in the Boulevard Wilson at the other end of the
city.

Almost the first man to see Reynaud in Bordeaux was de
Gaulle. Though he was only a junior minister, this did not
deter de Gaulle from speaking his mind.

'In the last three days I've realised the speed with which
we are rushing towards capitulation,' he said bluntly. 'I have
given you my modest assistance, but it was for making war.
I refuse to submit to an armistice.' As Reynaud listened
intently, de Gaulle rushed on. 'If you stay here you will be
submerged in defeat. You must get to Algiers as soon as
possible. Are you – yes or no – resolved on that?'

Reynaud answered with one word: 'Yes.'

'In that case,' de Gaulle urged him, 'I must go to London
at once myself to arrange for the British to help us with the
transport – either from here or anywhere else. Where shall I
rejoin you?'

'In Algiers,' replied Reynaud.

De Gaulle planned to leave that night, driving first to
Brittany, but before sending for his car he went to the Splendide for a quick bite of dinner with Lieutenant Geoffroy de
Courcel, his aide. Pétain was dining alone in a corner of the
restaurant, and de Gaulle made his way to the old man's
table to pay his respects. Pétain shook hands, but refused to
speak to him. The two men never saw each other again.

*

For members of the *corps diplomatique*, the arrival in Bordeaux was a nightmare never to be forgotten. Most ambassadors had not the faintest inkling where to go, but hung around for hours in a local schoolroom which had been hastily transformed into a 'diplomatic sorting-office' with hard-pressed clerks trying to discover which château or villa had been reserved for which ambassador. While they waited, there was nowhere for their families to go, not a spare chair on which to rest in the Splendide; indeed, there was nothing for it but to sit outside. As one diplomat observed, 'Meanwhile the ambassadors' wives, covered with sweat and draped with pearls, were being cooked by slow degrees in their Rolls-Royces on the Allées de Tournay.'

Campbell, the British ambassador, was more fortunate, though even he faced a snag when he arrived about seven o'clock – half an hour after Reynaud – and was told that he and his staff would be housed in the Château Filhot, nearly thirty miles out of the city. With memories of the single, ancient, hand-cranked phone at Tours, he demanded more central quarters, and Georges Mandel found an ideal 'embassy' in the Hôtel Montré at the corner of the rue Franklin – ideal because it was five minutes' walk away from where President Lebrun and Reynaud were staying.

The Hôtel Montré – facing a small square near the market – was modest, with bars on all the corner windows, a long corridor leading from the street to the reception desk, from which a short flight of steps, skirted by statues of immodestly clad ladies, led to a red-carpeted salon, with a glass roof, giving it the appearance of a winter garden. A few small potted plants struggled to add to the illusion.

But for the hard-pressed British embassy – or at any rate its senior staff – the Montré was ideal for another reason: the front door was opposite the Chapon Fin, undeniably the best restaurant in Bordeaux.

Tired though they were, both Campbell and Spears felt that it was urgently necessary to see Reynaud, to bolster his determination. They had a good excuse to visit him after the embassy notified Downing Street of their whereabouts and a cable from Churchill arrived renewing Britain's pledge to help France and, by giving this assurance, obliquely expecting France to give Britain a similar guarantee.

Churchill's message was magnificent: 'We renew to the French Republic our pledge and resolve to continue the struggle at all costs in France, in this island, upon the oceans and in the air, wherever it may lead us. . . . We shall never turn from the conflict until France stands safe and erect in all her grandeur. . . .'

The Dominions added their own moving message. From Canada, Mackenzie King cabled, 'We have followed, with the pride of blood, the heroic action of your soldiers. . . . The sacrifices and the devotion of France are an example to free men the world over.'

Armed with these stirring messages Campbell tried to telephone Reynaud. Strangely, there was no reply. He tried a dozen times, until finally after dinner the ambassador and General Spears set off for the rue Vital-Carles to see for themselves what had happened.

It was a dark night and the narrow street was ill-lit, but at the gates of Reynaud's residence stood a sentry in a tall, narrow box in front of heavy, spiked gates. Behind was a courtyard. Not sure that they had come to the right house, Spears asked if this was where the Prime Minister of France was staying.

The sentry looked puzzled, hesitated, then answered with the French equivalent of 'I dunno.'

The soldier did not, however, seem concerned when the two Britishers decided to find out for themselves. He made no attempt to prevent them from crossing the courtyard, which contained three chestnut trees, and walking up the steps leading to the double front doors, which were unlocked; the gloomy, pillared hall was empty, and as dark as the night outside. There was no sign of life. Spears made out 'tall columns supporting part of the upper floor on the sides of the hall, and a broad staircase'.

They walked up the stairs. There was no one on the landing, but then, as they made their way down a passage whose darkness reminded Spears of 'futility and desolation', they at last heard voices.

It is not difficult to imagine the feelings of the two men, striving against all the odds to keep France in the fight, the bearers of tidings which, if not of any concrete value, might at least give a kind of spiritual comfort to the sorely pressed Reynaud; Spears vividly records his sense of anticlimax as they entered the room.

'We opened a door, and there were Reynaud, de Margerie and a couple of secretaries eating poached eggs. It looked a convivial little gathering; the participants appeared to have banished the war for the moment, and as we entered, the faces of all at that table reflected clearly that we had brought a spectre with us into the brightly lit little room. We were, in fact, an awful bore.'

# Saturday, 15 June

## 1. *'This stinking city'*

As Saturday's dawn broke over the Gironde, fear born of ignorance struck terror into the hearts of a population swollen by hundreds of thousands of refugees. The swift decline of morale in high places, and the setbacks on the battlefield, presaged inevitable defeat. Only the brave or the foolish still dared hope for a miracle. For the rest, nothing could throw off the stupor that blanketed the city.

An ugly mood seized the people; the men and women of many nations who had been funnelled by circumstance into this one city could no longer disguise from themselves that they had reached the end of their tether. Besides, the people of Bordeaux resented this invasion by hordes of strangers whose presence summoned up the image of an enemy whose prowess and cruelty were magnified by report.

Riots followed in the wake of despair. Outside the Portuguese consolate, in the Quai Louis XVIII, men fought like savages as they vainly queued for a visa to freedom. Jews, Czechs, Poles, German and Austrian refugees – all knowing they were marked for the concentration camps – tried to storm the consulate building. The Portuguese officials phoned the police, who did not even bother to answer the distress calls.

Knowing the nature of their fate if the Germans caught them, these people did not realise that the Portuguese were issuing transit visas only, and these only to people whose passports were already franked with a visa for the country of ultimate destination. And for ninety-nine out of a hundred there was only one chance of getting this – unless they happened to know that the Republic of Haiti was prepared to stamp any passport with a resident visa for 150 francs.

The turmoil was just as bad at the United States consulate in the rue Esprit-des-Lois, temporarily elevated to the status of embassy. Freeman Matthews (who had to share a bedroom with nine people) found that 'the outer offices and hallway of the consulate were jammed like the subway at rush hour with frantic Americans anxious to get south to Spain and needing transportation, exit visas, advice, money and sleeping space; and frantic French and other foreign visa applicants, 90 percent Jews, who wanted to get out before the Germans came in. . . . The exodus was given impetus by the fairly heavy bombardment of Bordeaux we had one night which we watched from the consulate balcony.'

At the British consulate, near the Splendide, General Spears found 'the pandemonium outside and on the stairs was worse than ever. It was an appalling sight. The anxiety of people desperately anxious to get away was very comprehensible', but 'many were absolutely terrified' and 'going in and out of the consulate had become a real ordeal'. Most Britishers hoped to be evacuated by sea, but there was a snag: German aircraft had dropped magnetic mines at the mouth of the Gironde.

Many consulates – and the Splendide – faced on to a huge open square called the Place des Quinconces, which stretched from the road, with the Splendide set back behind its terrace of striped umbrellas, to the river. It was not a paved square or 'place' in the usual sense of the word, but an open space normally reserved for fairs or exhibitions. The authorities had obviously been preparing for some new exhibition when the first refugees arrived, for there were several abandoned pavilions, including one for 'Les Vins de France'.

Now the dusty open space was filled with troops, including a platoon of British soldiers with their trucks, though most came from other countries – Poles and Czechs who could not find their officers, their rations, their guns.

There were several fights in the Czech camp between officers and men on Saturday morning. One Czech soldier summed up the frustration of thousands when he shouted, 'I don't give a damn for your pips. What's a captain anyway? I'd like to bash your face in.'

For millions of people – soldiers and civilians alike – anger and frustration had mounted on the long journey across Europe. All over the continent brilliant chiefs of staff had planned the details of how to fight a war (though not how to win one), but none had foreseen the agony and misery of a rabble retreating before an implacable enemy. Now they were dumped in what the Czech soldier called 'this stinking city'.

Each man summed up the fearful, oppressive sense of doom, the intrigue, in his own way. To General Spears it was 'as if all the sewers in France had burst and their nauseating mess was seeping into the beautiful city like a rising flood of abomination'. To Percy Philip of the *New York Times*, the fatigue, the danger from bombing, the nerve-racking strain were 'nothing compared to the terrible sickness of heart. France had lost.' Worse still, to his mind, democracy was quietly disintegrating, with defeatist politicians playing on the vanity of a senile, one-time hero, and a woman playing on the frayed nerves of a distraught prime minister, while 'the mass knew nothing about it'.

A. J. Liebling criticised the double evacuation, first to Tours, then to Bordeaux, as a fatal psychological error, for 'the hunted pillar-to-post feeling that legislators get when they are evacuated twice in a week is an invitation to panic'.

Even the President of the Republic found that 'the atmosphere of the town is bad. The uncertainty of the news, the German advance, the influx of refugees, all these things created a great malaise, an obvious troubling of minds, of which the members of the Fifth Column will take advantage for their deadly propaganda. The Parliamentarians who have arrived from the different provinces are surrounded, isolated, lectured.'

Like thousands of others, Arved Arenstam, the Balkan

journalist, had spent hours searching for a room, only to be 'met with an impatient negative before one has had time to make the enquiry'. When he first arrived, he thought he was in luck, for he ran into his honorary consul and asked for help. The so-called diplomat brushed his advances aside and said he was 'merely a letter box'. Arenstam was furious with 'these ambitious businessmen who seek to bask in the sun of diplomacy, who are eager for decorations and long to sport a little flag on their cars . . . but are of no help whatever'.

Tired out, he walked to the Place de la Comédie. It was jam-packed. He had spent the night on a park bench and felt that his legs would give way at any moment. Suddenly, at the Café de Bordeaux, which had a huge terrace, a man left his seat. Arenstam pounced on the vacant chair and subsided thankfully. In the scorching sun, a waiter arrived with a drink and the cool sound of ice clinking in the glasses. Sitting there, watching, was like having a ringside seat. He caught sight of Élie Bois looking haggard and broken, and in the sea of cars crawling past he saw Maurice de Rothschild, Jean Giraudoux, Pierre Comert and Louis Gillert. Georges Mandel walked past, deep in conversation with another man. 'In fact everybody seems to be here.'

They included people from all walks of life. On the café terrace of the Splendide the piano player from Harry's New York Bar in Paris sat all day long, utterly exhausted, sleeping, head couched in his arms on the small table. He never seemed to stir, and to A. J. Liebling 'he typified all uprooted Paris packed into this city of indecision'.

Not far away Gordon Waterfield was making for the British consulate when someone hailed him, 'Well! We made it!'

Waterfield hadn't the faintest idea who the man was, yet at the sight of his puzzled face the stranger looked quite hurt.

'Don't you remember me?' he asked. 'We met outside the railway station in Paris after my friends and I arrived from Italy. When they wouldn't let us on the station, we got in round the back. We've travelled all the way to Bordeaux without a ticket.'

Britons and Americans who had to leave could at least deal with a consulate that functioned, but French people anxious to leave were in a far worse plight, for by now all pretence at organisation had vanished.

When Father Maillet, leader of the 'Petits Chanteurs' choir, began to fear for the future of his forty young charges at Rocamadour, he sent one of his teachers, twenty-six-year-old Marcel Chanfreau, to Bordeaux to discuss the possibility of sending the boys to north Africa. By now permits were required. Armed with a bundle of passports, Chanfreau tracked down the remnants of the Foreign Ministry to an old school, but 'no one had the time or inclination to bother whether or not a bunch of singing schoolkids went to north Africa'.

After a frustrating day trying to get some action out of unco-operative officials, the resourceful Chanfreau* finally found the necessary rubber stamps and himself franked the forty passports with the necessary visas.

There were really two worlds in Bordeaux during those last days before the Germans snapped the handcuffs on France. If refugees without rooms filled the park benches, shop-keepers filled the shelves of their windows. In the fashionable Cours de l'Intendance almost every imaginable article was on sale. Provocative dummies flaunted the latest fashions in dresses and hats for women; confectioners crammed their windows with mouthwatering displays of chocolates, the perfumiers with scents, the grocers with cheeses, rows of hams, mounds of pâtés, bottles of wine.

The choice was as varied in the dining-room of the Hôtel Splendide, behind the potted palms and the thickly carpeted foyer, though the company was not always of the best, as Jeanneney found when he dined there; he remembers how his meal was spoiled by the behaviour of a woman at the next table. After all, this was a critical moment for France, but time and again the woman complained to the harassed,

* Chanfreau now runs the 'Petits Chanteurs' booking-office at the Salle Pleyel, Paris.

overworked waiter because the pet dog on her lap had not received the cream she had ordered for it.

Alexander Werth fared better when he was lucky enough to get a table in the restaurant. It was packed, the service was slow, but the meal was delicious, and as he paid the bill Werth reflected that 'Bordeaux, now the capital of France, was not going to disgrace itself'.

The food was even better in the Chapon Fin, the Maxim's of Bordeaux, as Marguerite de Gelabert discovered when young Joffre took her there for lunch on the first day. As she walked in, the appearance was deceptive. The modest front door, with its framed menu in the lace-curtained window, led to a square room where hats and coats were divested in winter, but which was now furnished mainly by rows of naked, dangling hangers. Once past this, Madame de Gelabert walked along the short corridor into a splendid room that looked as though it had been devised for an under-water Cousteau film.

In front of her was a 'grotto', with huge artificial boulders along one wall, decorated with equally artificial seaweed and other marine flora. She could hear the vague tinkle of falling water as they made their way to one of the tables snuggling between the massive boulders (so that political diners could talk discreetly).

In one corner was the British embassy table. At the far end of the room she spotted the swarthy features of Laval, who lunched there regularly. And then Joffre pointed out to her a woman lunching with two men. It was the notorious Countess de Portes.

Madame de Portes was not the only mistress with political ambitions to reach Bordeaux. Quite apart from her arch-rival the Marquise de Crussol, Daladier's mistress, several ministers or deputies had arrived with their lady friends. Unlike Reynaud and Daladier, who had turned to the aristo-cracy (if once removed) for solace, most politicians were content to fish in the apparently inexhaustible reservoir of the Comédie Française, which provided attractive consorts for many of them. In the great tradition of French politics, the Countess de Portes and the Marquise de Crussol were simply (as the American Thomas Kernon put it) 'the drum majors of a long parade of women enamoured of politics'.

To the French Cabinet, racked by the need to make one agonising decision – to fight or to capitulate – there was one way of determining the wishes of those who were never consulted – the people of France: by letting their elected members of Parliament vote on the issue. By now more than enough senators and deputies of the two chambers had reached Bordeaux to form a quorum; they included Vincent Auriol, Paul Boncour, Charles Riebel, Ramadier, Bergery, Léon Blum to name only a few.

They had the constitutional right to decide – or at least to discuss – the fate of the voters; even the unusual locale was nothing new, for the Assemblies had sat in Bordeaux in the past. It seemed the logical step to take. At least Vincent Auriol thought so, and early on Saturday asked Reynaud if Parliament could be convoked. He found Reynaud sympathetic to the idea. 'Had I been able to call the Chamber together, I should have consulted it,' he remembered later, but Reynaud did not have the power. This rested with Herriot and Jeanneney, the leaders of the two chambers.

Auriol was not to be deterred. He asked Reynaud to lend him a car and drove out before lunch to see Herriot, leader of the Chamber of Deputies, who was staying at the Cours Xavier-Arnozan, which Jeanneney had turned down.

Without preamble, Auriol asked him, 'Aren't you and Jeanneney going to call an emergency meeting of senators and deputies?'

Herriot was so appalled at the prospect that he stared at Auriol 'in open-eyed amazement', and threw up his hands as he replied, 'What on earth for? What a spectacle *that* would be for the people of France!'

The truth is that, though constitutionally the French Parliament did have the power to decide the future of France, Herriot and Jeanneney refused to convoke Parlia-

ment because most members did not want to implicate the
parliamentary system – or themselves – in a dramatic decision which might turn out to be the wrong one. No one in
Bordeaux knew what would happen in a month, in a week,
even tomorrow; it was easier – and safer – to let others
assume those responsibilities, leaving the members free in
the future to insist if it suited them that their suggestions had
been ignored.

Around this time, Reynaud held the first of two painful discussions. Despite Madame de Portes' veto, Reynaud still wondered if troops could be embarked from Brittany – a reasonable strategy had the plan been implemented when first
mooted, but now too late – and de Gaulle was actually on his
way to London to ask the British to provide transport for any
French who could escape from Brittany (unaware that Brooke
had persuaded Churchill the Breton redoubt was not feasible). Reynaud did not know of Churchill's decision either,
so felt he should ask Darlan whether he could provide
additional vessels for troops wishing to fight on from Algiers.
The two met at nine a.m., with Darlan in a foul temper
having spent the night in a jolting train carrying him from his
new headquarters at Rochefort.

Darlan was uninterested in Reynaud's request for ships.
Despite the nautical jacket he affected, despite his bluffness,
despite the pipe that was a fixture into the corner of his
mouth, Darlan was more of a politician than a sailor, and
regarded the French fleet not so much as an instrument for
fighting as an instrument for bargaining. Behind his back he
was known as a 'rue Royale sailor'.* (Bullitt, the American
ambassador, in a weak moment described him rather differently: 'Darlan is the greatest military genius of the century,'
he said.)

When Reynaud told Darlan that he still hoped to mass
troops in Brittany, from where they could sail to north
Africa in ten days, Darlan said it could not be done and

---

* The Ministry of the Marine was at the corner of the Concorde and the
rue Royale.

asked how many men Reynaud had in mind. Reynaud replied that he hoped nearly a million men would follow the flag to Algiers.

Darlan was flabbergasted, 'You'll need two hundred ships,' he said. 'They're scattered all over the place. It's physically impossible to call them together in ten days.'

'Do your best,' Reynaud ordered him.

'Well,' conceded Darlan, 'I *do* have ten troopships available. Each one can carry three thousand men. So thirty thousand men can leave immediately if they're ready to embark.'

Reynaud had to admit that he did not even know where the troops were.

At this Darlan lost his temper. 'In that case,' he exploded, 'how can you ask me to evacuate nearly a million men in ten days?'

Without another word he stalked out of the room, banging the door behind him, 'furious at having his time wasted by an entirely nonsensical project'.

Darlan was an extraordinary man. Unable to resist the lure of high office, he felt that he must cover his actions for any eventuality. Almost as soon as he left Reynaud he met Herriot by accident in the Hôtel de Ville.

There were several people in the room, and Herriot remembered later how Darlan drew him aside into a bay window and then 'brusquely' asked him, 'Is it true that those bastards Pétain and Weygand wish to conclude an armistice? If this is so, do you hear, I am leaving with the fleet.'

Reynaud had only a short respite after Darlan left the rue Vital-Carles. Then Weygand arrived. He too was bad tempered, having spent sixteen hours in the train between Briare and Bordeaux. Even worse, he had just learned of Britain's decision to pull out nearly 200,000 troops. Coming on top of Britain's refusal to send aircraft to France, this was 'the last straw', particularly as Weygand had not been told of the decision – or so he said. (In fact communications had let the Allies down again. Brooke received categorical assurances that Weygand would be informed, but the message never reached Briare.)

Reynaud was equally staggered at the news, particularly after the reassurances he had received from Churchill and the Dominion leaders. It seemed absurd – all these promises that no one was prepared to honour.

In truth this was just another misunderstanding between allies who had never understood one another. Brooke insisted that, when they met, Weygand told him that French resistance 'had ceased'. Weygand now told Reynaud that he had not said anything of the kind: 'I told him that French resistance would not last much longer.'

Perhaps because for once both Reynaud and Weygand were equally annoyed with the British the discussion at first was on a fairly amicable level. Weygand even apologised for his bad manners on Thursday.

But what started as a *tête-à-tête* soon degenerated into a dispute. The nub of the quarrel was simple. Reynaud realised the French Army could no longer fight in France, and that it would be wrong to let the troops suffer unnecessary casualties. Yet he still wanted the French Government to go to north Africa, to raise aloft the standard and continue the war from the colonies. If the Government asked for surrender terms, it would be unable to fight on. To get around this dilemma, he suggested a compromise.

'I agree with you that we must stop the fighting,' Reynaud said, 'but the Government must carry on. Surely the best solution is a military capitulation. That would bind the Army, but leave the Government free to go to north Africa and rally the million troops in the French Empire.'

Weygand was horrified at the prospect of a soldier surrendering. That, he felt, was the duty of a government. 'Never!' he replied. 'I refuse and I shall always refuse, whatever may happen, to bespatter our colours with this shame.'

Reynaud was equally obdurate, for he wanted the French to behave as the Dutch had done in defeat. There, as the Germans overran Holland, the Army had surrendered, but Queen Juliana had fled to England, forming a government-

in-exile, which served as a rallying point for all Dutchmen
who wanted to continue the fight.

'You must obtain a ceasefire like the Dutch commander-
in-chief,' he said, 'and when the fighting has stopped and the
moment is ripe, leave for north Africa.'

Reynaud's plan seemed sensible, and had in fact stemmed
from Roosevelt, worried as ever about the future of the
French fleet, in a cable to Churchill. Churchill had passed
the suggestion on to Reynaud. It seemed feasible. The
French Army had hardly covered itself with glory (no more
than had the British at that time), so where could the shame
lie? If Holland had suffered terribly, yet felt it was honourable for the Army to surrender, why was it not also honourable
for the French Army? Weygand did not see it this way, even
when Reynaud protested that Algeria was not a foreign
country or colonial possession, but a part of metropolitan
France. There was no real difference (in theory anyway)
between the Government setting up a government in Tours
or Algeria. Both cities were an integral part of the mother-
land.

'It's not the same thing,' snapped Weygand. 'Anyway an
armistice is a governmental act, while a ceasefire is a military
act, and I refuse to assume responsibility for demanding an
armistice!'

'If that's all that's stopping you, I will take on the responsibility by giving you a written order.'

With 'an angry shake of his head' Weygand took refuge in
the remark that 'the honour of the Army is at stake'.

To Reynaud there seemed only one course open: the time
had come to dismiss his commander-in-chief, and even Weygand realised this, for, as he remembered later, 'The head of
the Government had ordered the army under my command
to lay down their arms and surrender, and I refused to obey.
On taking leave of M. Reynaud I certainly expected that an
order would follow relieving me of my command.'

Yet Reynaud changed his mind, even though, in his own
words, 'the dispute strengthened me in my resolve to relieve
Weygand of his command as soon as possible'.

Or did Reynaud instead decide on a more devious way of getting rid of Weygand – by, incredible though this may seem, resigning himself? Still fearful of public reaction if he insulted a national hero, Reynaud pondered, as he remembered later, 'on another possible outcome. President Lebrun could have accepted my resignation in order to entrust me at the same time with the formation of a new government which itself would be in favour of continuing the war.'

Preposterous though this may seem, we have not only Reynaud's thoughts at this crucial moment, but also confirmation from others who were thinking on exactly similar lines on this Saturday morning. De Margerie certainly felt this course was in Reynaud's mind, and was convinced that Reynaud believed he would be re-elected immediately if he resigned. And when Georges Monnet reached Bordeaux on Saturday morning he made straight for Mandel's office in the Prefecture where the two men had a curious conversation.

'There are at present a certain number of ministers who are clearly in favour of the armistice,' said Monnet. 'Others are beginning to waver. Is there any possibility of cutting down the numbers of ministers and keeping only those who are in favour of continuing the war?'

'I am convinced it could be done,' said Mandel, 'but everything depends on Lebrun. If Reynaud resigns, Lebrun can only entrust the formation of a new government to Reynaud or someone equally determined to carry on the war. Lebrun will consult with Herriot and Jeanneney, and it's unthinkable that they could hand over power to anyone who wishes for an armistice.'

In brief, if Reynaud resigned, it would ironically strengthen his hand.

One other factor would strengthen Reynaud's hand even more – a favourable reply from President Roosevelt. With a cabinet meeting due at four that afternoon, it was becoming increasingly clear to Reynaud that, if only Roosevelt could go further than he had so far done, Reynaud might still be able to sway the defeatists.

Certainly Drexel Biddle felt this to be the case. Before lunch he cabled Washington, 'I feel that I should make it entirely clear that the French Government is now faced with only two alternatives, namely to sue for peace, which of course would have to be unconditional, or to move to north Africa and continue the fight. The decision . . . will depend on the nature of your reply.'

Realising the critical nature of the developments, he also cabled Cordell Hull a brilliant summing-up of the pros and cons of carrying on the fight from north Africa.

Those that advocate surrender stress the very real likelihood of an uprising of an enraged people against the masters, both political and industrial, who have so criminally betrayed and deceived them. The innocent will suffer with the guilty and much blood will flow. They also point to German vengeance which will be wreaked on France for continuance of the struggle from Africa and loss of uncaptured fleet. They question the morale of a French evacuated army in Africa whose families are left to Nazi rule.

Then Biddle looked at the other side of the coin.

Those who urge removal of the Government to north Africa foresee that only thus can a free and independent France survive, for only thus can the symbol of a living France be maintained; only thus can the French fleet be kept afloat for the democracies.

It was a masterly analysis of the problems facing Reynaud, now almost at the end of his moral strength. Still, as Reynaud told Spears just before lunch, all was not yet over. 'With a smile that cost him an effort', he said, 'Everything depends on Roosevelt's reply.'

## 2.  *Roosevelt's dilemma*

Cordell Hull was always a little sceptical of Reynaud's im-
passioned appeals for help. He read hidden meanings into
them; reason told him that Reynaud *must* know that American public opinion was not only divided but changeable.*
He found some of the French appeals 'almost hysterical'.
They 'asked for the impossible' when Reynaud must surely
have known full well the congressional limits which shackled
United States foreign policy, to say nothing of Roosevelt's
delicate personal position.

With a campaign for re-election coming up, Roosevelt, in
the words of Robert Murphy, 'could see the advantage of
making American voters believe that he was not overlooking
any possibility of preventing all-out war'. Recent public
opinion polls indicated that, though sixty-seven per cent of
Americans favoured aid to Britain and France, only twenty-
seven per cent of those in favour of aid supported entering
a war 'now or later'.

As Arthur Krock, the distinguished columnist, put it in the
*New York Times*, 'Armed intervention not yet, and never if
it can be avoided without endangering our security; a desire
to aid Germany's foe or foes to the full point where depriva-
tion of our own defence needs begins; a belief that no official
voice, whether that of the President or Congress, should
appear to promise more than we can render, thus arousing
false hopes abroad.'

So, when Reynaud's last desperate appeal reached Washington, Cordell Hull felt that the French Premier, though not
exactly playing a double game, 'had carried out the intention
with which he had been toying since 18 May: he had covered
himself by appealing to America to come into the war,

---

* As Lord Lothian wrote to an American friend, 'Your countrymen are
very volatile. When the allies get a success they say, "Well, that's fine. They
can win without us." When Hitler is winning they say, "It's all over. There's
nothing effective we can do, so we'd better stay out."'

knowing that unless she did so, the defeat of France was inevitable'.

Count de Saint-Quentin, the French ambassador to Washington, did the best he could, but after spending an hour at the White House on Saturday he cabled Reynaud that there was scant hope of any military intervention.

'I backed your telegram in the most forceful terms,' he wrote. 'Mr Sumner Welles assured me that the United States Government was determined to go as far as it could on the Allies' behalf short of entering the war, for neither Congress nor public opinion would follow it that far. In the event of war, the President would have against him not only the Republicans, but also the top unions and a number of dissident Democrats, who would be only too happy at finding grounds for a favourable attack.'

This was only too true, though it might have been difficult for the hard-pressed French to understand how it was possible for a friend as sympathetic as Roosevelt to be the leader of his country and yet, at times, seemingly powerless.

Before the war Roosevelt had asked Congress for a law to allow him to embargo arms to any aggressive nation but Congress refused unless the embargo applied to everybody. This ended any possibilities of collective security. When war did break out, all Roosevelt could say was, 'This nation will remain a neutral nation, but I cannot ask that every American remain neutral in thought as well. Even a neutral has the right to pay heed to the facts. Even a neutral cannot be asked to close his mind or his conscience.'

Roosevelt not only had to heed Congress; he could not ignore the huge isolationist element in the country – the pacifists, the America First Committee, the anti-New Deal businessmen. Week after week the Hearst Press branded Roosevelt a warmonger prepared to sacrifice American youth in Europe once again. It was a threat that struck home.

Most Americans were anti-Nazi, but a certain number felt that the Germans had some case against the French. Others felt that they had been dragged into World War One by British propaganda and Wall Street, that ideals had been betrayed at Versailles and they had received no thanks for their intervention. They saw no reason why they should become involved again in a far-off war, when the Atlantic and the Pacific provided all the protection they needed.

The Communists, who had generally supported Roosevelt in his New Deal policies that had lifted America out of the Depression, swung against him when the Germans signed a pact with Russia; they now cried that the war in Europe was imperialist and accused Roosevelt of plotting to plunge the United States into it.

Though few in number, the Communists were vociferous and well organised. When the American Youth Congress made a pilgrimage to Washington in January 1940, ostensibly to support the President, Communists and isolationists managed to manipulate the marchers, who chanted 'Schools, not battleships' and sang a verse which ran:

> 'No, Major, no, Major, we'll not go;
> We'll wager, we'll wager this ain't our show.
> Remember that we're not so green
> As the boys in '17.'

Roosevelt was under pressure not only in America and from France but from Churchill, who sent him two cables on this Saturday. In the first he said he was convinced that America would in the end go to war, but at this critical moment for France 'a declaration that the United States will if necessary enter the war might save France. Failing that, in a few days French resistance may have crumpled and we shall be left alone.'

A few hours later Churchill reinforced Reynaud's last appeal with one of his own, in which he said, 'I have heard that M. Reynaud has practically said that the decision of France to continue war from overseas depends on your being able to assure the French Government that the United States of America will come into the war at a very early date . . . I am afraid there is no getting away from the fact that this is the choice before us now.'

Churchill even asked Lord Lothian, the British ambassador in Washington, to see Roosevelt. The two men had a long talk, during which they discussed among other things the dangers facing America if some part of the *British* fleet fell to the Germans in the event of a Nazi victory. Finally Lothian asked Roosevelt a blunt question: 'What are the chances of the United States being at war with Hitler before these final and critical decisions have to be made?'

No one could answer that question, said Roosevelt. Much depended not only on American public opinion, but also 'on whether before that time the dictators had taken some action which compelled the United States to go to war in self-defence'.

So, even while Reynaud was hoping against hope, even while Churchill was adding his pleas to those of the French Premier, Roosevelt could offer no prospects of active participation. At 11 a.m. Washington time, he cabled Reynaud. The message contained a pledge that America would make redoubled efforts to supply all possible moral and material assistance 'so long as the Allied governments continue to resist'. And Roosevelt added, 'I believe it is possible to say that every week that goes by will see additional *matériel* on its way to the Allied nations'. Nor would America recognise 'the results of conquest of territory acquired through military aggression'. But despite the very real sympathy, despite the genuine promises, nothing could hide the bleak conclusion of the President's message: 'I know that you will understand that these statements carry with them no implication of military commitments. Only Congress can make such commitments.'

3. *'Never shall I inflict such ignominy upon our colours'*

Shortly before 4 p.m. the French ministers started to trickle into the gloomy, colonnaded hall of the Prefect's house, next door to Reynaud's in the rue Vital-Carles, and now the temporary home of the President of the Republic.

The cabinet meeting was held in more cheerful surroundings – the spacious ground-floor sitting-room, beautifully proportioned and furnished in the Empire style. At one end french windows gave out on to a large winter garden, at the other end panelled double doors led to an outer drawing-room where the politicians now congregated.

Despite Weygand's antagonism, Reynaud was still determined to try to implement the 'Dutch plan', so that, almost as soon as the meeting proper started and the inevitable question of seeking an armistice arose, he said, 'I am going to do something better than conclude an armistice. I am going to order a ceasefire and the shooting will stop at once.'

Nothing could have delighted the cabinet ministers more, but how could it be achieved? In fact Reynaud hit on a brilliant debating-point: if France requested an armistice, fighting would continue for several days while it was discussed with the Germans. But, if the Army were to lay down its arms now, the slaughter could stop immediately, this very day.

Reynaud was so eloquent that he virtually persuaded the Cabinet to agree to a purely military ceasefire. No one knew of the harsh words that had passssed between premier and commander-in-chief a few hours earlier; it seemed a neat arrangement. Even Pétain was inclined to favour it. There was still one stumbling-block – in the shape of Weygand, cooling his heels in the ante-room – but Reynaud felt that with Pétain on his side he might be able to deal with the obdurate commander.

Now Reynaud hit on another, less happy, idea. Knowing that he himself could never persuade the hysterical Weygand, he suggested, 'Nobody is more qualified than Marshal Pétain to explain to General Weygand that this solution in no way conflicts with the Army's honour.'

It seemed sensible to ask Pétain to mediate; even Lebrun felt that 'Marshal Pétain seemed convinced'. But he was frail; he was a soldier talking to another soldier; they both heartily despised politicians. In fact Reynaud could not have chosen a worse envoy.

After fifteen minutes Pétain returned and said that Weygand would not change his mind. Had Pétain now stood by Reynaud, the Premier could have dismissed Weygand on the spot because to the people of France Pétain could do no wrong; but worse was to come: Pétain went on in his slow, pontifical way to make it clear that he believed Weygand's concept of military honour was right.

Reynaud was mortified, the more so as Pétain refused to explain why he had changed his mind. 'Only they knew,' Reynaud wrote later, 'and they preferred to keep silent.'

Reynaud was thrown back on the defensive and Camille Chautemps, the Vicar of Bray in French politics, was just the man to take advantage of him.

For twenty years Chautemps had managed to be a member of every French government, despite their different political leanings, and, as Theodore Draper put it, 'even to be Premier himself when all the leading contenders cancelled each other out', though he was 'unlucky enough to fall into crises which forced him to betray his lack of character and policy – notably when he resigned just in time to leave France without a government when Hitler seized Austria'. A silver-tongued orator, at his best when retailing tragic events in 'a rhythmical wail', Spears felt that 'Chautemps could have made a stone weep'.

He described the plight of the refugees, then of 'the brave soldiers of France who are being exterminated in a rabbit drive'. Taking the greatest care not to side openly with Pétain and Weygand, he insisted that it would be impossible to ask for an armistice because of the treaty binding Britain and France.

Instead he made a sinister proposal. 'You are asking us to leave France,' he said to Reynaud. 'It is an unprecedented action and you, like us, are aware of its extreme gravity. We do not refuse. But if the Government is prepared to follow you to north Africa, it must be protected from adverse public opinion. I am convinced that the Germans' conditions for

an armistice will be unacceptable; but we must prove it, and
to prove it we must ask what they are. Once this proof has
been offered, the French people will realise that the Government had no choice but to leave France, and all the ministers
will follow you to north Africa.'

The room, crowded with ministers, had, as Léon Blum
remembered later, been hushed by what Blum described as
'this *coup de théâtre*'. After a pause to allow his words to
sink in, Chautemps added, 'Let us therefore ask the Germans
what their *conditions* would be. And, because of our obligations, let us inform the British Government that we are
taking this step. Mr Churchill, who has shown us understanding and sympathy, would surely not withhold his consent.'

Again he stressed that he was not in favour of *seeking* an
armistice, but only of asking for conditions under which
an armistice might be possible. To ask for the *terms* of an
armistice was not the same as to ask for an armistice. The
idea seemed on the surface brilliant to politicians clutching
at any straw, for it did not (in theory, anyway) commit them.
It procrastinated at a critical moment when every hour gained
was precious. Spears felt, when Mandel told him what had
happened, 'There was another point in favour of his crafty proposal: it meant casting a share of responsibility on the British
government; either they agree and the French are covered,
or they disagree, when the French would have a grievance.'

The idea that the Germans would stop fighting while
arguing about whether or not to discuss an armistice was
preposterous. Churchill later wrote, 'It was not of course
possible to embark on this slippery slope and stop,' yet 'the
Chautemps suggestion had a deadly effect on the majority'.

Shattered as he realised that 'the Pétain–Weygand clique
is joining hands with the Chautemps clique', Reynaud
picked up a piece of paper and down the middle drew a
straight firm line with his thick, black pencil. On the right of
the line he wrote down the names of those who favoured the
Chautemps proposal, on the left the names of those on whom
he felt he could count for support. There were thirteen
names on the right of the line, six on the left.

With hardly a moment's hesitation, Reynaud rose to his feet, turned to Lebrun and said, 'I have no choice but to hand in my government's resignation.'

Lebrun, without thinking, protested, 'If you go – I go too.' (He could not, of course. As President he was not free to leave office.)

Reynaud now faced what he remembered as 'perhaps the gravest moments in my political life'. Perhaps the moment he had hoped for, when he could get rid of Weygand, had arrived. But would Lebrun in fact summon him back if he resigned? He could not be sure. Chautemps' proposal, coming out of the blue, had changed everything. Now Reynaud was no longer sure that he would be able to form a new government. An astute politician, Reynaud realised that timing was all important, and at this moment the timing was somehow wrong. When Lebrun insisted, Reynaud agreed to remain in office.

The cabinet meeting had lasted four hours, but there was more drama to come. As Reynaud walked into the ante-room at five minutes to eight, he saw Weygand. He came straight up to him and said, 'General, as we agreed earlier, I want you to seek the surrender of the Army.'

'I have never agreed to anything of the kind,' cried Weygand. 'Nothing will compel me to perform an action of which I thoroughly disapprove! No force can make me sign the surrender of an army that has fought like ours.'

'Calm down,' said Reynaud.

'I shall *not* calm down,' shouted Weygand, 'nor shall I hold back what I have to say! The Government can dismiss me if it likes, but never shall I inflict such ignominy upon our colours! You were mistaken if you supposed that you found in me a man ready to stoop to any task! The cessation of hostilities, like the decision to go to war, is the Government's business. Let it show itself capable of facing up to its responsibilities!'

'Don't worry, it will,' Reynaud answered.

Weygand quickly went into the makeshift cabinet room,

where Lebrun was talking to some of the ministers. Beside himself with rage at what he considered a public insult, Weygand turned on Lebrun and shouted, 'Do you take me for a child? Was this what I was recalled from Beirut for – to walk into a trap? I have been involved in the nation's affairs for too long not to know how far everyone is to blame for the present tragedy.'

'Kindly be quiet,' replied Lebrun, with great dignity. 'The acrimony of your remarks is really too much.'

Reynaud, returning to the cabinet room, was appalled. He would have been even more shattered had he known that this very morning his commander-in-chief had been the main instigator in hatching a plot to depose Reynaud by force if necessary.

Convinced that he was about to be relieved of office, Weygand decided to turn his two-day-old threat, 'it will be necessary to arrest them', into fact, by using French air force cadets training at Mérignac airfield, near Bordeaux. The plot came to light only by the merest chance.

During the morning the cadets were suddenly summoned for a major parade. As Christian Foucher* remembered, they stood to attention while an officer told them, 'Marshal Pétain and General Weygand are determined to carry on with the war by all means, but the civilians wish to capitulate. It is very possible that they will have the Marshal and General Weygand arrested with the help of a Senegalese Regiment stationed near Bordeaux. You will be entrusted with the glorious duty to watch over the safety of the great leaders.'

It may seem incredible that the Commander-in-Chief could dare to hope that such a twisted story – a complete reversal of the facts – would be accepted. Yet any doubts were quickly dispelled by the sight of General Weygand himself. Soon after the youngsters were marched to the arsenal and issued with automatic weapons, then formed

---

* One of the cadets, Christian Foucher, later to become a secretary in the diplomatic service, wrote a full account of the plot in *La Marseillaise* of 15 June 1943.

into small, mobile detachments, and told to prepare to guard various key points in Bordeaux later in the day.

About this time Jean Daney, the young cadet who had given Madame de Gelabert a lift, drove her out to Mérignac to meet Jean-Paul Joffre. They were both puzzled to find that the normal free and easy atmosphere at the entrance to the airfield had suddenly disappeared. The place was on a 'war footing', buzzing with excitement. When Daney explained to a sentry that Madame de Gelabert wanted to see her relative ('I thought I'd better stretch it a bit') he was met with a blank refusal by guards who, he noticed, were now armed with sub-machine guns.

'All cadets are being confined to barracks,' she heard one guard tell Daney.

As they stood by the main gates, pondering what to do, the sentries snapped to attention, a shiny black Citroën drove up, the gates opened to a flurry of salutes as the car drove through. Madame de Gelabert caught a glimpse of a huddled figure, half-hidden in the back. It was General Weygand.

Finally Daney – crestfallen because he had arrived too late to be assigned duties in the plot – discovered what had happened, and explained to Madame de Gelabert why Joffre could not see her.

Daney was appalled at the prospect of missing the 'fun'. Madame de Gelabert was appalled for another reason. 'It seemed to me that something was wrong somewhere. Everyone knew that Reynaud wanted to fight.' According to all the rumours she had heard, 'it was the generals who didn't want to fight'. Though she was puzzled, it seemed at first that there was nothing she could do about it. She had met Madame de Portes once and it crossed her mind that she should go to see her. But she didn't even know where she was staying 'or for that matter if she were even in Bordeaux'. Anyway, she would be far too frightened to confront 'that witch' – and there was probably nothing in the story anyway.

She might have done nothing had not Gabby, her husband, given her a letter of introduction to a Madame Coudray, an ex-actress and family friend who, Gabby felt, might help his wife. Madame de Gelabert went round to see the old lady, really to discuss the simplest way of reaching the Spanish frontier, but finished up by telling her what she had seen at Mérignac. Madame Coudray was horrified.

'But everyone knows it's Reynaud who wants to fight,' she cried. 'I don't believe a word of what Weygand says.'

Finally, she persuaded Madame de Gelabert to go to the Prefecture. It was the only place they could both think of. 'I'll come along with you,' said Madame Coudray.

Neither knew that the Prefecture had been virtually taken over by Georges Mandel. When they reached the crowd of milling people, a gendarme told her, 'Monsieur le Prefet is out, and I am sure that Monsieur Mandel is too busy to see you.'

'Mandel!' cried Madame Coudray. 'But I know him. He's a close friend of someone who was on the stage with me before I married.'

At that moment Mandel walked down the stairs. Madame Coudray asked if he remembered her. Madame de Gelabert told her story.

All these coincidences – Marguerite de Gelabert meeting Daney at Tours, Madame Coudray having met Mandel and Béatrice Bretty, with whom Mandel was in love, the fact that Mandel appeared in the Prefecture at that one particular moment – may well have combined to save Reynaud's life. Certainly the chain of events was so bizarre they would never have been tolerated in a work of fiction.

How the plot was quashed has never been divulged, but certainly Mandel took immediate action. Later that day Joffre telephoned Madame de Gelabert. The orders confining the cadets to barracks had been cancelled, he said; he fixed a time to meet her. But it also seems that, though Mandel acted quickly, the speed of events was so pressing that he only gave Reynaud the barest outline, for Reynaud later wrote that he did not learn the details for five years.*

* Years later Reynaud met Madame de Gelabert in Greece and, with typical French gallantry, apologised 'for not having thanked you personally'. Reynaud also told the author that had he not been warned he would probably have been arrested or assassinated.

Weygand was not the only one plotting behind Reynaud's back. On this same afternoon Madame de Portes took the ultimate step of going to the United States temporary embassy in the rue Esprit-des-Lois and begging a top official to persuade 'cher Paul' to give in. The man chosen as the target for her appeal was 'Doc' Matthews, who probably had more experience of French affairs than any other American official in Bordeaux; but nothing had prepared him for the sudden arrival of this hysterical lady at the embassy, or the tactics she used to try to win his sympathy.

It is a measure of her panic that, though she must have known that America was doing everything possible to encourage France to stay *in* the fight, she still had the temerity to believe she could make American officials change their minds. Though she might have been able to storm and threaten Reynaud, she had to employ more subtle methods with Matthews, so resorted to woman's oldest guile: she burst into floods of tears, and for an hour wept on his shoulder, hysterically entreating him to bring pressure on 'poor Paul' to surrender.

The truth is that she was terrified by the time she reached Bordeaux. There had been several air raids, and Vincent Sheean told how 'she lived in chattering fear from the moment the first German bomb fell and ... was afraid to travel except under the protection of the American flag. Her face at Bordeaux, towards the end, was not recognisable. All the make-up had fallen off and the natural pale green skin of the frightened woman appeared.'

No wonder that, after she left, Matthews cabled the State Department that 'I don't think her role in encouraging the defeatist elements during Reynaud's critical last days as prime minister should be underestimated. She spent an hour weeping in my office to get us to urge Reynaud to ask for an armistice. She knew that our efforts were all in the opposite direction but she was in such a state of panic that she would leave no stone unturned to get Reynaud to surrender.'

### 4. *'The last quarter of an hour'*

Within an hour of the cabinet meeting's end, Reynaud sent for Campbell, the British ambassador, and General Spears. The latter noticed that 'Reynaud looked pale – washed out would be the right description, a starched collar that had fallen back into the tub.' The two Britishers sat down at the imitation ebony and ormolu table that served as a desk, with Campbell on Reynaud's right, while the Prime Minister gave them details of the cabinet meeting.

Such was the importance of the occasion that Spears felt it only proper to keep a written record of what was said, and looked round for some scrap of paper on which to make notes. Finding none, he seized a few sheets of foolscap headed 'République Française'. He had hardly written a dozen words when Reynaud said, 'As Churchill stated at Tours that he would agree that France should sue for an armistice. . . .'

'But that's not true,' Spears cried.

Reynaud looked surprised. 'Baudouin asserted at the cabinet that he *did* say so,' he replied.

Spears answered sharply, 'All three of us were at the meeting and all three of us know that the Prime Minister never said anything of the sort.'

Reynaud finally rang his bell for de Margerie, and asked him to bring in the minutes of the Tours meeting. They did not contain a single word that in any way could be construed or twisted into the statement that Baudouin had claimed Churchill uttered.

Reynaud thanked de Margerie. Then without another word he took several sheets of paper and started to write a message for Churchill. It read:

At the meeting of the Cabinet this afternoon it was held that at a moment when the enemy is on the point of occupying the entire country, which will mean inflicting cruel privations and suffering on the French nation, the departure of the government would be considered by the people as desertion.

This might give rise to violent reactions on the part of the public unless it had been established that the peace conditions imposed by Herr Hitler and Signor Mussolini were unacceptable as being contrary to the vital and honourable interests of France.

The Cabinet does not doubt that these conditions will in any event be unacceptable, but has decided that it is indispensable that this should be proved beyond doubt. If this course is not adopted the government will break up, as many of its members would in that case refuse to leave the soil of France.

With a view to ascertaining German and Italian conditions, the Cabinet decided to seek leave of the British government to enquire through the United States government what armistice terms would be offered to France by the German and Italian governments.

The Prime Minister is authorised, if the British government will agree to the French government's taking this step, to declare to the British government that the surrender of the French fleet to Germany would be held to be an unacceptable condition.

Should the British government withhold its consent to this step, it seems likely, in view of the opinions expressed at the Cabinet meeting, that the Prime Minister would have no alternative but to resign.

Reynaud had just finished writing what he thought was the final paragraph when a messenger entered and handed him a sealed envelope. It contained Roosevelt's answer. As Spears watched closely, Reynaud 'grew still paler, his face contracting, his eyes became just slits'.

In a 'small, toneless' voice he said, 'Our appeal has failed. The Americans will not declare war.'

It is not difficult, looking back, to imagine the drama of that moment in the upstairs room in the rue Vital-Carles, but

it is difficult to understand how a man of Reynaud's perception and political knowledge could have expected any other
answer.

He must have known that, though Roosevelt had gone as
far as possible to sway American public opinion in support
of France and Britain, he could not at that time have brought
a united country to the point of declaring war. Many Americans were afraid of Nazi Germany, and thought that if
France fell the United States would not be invulnerable.*
But the United States was half a world away from darkened
France, with the street lights burning, a world where the
agony of France was remote, a world where newspaper
readers were still reading details of a New York première:
Ray Milland and Loretta Young in *The Doctor Takes a Wife*.

Certainly in this case Madame de Portes cannot be blamed
for Reynaud's illusion; it can only be explained by the fact
that even when all is lost men have to go on hoping.

As Campbell and Spears read the text of Roosevelt's reply,
Reynaud added a postscript to his message to Churchill:

> It was agreed last Thursday, at your suggestion, that the
> question of authorising a request for an armistice would
> be reconsidered if President Roosevelt's reply was neg-
> ative. This eventuality having materialised, I think the
> question must now be put afresh.

Handing the message to the British ambassador, he asked,
'Please send this to Mr Churchill as soon as you can. Make
it clear that the decision was not taken by me, but by the
Cabinet. It is essential that I get an answer, telephoned if
possible, early tomorrow morning.'

'That doesn't give us much time,' said Campbell.

'I know – but think how those in the Cabinet who want an

---

* In a recent conversation with the author, an articulate and politically
conscious friend said, 'I remember as a girl in Omaha, Nebraska, being more
concerned about the fall of France than I was about Vietnam until the later
years of that war. We felt that if France fell, we might. We never felt that
way about Vietnam.'

armistice are going to exploit the President's reply,' said Reynaud. 'I should like to face them tomorrow morning with a British answer that will somehow offset it.'

Herriot and Jeanneney now arrived, to be told the latest news. There was little they could do about it, and after staying only a few minutes they left. Since Lebrun's residence was only a couple of steps away in the same street, they decided to acquaint him with the details of Roosevelt's reply.

They were too late. Though it was only a few minutes past ten, Jeanneney remembered later that for some time their knock on the heavy old door was not answered. Finally the door handle was turned – but not by a servant. André Magre, Lebrun's sixty-two-year-old Secretary-General, stood there in his pyjamas. The whole household, he whispered, was asleep.

Meanwhile Campbell and Spears had reached their hotel to despatch the message (which reached London at 4 a.m.), and at midnight Drexel Biddle arrived to see Reynaud at the rue Vital-Carles. However much Reynaud tried to put a brave face on it, he could not disguise his 'profound disappointment' at Roosevelt's reply, and told Biddle that without some guarantee of more help from America it was going to be difficult to prevent the Cabinet from sounding out the Germans for armistice terms.

Biddle asked Reynaud just one question: how could he have agreed to such a 'risky enterprise'? Reynaud brushed aside Biddle's fears, insisting once again that when the French people realised the severity of the German terms their anger would be so manifest that the Government would be able to justify its decision to fight on from north Africa. He made no attempt to explain just how the people of France – as cut off from reality as their premier – would be told of the terms, or why he thought the Germans would permit them to voice their displeasure.

All Reynaud added, with a certain irony, was, 'I hope the armistice conditions won't be too moderate.'

There was little Biddle could do but return to the embassy

and cable Roosevelt that Reynaud felt the armistice terms would be so harsh that France would have to reject them, but that only by publishing the German terms 'could [he] show the French people, who had been kept in utter ignorance of the real gravity of the military situation, the severity of the German terms, and justify the flight of the Government to Africa or England'.

France had now reached, in Weygand's words, 'the last quarter of an hour'. In the early hours of the morning, most people in Bordeaux were preparing to try to sleep for the rest of the night – the refugees in their cars or on park benches, or in the lobbies of the more hospitable hotels, the more fortunate in their suites in the Splendide.

Reynaud was exhausted and – who knows? – might even have been secretly grateful that Madame de Portes was safely out of the way in her hotel room and so could not torment him.

Not all were asleep. Spears spent two hours sitting on the edge of his bed in the Hôtel Montré making a telephone call to Churchill. In a room below cipher clerks were 'translating' Reynaud's message and the night's cables.

The Chapon Fin was still crowded long after midnight, and at his usual corner table sat Pierre Laval – dark face above white tie – talking earnestly to his crony Marquet.

In a small studio off the Place Gambetta, Drue Tartière, the American actress, was still broadcasting to America on Radio Mondiale, telling listeners of 'the heartsick mob, the new population of the town, jammed into three cafés in the Place de la Comédie, or walking restlessly up and down'.

When she had finished an American nicknamed Smitty took over. Just as he started, the sirens wailed, and as the first German bombs whistled down he yelled into the microphone, 'Hear that, America? The goddamned sons of bitches are bombing us now!'

In Paris, Jimmy Ashworth, safely back from Tours, had arranged for his daughter's piano tuition, and went to sleep. It would be the last night in five years that he slept in his own bed. He had been warned that the internment of Britishers would start the next day.

In England, General de Gaulle had landed from a French warship at Plymouth before midnight, and was being driven through the night to London.

One wonders what all these people, each involved in differing ways in what Sartre called 'a phantom war, a phantom defeat, a phantom guilt', would have thought had they known that far away, on the other side of the Atlantic, in a country at peace, a man sitting in his oval-shaped study, picked up a pen and scrawled his signature to a document of profound significance, one that would change the history of the world.

For in Washington that night Roosevelt, after many misgivings, finally gave the executive order which led to the manufacture of the atomic bomb.

# Sunday, 16 June

## 1.  *The Gestapo moves in*

As Bordeaux writhed in its death throes, the corpse of Paris
was slowly stirring to life. It was not life really, but a twilight
existence that reminded Jimmy Ashworth of a car crash
victim who experienced all the emotions of death, only to
awake a cripple for whom no cure was possible. Like many
other British people, Ashworth felt it would be impossible
to escape with his family, so had decided to take his chances
with internment.

The German entry into Paris was not so much the kiss of
death to a great and beautiful city as a stamp of bondage on
a proud and independent people, suddenly become slaves;
and 'the terrible thing', Ashworth remembered later, 'was
the feeling that there was no way this slavery could ever end.
Being British I suppose I was sure the British would win, but
I tended to think like a Frenchman, and remember wondering, How can *anybody ever* cross the Channel and kick the
Germans out?'

Sunday was warm, with the sun dusting the boulevards,
and many people were drawn to church, not merely pilgrim-
ages to Notre-Dame or Sacré Cœur – though both were
packed – but to their own small churches just around the
corner, which many had not visited for years.

The city was filled with the desolation that comes to
people kept in ignorance, for none knew that the moment of
decision was about to be reached in Bordeaux. Indeed, no-

body knew anything except what the Germans allowed them to read in *Le Matin,* which had been restarted with the help of liftman Schliess. Its first and second issues dealt mainly with German victories, Hitler's 'humane' plans for the French people, together with vitriolic attacks on the British, who, the newspaper predictably announced, were responsible for the tragic situation in which the French people found themselves.

Above all else, nothing could disguise the feeling of desperate unhappiness, as William Shirer found when he arrived with an ache in the pit of his stomach at the sight of the empty streets. 'I wish I had not come,' he wrote. 'My German companions were in high spirits.' As he reached the Place de l'Opéra, he remembered, 'For the first time in my life, no traffic tie-up here, no French cops shouting meaninglessly at cars hopelessly blocked. The façade of the Opera House was hidden behind stacked sandbags. The Café de la Paix seemed to be just reopening. A lone *garçon* was bringing out some tables and chairs. German soldiers stood on the terrace grabbing them.'

To the Germans, Paris was no longer a battlefield, but rather a rest and recreation centre, and Shirer, who noticed a certain amount of 'open fraternising' between German soldiers and Parisians, remarked that 'it seems funny, but every German soldier carries a camera. I saw them by the thousands today, photographing Notre-Dame, the Arc de Triomphe, the Invalides.'

The first German women had appeared. Ninetta Jucker, who had returned to Paris after her car overturned, thought they were 'tough-looking young women' who drove up to Maxim's or the Tour d'Argent in expensive cars, the mistresses of German officers who had come for a whiff of conquest.

Many Parisians were now returning, drifting into the city, footsore, the children so tired they could neither eat nor sleep. Many refugees had ditched their cars – literally – and made their way back as best as they could on foot. They collapsed on the pavements or on the roads. Whenever she could Mrs Jucker took children into the concierge's lodge in the courtyard and fed them with condensed milk.

Hundreds of French soldiers were also flooding back to the capital. Too tired to search for civilian clothes, they had simply torn the buttons off their tunics to 'prove' they had become civilians. One told her, 'We had the guns, but the wrong ammunition.'

Many shops had reopened, for Sunday morning was a busy day for thrifty housewives. True, stalls were half-empty in the open-air street-market that stretched along the centre of the Boulevard Raspail, but there was an echo of the old bustle as shopkeepers offered their clean, well-packed vegetables and the herbs for which this market was famous.

Though in some areas of Paris the shelves in the shops were bare, in others there were still good stocks, particularly of expensive foods, as Dynevor Rhys discovered when he decided to lay in some provisions. Around 9 a.m. he strolled to his usual grocer, a small shop in the rue de Rennes. All seemed quiet. German vehicles were parked in the small square by the requisitioned Hôtel Lutétia. A tall, slim German officer who spoke French asked politely to see his papers, and when he discovered that Dynevor Rhys was a neutral American insisted on airing his knowledge of the English language. Rhys remembers little of the conversation, except the officer's puzzled, bewildered remark, 'I just can't understand it – it's all been so easy.'

Rhys was anxious to shop early, certain there would be a rush for food. But the rue de Rennes was almost empty, and he was amazed that 'it didn't seem to occur to people what was going to happen. I was the only person in the shop and the grocer was delighted to have a customer.'

In fact, most residents had left, and the few remaining on the Left Bank probably did not have enough money for expensive canned food. In all Rhys made five trips to the Épicerie Bec Fin, bringing back all the flour, rice and canned goods he could carry.

Someone else was pleased to see him – Veillard, the local carpenter, who years before had put up the bookshelves lining one wall of Dynevor Rhys's apartment, and was now delighted to get a small cash-on-the-nail job to do. There was not enough room in the apartment to store all the food. However, on the tiny landing opposite the fifth-floor front door – the top storey of the building – was a small room that had been a separate toilet before Dynevor Rhys installed a bathroom. In a few hours Veillard lined the cubicle with shelves, produced a heavy padlock and locked up the store of food.

Though Dynevor Rhys was able to lay in a supply of food, his colleague Iris Schweppe in Vaucresson was not so lucky. She had, it is true, ransacked her neighbour's garden, but when she went to buy canned food at her local grocer she found a polite German standing in the shop with something that looked like a small knife in one hand. She was told she could buy what she wanted within reason, but on one condition: as a precaution against hoarding, the German sergeant had orders to puncture a hole in the lid – which meant that the contents had to be eaten or drunk fairly quickly.

The Germans demanded strict obedience to all the rules they laid down, and within forty-eight hours closed three shops in the community for overcharging. Soldiers marched up to one grocery shop, unceremoniously padlocked the doors and stuck a notice in the window: 'Closed for one week because of attempted speculation.'

Other troops, armed with spades and hoses, started studying the back gardens – including the tiny patch of ground belonging to Iris Schweppe. Whenever the Germans suspected that the ground had been disturbed, they poured water on it. If the soil settled, if it made even a slight depression, the Germans took it as evidence of a possible hole, perhaps a cache of hidden money or jewels. In half a dozen gardens Germans found buried treasure in the form of silver, cutlery, plate and other valuables too heavy for the refugees to carry with them when they fled.

It was on the Sunday that the Germans made their first arrest in Vaucresson – an inoffensive English widow of at least eighty called Mrs Joyce Wilkinson, who had lived in

Vaucresson for thirty years. Iris Schweppe heard she had been arrested with hundreds of others in the Paris area during a round-up of 'dangerous newspaper agitators'. The sobriquet was laughable. Mrs Wilkinson was the mildest of women. She had never been a journalist – or had she? In fact, Mrs Wilkinson had written occasional articles for a York-shire newspaper, the *Doncaster Gazette*. She had received no payment, but as a journalist (and a widow in straitened cir-cumstances) she was entitled to get her French *carte d'identité* for eighty instead of the normal 400 francs. To the Germans, she was a newspaper reporter – and suspect.*

The German zeal resulted in some curious situations. During the afternoon Iris Schweppe heard a knock on the door. A German sergeant, good-looking and smiling, gave her a swift, stiff bow from the waist and asked, 'Miss Schweppe?' Iris nodded.

'You are English, Fraulein?' He did not wait for a reply, but, consulting some documents, added, 'I understand you have a radio set and a telephone. This is forbidden for all English people. I must ask you to hand over your radio set. I will give you an official receipt. Arrangements will be made for your telephone to be cut off.'

Iris Scheweppe, who had a sense of humour, replied, 'You'd better speak to my mother.' To a German soldier it seemed an odd remark from a woman of thirty-eight. He 'looked puzzled' and started, 'But, Fraulein—'

'Mother,' shouted Iris and waited. Seventy-year-old Mrs Schweppe trundled down the stairs to the front door.

'Well, young man?' she glared at the sergeant.

'Your radio, madame,' started the sergeant, who obviously had not done all his homework.

'And since when has it been illegal for a German national to own a radio set?' snorted Mrs Schweppe, brandishing her passport.

The startled sergeant left, returning with an officer, who compromised by warning Mrs Schweppe, 'You can of course keep the radio and the telephone, Frau Schweppe, but on the

---

* Mrs Wilkinson was released three months later.

strict understanding that your daughter does not listen in or use the phone.'

By Sunday afternoon, the Gestapo was in action, and started a series of 'spot checks'. Many Americans were questioned, ostensibly to make certain they were not suffering undue hardship, but in reality to make certain they were not hiding people.

Armed with lists of addresses where Americans were known to be living, they visited apartment after apartment, including the one in which Madame Beaurepos and Mrs Etta Shiber were living – and hiding William Gray, the R.A.F. pilot, who had been there for two days, while Madame Beaurepos and Mrs Shiber tried to think of a way to help him to escape.

The two ladies and Gray were sitting in the living-room at the rue Balny d'Avricourt, with its large leather-backed divan and gay warm rosy colours, drinking the last of Madame's genuine coffee, when the doorbell rang.

Mrs Shiber bundled Gray into her bedroom and whispered, 'Quick! Get off your clothes and into bed. Pretend you are ill. Leave the talking to me.'

More than once Gray had reminded Mrs Shiber of her brother Irving, who had died on holiday in Paris several years previously (and was in fact buried in the Père Lachaise cemetery). Her brother's photograph was on the dresser and she remembers, 'I could not help noticing again how much this picture of my brother looked like the young man waiting for his executioners.'

Gray was in bed in seconds. Mrs Shiber tied a towel around his head – just as she heard Kitty Beaurepos call out, 'Etta – where are you? This gentleman wants to see your room.'

As Mrs Shiber walked out into the living-room, it seemed to her 'that the piercing glance of the Gestapo agent bored right through me'. Two plainclothes men stood in the doorway. The remarkable Mrs Shiber opened the bedroom door for the Gestapo man, saying, 'You'll have to excuse the mess.

My brother is quite ill with intestinal flu. I hope you won't have to disturb him.'

As the German walked in she said, in what she hoped was a soothing voice, 'It's all right, Irving, don't try to talk,' and turning to the agent added, 'This is my brother.'

'His papers, please,' the German asked.

She had kept all her brother's papers in a red wallet and now took out his American passport. The Gestapo man flicked through the pages casually while Mrs Shiber 'thanked God for William's unshaven face and also for the fact that the passport, issued some years back, carried a picture taken when Irving was nearer William's age'.

It seemed to satisfy the German, for he walked back into the living-room, asked Madame Beaurepos a few noncommittal questions and left. Within seconds the two women heard the peal of the next-door bell and 'in the doorway of our room appeared a pale-faced, unshaven young man in his underclothes, a towel tied round his head'.

'What happened?' asked William Gray.*

While one group of the Gestapo started house searches, another was engaged in the systematic looting of Jewish property. Armed with lists of where to go, what to take, even what to discard as worthless, they missed nothing.

Shortly after lunch on Sunday, two removal vans, with Cologne number-plates, pulled up outside the famous art gallery belonging to Paul Rosenberg in the rue Faubourg St Honoré. The movers took out every single picture and *objet d'art* they could carry.

If looters did not pillage the beautiful statues of Paris, it was only because they could not be removed from their

---

* These two extraordinary women hid Gray until they found someone who smuggled him into unoccupied France, from where he escaped to England. It was the start of an incredible five months in which they helped 150 British flyers to escape before they were caught and tortured by the Gestapo. Madame Beaurepos was sentenced to death, Mrs Shiber (as an American) to three years' hard labour. In 1942 Mrs Shiber was freed in exchange for the notorious German Johanna Hoffman, who was held by the Americans. Madame Beaurepos was never heard of again.

bases, though there was one exception. A German squad, with a demolition machine, drove up to the bronze statue of General Mangin in the Place Denys-Cochin in the seventh *arrondissement*. Mangin had guarded the Rhineland in 1920 with Senegalese troops; every German 'knew' that he ordered German mayors to provide brothels for his soldiers, and when the mayors protested at 'providing German women for Senegalese gorillas' Mangin was alleged to have replied, 'German women are none too good for my Senegalese.' By Sunday evening, his statue was a mass of rubble.*

The Germans had made meticulous preparations; Robert Murphy of the American embassy was 'amazed to discover how thoroughly they had prepared for every phase of military government'. It was soon apparent to him that they had blueprints to cover any conditions they might encounter. 'The U.S. Government might have practised to advantage some of the German foresight,' he observed later.

Though the Germans prided themselves on their 'correct' behaviour – indeed it was a stringent order – they lapsed frequently as when one German colonel, rummaging about the customs sheds, found a shipment for the American embassy which had not been delivered by the time the Germans entered Paris.

When he saw that the package was addressed personally to the ambassador, the German colonel cried, 'So, these are Bullitt's cigarettes! Well, he won't get them. I used to live in Philadelphia and I never did like Bullitt! Take them away.'

Yet Bullitt stood no nonsense from the Germans. As soon as von Studnitz was installed in the Hôtel Crillon his staff began fixing up special telephone wires on the roof of the hotel. They had to be slung to a point some distance away to operate a direct line to Berlin and, as there was apparently no place on the Crillon roof to which the far end of the wires could be attached, an engineer started to string them along the American chancery roof – the nearest building to the Crillon.

The German engineers were helped by a coloured

* The bronze was melted down and used for German bullets.

American doorman with the picturesque name of George Washington Mitchell, who was born in North Carolina and ended up in Europe in a Buffalo Bill show. Before 'graduating' to the embassy, Mitchell had toured many countries and, though illiterate, spoke a smattering of German. When the engineers climbed on the high, locked metal grille of the chancery fence, George Washington Mitchell started to help them. Horrified, Robert Murphy saw the scene from his office window and ran down the stairs to discover what was happening.

'Why, Mr Murphy, they's from Hamburg,' drawled George Washington Mitchell. 'They know people ah know in Hamburg. They's very nice fellas.'

Bullitt took a different view. Angrily he sent a message to the German general: 'If everything is not removed in one hour I will consider it an inroad on American soil and I will personally open fire on all Germans who are still there.'

They vanished in a matter of minutes.

Bullitt also helped General Dentz, after von Studnitz ordered the French commander to report to him at the Crillon. Dentz arrived, was shown up to the Prince of Wales suite, and left standing outside until the German general sent for him.

'Now that we are in control,' von Studnitz told Dentz, 'please hand over your instructions from the French command.'

Dentz was a tough, burly man of Alsace who did not relish being bullied.

'I have no orders to pass on to an enemy,' he replied.

Von Studnitz, sitting behind his carved, gilt-embossed desk, dropped his monocle in surprise. 'Explain yourself,' he asked.

'There's nothing to explain,' retorted Dentz. 'My mission was to maintain order until you arrived. I accomplished it. Do you agree? Well, the mission is now completed.'

Von Studnitz, flushed with anger, snapped out another question, 'Who was responsible for setting fire to the petrol supplies just before we took your city?'

'I was,' said Dentz coolly.

'You can face a court martial for breaking undertakings given by the French Government,' von Studnitz threatened.

'With all due respect, that is not true,' said Dentz. 'You only have to study a map to see that the dumps were outside the Paris boundaries. No hostile act has been committed inside Paris.'

Von Studnitz was not in the mood to argue. Dentz was ordered to return to Les Invalides, where he was placed under house arrest. Only after vigorous protests by the American ambassador was he released.

The pity is that the people of Paris had no knowledge of the way in which Bullitt did protect certain Frenchmen from the Germans. Instead, at the outset, they received a most unfortunate picture of the American ambassador, which so outraged them that those who saw it never forgave him. It was the result of a stupid error of judgment difficult to credit to a man who prided himself not only on being a good diplomat, but also on his love of all things French.

Bullitt had a country house of his own at Chantilly, thirty miles or so outside Paris, and was anxious to find out if it had been damaged during the German advance. On the Saturday, the day after the Germans entered Paris, he sent Commander Hillenkoetter, his naval attaché, to ask von Studnitz if it would be in order for the ambassador to drive out to Chantilly and inspect his property. Hillenkoetter remembers that General von Studnitz was 'very perturbed'.

'Of course the ambassador can go,' he said. But a moment later he changed his mind and asked if the visit could be postponed until Sunday. Von Studnitz explained to Hillenkoetter, 'There has been some fighting around Chantilly – and I would like to check that the house is all right.'

It was all right, and at 11 a.m. on Sunday those people of occupied Paris who were not behind their shutters saw Bullitt set off. He reclined in the back of his shiny black car, with his Stars and Stripes fluttering from its diplomatic mast, guarded by a posse of motorcycle outriders with swastika armbands, clearing a way through non-existent traffic.

## 2. *The rout*

All over the country, the soldiers of the once-mighty French Army were now in pell-mell retreat. Indeed, the German legions occupied a quarter of the country, and in Berlin Goebbels congratulated the Führer's troops, 'You have just one more battle to win, then the bells of peace will ring.' That peace, Goebbels promised, would be dictated to the Allies in London.

In the north, Rommel started his advance on Cherbourg on Sunday morning. Astonishingly, he had rested only two days since taking Le Havre on the day Paris fell.*

Everywhere the story was the same. For the second day running, German planes bombed virtually every bridge over the Loire, causing enormous losses among the endless columns of refugees and the massed troops choking the crossing-points. 'We are making superhuman efforts,' one officer telephoned General Georges, but complained that 'innumerable convoys of refugees conspired to make the situation truly tragic'.

It was catastrophic. Ever since the exodus started, refugees had from time to time been dive-bombed or machine-gunned, but now they were in the midst of disorganised French troops, fighting for their lives, or in turn becoming hapless refugees. Those who passed along the beautiful banks of the Loire and lived through that French rout on Sunday remember only fragments of the terror they survived – the stale stench of bodies, the dust, those in cars punching at people, shouting, 'Get off, keep clear!' even when no harm was intended; the endless streams on foot, plodding painfully, according to one witness, 'all beginning to look more and more like the one in front and the one behind'; he saw a soldier ask one tottering old woman if he could carry her bundle for her but, suspicious, she hugged

---

* In six weeks Rommel captured 97,648 prisoners, 227 guns, 458 armoured vehicles, 4000 trucks. He lost only 682 killed, 296 missing and 42 guns.

it to her chest and shouted at him. And far above, like
background music, was the terrifying noise of the Luftwaffe.

As the bombing increased on the banks of the Loire, the
confusion was total along roads lined with the charred carcases of cars and trucks, with the occasional tank still smoul-
dering. Near Gien, the roads were lined with bodies, and
nothing could be done for the wounded. Their families were
faced with the terrible choice of whether to stay behind and
nurse them or find their own way out of the morass. By now
hundreds of thousands of civilians were trapped. Most of
them were women and children, some screaming in terror,
others 'dumb with horror' as the battle-weary troops tried to
force a way through, searching for lost units. And as always
the Germans were hard on their heels, so that by nightfall,
as Jacques Benoist-Mechin wrote, 'Nobody knew where our
units were, or where the Germans were, with the result that
hundreds of our batteries, imagining they were encircled,
were inadvertently opening fire on our troops.'

Many of the towns and villages through which the earlier
refugees had streamed were now in enemy hands. A long
German armoured column was calmly advancing along the
main road to Orléans and by evening fighting had started on
the outskirts of the city. Other German units had reached
Alsace and were threatening Colmar. General Pretelat reported, 'I do not know whether the Germans are in Dijon,
but the local commander has fallen back to Châlon-sur-
Saône. Dôle is not occupied, but Besançon is.'

At least Frances Kay, the twenty-two-year-old English girl
cycling to Lyons, was ahead of the Germans. She had joined
forces with a young Besançon university student she knew,
and they cycled together, but to Frances 'The days are all
jumbled up in my memory. I can remember seeing across
the fields the main road being bombed. I slept in barns and
farmhouses at night. And I can remember waking up early
each morning, terrified, and how it always felt better after
we had cycled a bit and found something to eat. There is

something about waking up hungry and shivering which is very demoralising.'

She had promised to try to reach the consulate in Lyons by midday on Sunday. Fortunately, she was ahead of time, reaching the outskirts of the city before 10 a.m. From the direction of Besançon, the approach to the heart of Lyons is by the long downward slope, with the hills on one's right and the river far below on the left, until the road ends by one of the bridges. At least Frances Kay did not have to pedal the last few miles, but she was nevertheless exhausted by the time she reached the consulate shortly before 11 a.m.

It was closed, locked and barred, 'and that was the moment when my heart really sank — all that ride for nothing!'

She rang the bell for the concierge. She seemed to take an age before waddling out. But she did have a message. Ledger, the acting consul who had left Besançon with the honeymooners, had gone to the private residence of the Lyons consul-general. He would wait there until midday. And the consul-general lived, as Frances Kay still remembers, 'right at the top of the long, never-ending hill down which I had free-wheeled. There was nothing to do but go all the way back.'

The hill was too steep for cycling. Frances Kay – who had packed a bottle of brandy in her saddle bag – started to wheel her bicycle all the way back up the hill again, swigging neat brandy from the bottle which until then had been unopened.

As she turned into the gate of the consul-general's garden, Ledger was actually piling his wife and passengers into the car ready to leave.

This time there was room for Frances Kay, when the car set off for Bordeaux.

## 3. Laval waits to be crowned

The tall, graceful windows of the Hôtel Splendide's royal suite had a magnificent view, looking across the Place des Quinconces to the river curling away to both left and right. Old-fashioned the hotel might be, but it lacked nothing in ostentatious comfort. The silk curtains and the thick blue carpet in the bedroom effectively deadened the sounds from the busy square outside, while the adjacent sitting-room was elegantly and comfortably furnished (not always synonymous in France). A cut-glass lamp stood on the small writing-desk of polished inlaid wood. On a coffee table in front of the brocade-covered sofa *café complet* rested on a silver tray. It was 7 a.m., breakfast time for one of the many illustrious clients of the Splendide, Pierre Laval, arch-betrayer of France's honour.

Laval hoped this Sunday would see the culmination of years of scheming endeavour. If France had reached the last quarter of an hour before defeat, Laval had reached the last quarter of an hour before victory.

Laval had come a long way since the days when, instead of being served by a deferential waiter, he himself was serving the coffee in his father's modest café in the small Auvergne town of Châteldun. Charmless, ugly, swarthy, his pudding face almost always marked by a scowl, he had had an insatiable ambition, since, as a penniless lawyer, he started working for the C.G.T. – the Confédération Générale du Travail – finally becoming in 1914 left-wing socialist deputy for the labour stronghold of Aubervilliers near Paris. Since then he had served in eight governments, been prime minister twice, and had changed his political colours from Neo-Communism to Fascism, becoming a fervent admirer of Hitler in the process. Matthews of the United States embassy cabled Washington on one occasion, 'Laval . . . was the strongest believer in a complete and early German victory, and . . . based his entire policy on that theory.'

Though Laval had risen from humble beginnings, he still did not count his achievements as 'success', perhaps because he thirsted for absolute power. Possibly another reason spurred him, an inferiority complex born of the knowledge that, even though he had successfully married his daughter Josée to the Count René de Chambrun in 1935, he was never really accepted, either by French 'society' or, even more, by the French political world. To them, Laval was an outsider, despised for, as Theodore Draper put it, 'his intellectual cheapness ... his mania for scheming. ... He was not the kind who developed a political machine by winning people; he was a master of "combinations".'

The man who helped to arrange these 'combinations' was Adrien Marquet, mayor of Bordeaux, to whom Laval was indebted for occupying his present suite. If Laval saw himself as Führer of France, then Marquet was content to play the role of local political boss, master of Bordeaux, a man whose word was law in his corrupt political kingdom, which he now placed at the disposal of the man conspiring against the State. It was Marquet who sent for Laval, who sensed that Laval's moment of destiny had arrived.

The key to his ambitions, as Laval saw it, lay with the waverers who had not yet made up their minds whether to follow Pétain or Reynaud, but who were waiting, anxious not only to back the winning side, but to be *seen* to have backed the winning side when the moment of retribution arrived.

No city in France could offer Laval a more sinister breeding-ground for plot and counterplot than Bordeaux, for each exhausted senator or deputy who arrived found a government in the last stages of disintegration. Theodore Draper was not alone in finding that the Government 'was no more than a collection of weary, terror-stricken individuals who did not even enjoy the physical symbols of power which they had left behind in Paris'. President Lebrun in an office in the local police station in a provincial city was hardly as impressive as President Lebrun in the Élysée Palace.

The atmosphere of hopelessness made it all the more easy

for Laval's shock troops to play on the frayed nerves of those torn by doubt. Victory for the defeatists was made surer by the fact that several of the senators and deputies who arrived on Saturday and Sunday were already half-convinced that France must capitulate, possibly because many lived near Bordeaux and had already been influenced by Marquet's political machine.

When they did arrive, they were brainwashed. On Sunday morning, Laval was on the telephone to Marquet with a request: 'Could I borrow the large committee room in the Hôtel de Ville?'

This was the main room of the Bordeaux town council, but the town council was the heart of Marquet's empire, and this was just the sort of service a local political 'boss' could offer. Early on Sunday, Laval held the first of several meetings in the large committee room, where he met all the waverers as they arrived. According to his protégé Jean Montigny, 'Tirelessly Laval received the parliamentarians who arrived and repeated his arguments to convince them that it was their duty to stay in France and share the ordeals of the people.'

To each one Laval repeated the words he had used to Senator Jacques Bardoux, 'Let Reynaud bear the shame of asking for a capitulation, but he must not be allowed to negotiate it. He has insulted Hitler and Mussolini, and will receive the hardest conditions. I am going to ask Marshal Pétain to let me do it.'

By Sunday, Montigny found that 'little by little, by virtue of the bankruptcy of the President of the Senate and the President of the Chamber, there was formed a kind of "commune" in Bordeaux which influenced events in a decisive way'.

One wonders whether Reynaud was aware of the extent of Laval's sinister plotting; probably not, for sharply at 10 a.m. Herriot and Jeanneney arrived at the rue Vital-Carles. Reynaud had asked them because constitutionally the Government could not leave metropolitan France without their consent. Reynaud wanted to sound out their views, to make certain they would agree to this course in front of his cabinet colleagues at the eleven o'clock meeting. Both did agree immediately to authorise the Government to move to north Africa.

Jeanneney, a frail, thin invalid who found difficulty in getting out of a chair, rose painfully, swayed a little, then said, 'You can count on me for any action that can save the honour of France.' Herriot was more down to earth. As he left he turned to Reynaud and said, 'I'd rather be shot by the Boches than despised by the French.'

Hardly had they left before Campbell, the British ambassador, arrived with General Spears. They had to wait for a few moments in the secretaries' room, where Madame de Portes was flitting from one person to another, talking at the top of her voice. She pretended not to see the two British visitors.

When Campbell and Spears entered they found Reynaud 'nervously exhausted' and desperately anxious to learn Churchill's reaction to his telegram of the previous night. Churchill, of course, had not had time to consider it, let alone place it before the War Cabinet. For half an hour the British ambassador and Spears did all in their power to bolster Reynaud's flagging morale. The agreement not to make a separate peace was not, as Spears put it, 'just a polite formula'. It had been drawn up for just such a contingency as France now faced. Campbell asked Reynaud point-blank if Pétain could be forced to resign, but Reynaud said that he was afraid of public opinion; he did not change his attitude when Campbell pointed out there could be no public reaction as there were virtually no newspapers and the radio was controlled by the Government.

Spears felt that 'a military Commander might sue for an armistice without dishonour', but it was a very different matter for a country to sue for an armistice while it was still master of the world's second largest colonial empire and possessed a powerful fleet. Reynaud himself had bitterly criticised the King of the Belgians for giving in. Did he want

France to behave like Leopold, or would he follow the example of the Queen of Holland, who had cried as she transferred her government to England, 'Where there is no liberty, there is no place for the House of Orange.'

Spears even offered the ingenious suggestion that, if the French Government moved to north Africa, Pétain could remain behind to negotiate the surrender of the armed forces.

In fact the role of Campbell and Spears was not so much to persuade Reynaud, who clearly agreed with the British viewpoint, but rather to encourage him, to sustain him for the stiff political fight that lay ahead.

Discussion was not made any easier by frequent interruptions by Madame de Portes. Several times she opened the door to Reynaud's office without knocking and was so angry at the never-ending talks that she stamped her foot in rage as she slammed the door. A few minutes later she was back again, head round the corner of the door, making faces at Reynaud as though to say, 'Hurry! I've got important news for you.'

Campbell – the epitome of correct diplomatic behaviour – was shocked, but as Spears remembers, 'We managed to hold our tongues.' Reynaud looked embarrassed but said nothing.

It was left to de Margerie to sympathise, when, on the way out, Spears told him what happened.

'She is ugly, *mal soignée*, dirty, nasty and half-demented and a sore trial to me,' de Margerie said.

As Spears drove away to the consulate – besieged by anxious Britishers – he could only reflect that 'Hélène de Portes had done Paul Reynaud more harm than anyone, for it was she that had imposed on him as collaborators the men who were now his bitterest opponents'.

How could a woman behave like that to the man she loved? Or did she love him? Presumably she did, thought Spears, 'unless she was really infatuated with the power her hold over him gave her'.

At the very moment when Campbell was trying to bolster

Reynaud's morale, Weygand was trying to undermine it. Reynaud at this time cannot have known anything of Weygand's abortive plans for a coup; he was still at liberty – and still undeterred. He chose a curious, roundabout method for his new attack. For reasons never explained, he decided not to attend the cabinet meeting scheduled to start later in the morning, but he did know, of course, that the French President would be there. So Weygand sent for one of his supporters, Senator Charles Reibel and told him of 'the pitiful plight' of the French Army, suggesting that he pass the details of the news directly to Lebrun.

'Within a matter of days, or even a matter of hours,' Weygand told Reibel, 'the French Army will be cut to ribbons. Is it humane, is it reasonable, to treat the French Army this way? If the Government leaves what will be left of France and the French people? Will the latter accept such an act of desertion?' Weygand told Reibel that this was the attitude of 'attack' he should place before the President of the Republic. 'Make the President and the ministers realise', Weygand added, 'that things cannot go on as they are without the deadliest perils for France. And, whatever you do, act quickly, quickly, quickly!'

Reibel almost ran to the President's residence to pour out Weygand's fears.

'Ah, my dear Senator,' replied Lebrun, 'what a curious situation. It is the military – Pétain and Weygand – who want to end the war, and the civilians – Reynaud, Louis Marin and Mandel – who want to continue it.'

A few minutes later President Lebrun opened the morning cabinet meeting, held in the ground-floor sitting-room with its rose-coloured satin chairs. When the ministers had assembled, Jeanneney – on behalf of himself and Herriot – repeated their formal agreement to allow the Government to move to north Africa, then left the room.

Almost before they had withdrawn, Reynaud braced himself for the unenviable task of reading out Roosevelt's reply. Lebrun realised that it had 'a profoundly depressing effect on the Cabinet' for, however sympathetic, 'it cannot be said to have contributed anything new to the situation'.

There was, however, no time for discussion, for, as though relishing the grim news, Pétain rose to his feet, and with a fine sense of the dramatic announced baldly, 'I can no longer remain in the Government. Our armies are disintegrating more and more. The inevitable solution has been put off too long. I do not wish to be associated with this delay, for which all France is paying.'

Even as he ended the first sentence, there was a 'gasp of dismay' and, when the aged marshal turned to walk out of the room, Lebrun – not for the first time over-emotional – cried, 'Mais non! You can't do *that* to us now!'

The ministers joined in the protestations. Even those who backed Reynaud, who knew Pétain would settle for nothing short of capitulation, were so spellbound by Pétain's mystique that one shouted, 'You've got to give the Government the benefit of your prestige.'

This was the stuff on which vanity thrives, and no one was vainer than Pétain. He waited by the door until Reynaud had calmed the hubbub, then slowly walked back to his place. However, to signify his displeasure – and really, what a silly old man he was – he refused to sit down in his chair. He remained standing while Reynaud explained that he could do nothing until he received Churchill's reaction to the Chautemps proposal.

'After all,' added Reynaud mildly, 'when you approach an ally on a serious matter like releasing you from your word, surely etiquette demands that at least you wait for a reply.'

At the sacred word 'etiquette' Pétain pricked up his ears. 'When is the reply supposed to arrive?' he asked.

'I think I shall be able to communicate it to the Cabinet this afternoon. Until then, please be patient.'

'Very well,' Pétain agreed grudgingly, 'I will stay – but only on condition that you hurry up and come to a decision.'

In fact Churchill's reply reached the British embassy as the cabinet meeting was sitting, and the British ambassador was dismayed when he read it.

Our agreement forbidding separate negotiations, whether for armistice or peace, was made with the French Republic, and not with any particular French Administration or statesman. It therefore involves the honour of France. Nevertheless, provided, *but only provided, that the French Fleet is sailed forthwith for British harbours pending negotiations*, His Majesty's Government give their full consent to an inquiry by the French Government to ascertain the terms of an armistice for France. His Majesty's Government, being resolved to continue the war, wholly exclude themselves from all part in the above-mentioned inquiry concerning an armistice.

Spears, too, was very upset, feeling that it was 'a mistake to do anything in the nature of releasing the French from their agreement'. Not only that, the peremptory order to send the French Navy to British ports was an insult, a sign of mistrust; it would infuriate the French, specially the anti-British Darlan. Spears felt so strongly that he offered to phone Churchill and tell him so, though 'he would no doubt bite my head off'.

'After all,' he told the ambassador, 'we are in the last resort dependent on the decision of the French themselves, and if they get it into their heads that we wish to hold their fleet as hostage, the outcry concerning the honour of the French flag raised yesterday by Weygand may be renewed by Darlan today.'

Whatever the ambassador felt, the message was, he pointed out, a cabinet decision. His duty was to deliver it to Reynaud. He took Spears along with him. They walked the short distance down the rue Vital-Carles and were taken in to see Reynaud immediately. He had just returned from the cabinet meeting. When the French Prime Minister read the message he was extremely annoyed and made no effort to disguise the fact.

'What a very silly thing to do, to ask that the French fleet should go to British harbours when at this very moment it is protecting Algeria and the western Mediterranean,' he exploded. 'And you ask me to do this at the moment you are inviting us to go to north Africa. Non! Vraiment, c'est trop bête.'

At that moment the door of his office opened and Madame de Portes popped her head round. This time Reynaud *must* have been angry at the interruption, for instead of raising his eyebrows as he usually did when she appeared he glared angrily at her and, in Spears' words, 'the door closed with unwonted severity'.

When the door had closed, Reynaud added a little more quietly, 'It is really too silly. The French fleet is relieving the British in the Mediterranean. To send ours away would place a fresh strain on yours.'

That was not true, for the French fleet could have operated easily from British bases in the Mediterranean, but Campbell could not emphasise the real reason for the suggestion: the growing concern in London and Washington that the French might use the fleet for bargaining with the Germans when armistice terms were discussed. Roosevelt himself had made clear to Reynaud how vital it was for the French fleet not to fall into enemy hands. If the fleet were anchored in British waters – even if it never left port – its denial to Germany would represent a major Allied victory. Reynaud must have realised this, but he said nothing. Instead he switched the conversation. He had spoken on the phone earlier in the day with Churchill, who had suggested a meeting. Reynaud asked Spears if he would make the arrangements – to meet at sea off Concarneau. Churchill would arrive from England by destroyer.

Campbell had one more message to deliver from Churchill. It was an aide-mémoire to Reynaud: 'Do not forget your promise to send the captured German flyers to England.'

Reynaud had already given the order, as he had promised Churchill he would, but he wrote in red pencil on the side of Campbell's message, 'Say where they will be embarked.'

It was too late. Reynaud later remembered that 'My staff immediately sent my instruction to the competent authority which was intended to speed up the execution of the operation.' But the French were now sliding so swiftly along the road to defeat that Reynaud's order was never carried out, whether or not deliberately we shall never know, and so the 400 German pilots became available for the Battle of Britain with the result that, as Churchill grumbled, 'We had to shoot them down a second time.'

Reynaud was now on the point of despair. While Campbell and Spears tried to encourage him in private, Biddle tried to bolster his image in public, for a display of American interest and support was invaluable, even if it were a charade.

Biddle made certain that he and Reynaud were regularly seen together, talking seriously, smiling confidently, as though some new offer from Washington might be winging its way across the Atlantic cables. The two men had little to say to each other beyond exchanging pleasantries. Biddle could only say, 'Bonjour, mon pauvre vieux.' Reynaud usually replied briefly, 'Bonjour.' But they would then remain closeted together in Reynaud's office for ten or fifteen minutes so that callers impatiently waiting in the ante-room would imagine them discussing matters of vital import. Then, with 'a busy, important look', Biddle would leave the rue Vital-Carles for the United States embassy.

### 4.  De Gaulle lunches with Churchill

The drive from Plymouth to London, in the blackout, with only the smallest slits of light piercing shuttered headlamps, had been slow and tiring, the more so for a man so tall that his long legs were cramped. But de Gaulle, who had arrived

at Plymouth on the French warship *Milan* just before midnight, was in good spirits when the car finally drew up,
shortly after dawn, in front of the Hyde Park Hotel.

He had barely unpacked his grip, and was swilling his
face, when there was a knock on the door.

André Corbin, the French ambassador to London, a
dapper man with a neatly trimmed moustache, Jean Monnet
and René Pleven of the French economic mission to London
had walked round the corner from the French embassy in
Albert Gate.

Corbin reeled off a list of appointments made for de Gaulle
with British shipping experts, and told him that Reynaud
and Churchill planned to meet the following day. De Gaulle
sensed an undercurrent of tension in his visitors. Finally it
came out.

'It occurred to us', said Corbin, 'that some sensational
stroke – if we could throw a new factor into the situation –
might be what's needed to strengthen M. Reynaud to go to
Algiers.'

'We know the mood for surrender is making rapid progress
at Bordeaux,' interrupted Monnet. 'Today's cabinet meeting
could be decisive.'

The three men sat down, the lanky de Gaulle on the edge
of the bed. Coffee arrived. Only then did Corbin, with a note
of suppressed excitement, reveal what they had in mind – a
plan so bold and dramatic that de Gaulle could only describe
it as a *coup de théâtre*. In brief, Corbin suggested forming an
indissoluble union between Britain and France which – if
Churchill could be persuaded to agree – would be solemnly
proposed by the British Government to the French Government in Bordeaux.

For several days Corbin and his colleagues had been
lobbying the project with Sir Robert Vansittart, Permanent
Under-Secretary at the Foreign Office, who was as excited
as they were. But the first hints had been dropped to Churchill only the day before, when he lunched with Corbin,
Monnet and Pleven at the Carlton Club, and Churchill had
grave doubts. 'My first reaction', he remembered, 'was

unfavourable.' When de Gaulle read the proposed draft, he too was doubtful. The idea was magnificent, he agreed, particularly the significance in Bordeaux of such 'a manifestation of solidarity', but was it not, he asked Corbin, too historic a decision to be realised 'by a simple exchange of notes'?

'But if we could get it proposed this afternoon', cried Monnet, 'at least it may postpone surrender.'

'The only problem', admitted the French ambassador, 'is that we shall have to get the plan adopted by the British.' And time was running out. Turning to de Gaulle, Corbin added, 'You alone can persuade Churchill to do it. It's been arranged for you to lunch with him. That will be the supreme opportunity.'

Churchill and de Gaulle lunched at the Carlton Club, and when de Gaulle introduced the subject Churchill's first comment was 'Lord Halifax has spoken to me about it. But it's an enormous mouthful to chew on.'

'Yes,' agreed de Gaulle, 'that means that its realisation will involve a great deal of time. But the gesture can be immediate. As things are now, nothing must be neglected by you that can support France and maintain our alliance.'

Thinking back to that momentous lunch, Churchill remembered that 'I asked a number of questions of a critical nature', but before the two men reached the pudding he realised that de Gaulle had a good case. 'He impressed on me that some dramatic gesture was essential to give Reynaud the support he needed to keep his government in the war.' For his part, the persistent de Gaulle felt that 'Churchill came round to my point of view'.

Churchill could not make such a decision on his own, but called an immediate cabinet meeting. Meanwhile de Gaulle tried to telephone Reynaud, only to be told that he was in a cabinet meeting. He spoke to de Margerie. 'Tell him to hold on, to keep the meeting going as long as possible,' he told him. Later he telephoned again. Reynaud was still unavailable but, though de Gaulle could not even hint at the momentous news that might occur, he did tell de Margerie,

'M. Reynaud might by tonight be prime minister of France and Britain.'

In London the Cabinet was so enthusiastic that even Churchill 'was surprised to see the staid, solid experienced politicians of all parties engage themselves so passionately in an immense design whose implications and consequences were not in any way thought out. I did not resist, but yielded easily!'

As the Cabinet debated, de Gaulle, waiting in an ante-room, again telephoned France. This time he spoke to Reynaud, and begged him to stand by for an important announcement, the details of which he could not divulge. Reynaud promised he would try to delay his second cabinet meeting, timed to start at 5 p.m., but warned de Gaulle, 'I shan't be able to postpone it much longer.'

It was not necessary. The British Cabinet voted over-whelmingly in favour of union, and despite his reservations Churchill felt that 'we must not let ourselves be accused of lack of inspiration'. He did, in fact, contribute to the final draft. When it was agreed, he himself took it to de Gaulle in the next room, noting that 'the general read it with an air of unwonted enthusiasm'.

Then de Gaulle picked up the telephone and asked for Bordeaux.

## 5.  'Better be a Nazi province'

Sadness more than fear was the predominant emotion among the hundreds of Britons crowding round the consulate steps in Bordeaux. To many who had lived half their lives in the country, France really was 'every man's second country', and many were tortured by the same thoughts as Alexander Werth, that 'this lovely, gentle land of France which we had all loved, was, we felt, rapidly disintegrating. This endless sitting about in cafés round the Hôtel Splendide with the question hammering at our brains: "Is France capitulating?" was like an intolerable mockery of the past. Here we were, witnessing the end of France in the happy-go-lucky atmosphere of a provincial *café du commerce.*'

The only Sunday paper – the *Petite Gironde,* by now reduced to a single sheet – offered no comfort in its latest war communiqué, with its carefully worded sentences like 'enemy pressure became more marked' and 'German advance units...' or 'German detachments succeeded....'

Sunday was very hot, and during the afternoon Werth went for a walk along the *quais* of the Garonne, feeling 'I was still in France; why was everybody looking so unhappy? Here were the cranes, and the large ships, all intact; and tramcars were running along the *quais* and over the wide bridges across the Garonne. Was the war real, or was it only a bad dream?'

It was real enough, and the atmosphere of fatalistic acceptance was like a dead hand over the city. General Spears asked himself, 'Who would resist when the great Marshal preached resignation? Who would fight when that redoubtable warrior Weygand proclaimed fighting to be a folly?'

Everyone looked desperately sad, defeated. When Werth returned to the Splendide he saw 'Pertinax', the famous French columnist, 'haggard, in a state of mental distress'. Geneviève Tabouis, equally famous, pressed his hand 'with her frail little fingers', but said no word. Only Weygand appeared to Werth 'extraordinarily unperturbed – almost pleased with himself'.

Apart from that curious exception, 'it was like a funeral', or a black comedy, for at the Splendide Werth had the greatest difficulty in finding a table on the crowded terrace, where people were shouting 'Garçon! Un pernod! Garçon, un demi!'

Nearly 2000 Britons had reached the Bordeaux area now. Luckily for them the energetic Captain 'Ned' Pleydell-Bouverie, naval attaché at the embassy, was looking after them, bullying the Spanish and Portuguese for urgent visas, arranging shipping, either from Le Verdun, the port at the extreme end of the mined Gironde estuary, or from La Rochelle, where a ship that could take some hundreds of deck passengers was expected hourly.

Spears found Pleydell-Bouverie a model of 'cheerful efficiency', who put an end to the 'confusion and general helplessness' at the consulate. He had to elbow his way through the refugees as they struggled to force their way in past two military policemen. More people packed the stairs and waiting-rooms, and Spears felt his sleeve being plucked by people he knew as he forced his way through.

Pleydell-Bouverie's task was not made any easier by the pathetic queues of foreigners – many of them Jewish – trying to get visas for England; not only men, but mothers with children tugging at their skirts, who realised they were doomed if the Germans caught them.

There was no time for screening strangers whose characters and lives were closed books, who might be genuine refugees from the Gestapo, but who equally could be spies. Pleydell-Bouverie had to use his judgment.

He particularly remembers a frantic Dutchman who cried, 'You *must* get me away! You *must!*' When the naval attaché said there was nothing he could do, the Dutchman tore open his jacket, which contained a voluminous 'poacher's pocket', and produced a parcel of commercial diamonds. 'They're worth half a million pounds,' he cried.

To Britain, industrial diamonds were an urgent priority. Captain Pleydell-Bouverie made him an offer.

'I'll get you to England if you give me the diamonds, to be returned to you after you've been screened at the port of arrival,' he said. Gratefully the Dutchman agreed.

Some of the journalists were also getting worried. Geoffrey Cox and George Millar of the *Daily Express* were making the rounds of seamen's hostels to try to glean news of possible ship departures. H. R. Knickerbocker, the American writer, suggested that all the newspapermen club together and buy a boat.

Some had difficult personal problems that were resolved

only at the last moment. Gordon Waterfield and Harold King were issued with tickets to board a ship, together with the pretty young English journalist Joan Slocombe, daughter of a well-known political writer. But Joan was engaged to Paul Bouchon, a French journalist, and she had no idea where he was. She was terribly torn and decided in the end to stay.

'You're crazy,' said Waterfield. 'The last we heard of him, he was with the French troops. He could be anywhere.'

Most newspapers had, of course, been evacuated from Paris, but to different regions. 'At least we know that Paul's paper has moved to Clermont-Ferrand,' said Joan. 'If I have to, I will go there and wait.'

Again Waterfield tried to persuade her to leave with them; but Joan Slocombe found an unexpected ally in Harold King. 'Don't try to persuade her,' he warned Waterfield. 'She's right. If she doesn't do this, she'll have a complex for the rest of her life.'

Then a minor miracle occurred. Joan Slocombe managed to get through to the editor at Clermont-Ferrand. 'He's standing next to me now,' said the editor in reply to her urgent question. Paul had arrived at the office ten minutes previously. As Waterfield and King prepared to leave for England, Joan Slocombe travelled to Clermont-Ferrand to marry Paul.

The British ambassador and General Spears lunched at the Chapon Fin, sitting at their usual large table reserved for senior members of the embassy staff; they were so busy that they arrived at different times. Some were toying with their cheese as Campbell walked across the street from the Hôtel Montré, others arrived as the ambassador sipped his coffee.

The famous restaurant was more crowded than ever, with deputies and senators, many of them known to the Britishers. They stopped and talked to some of them but Spears, who felt that by now 'my British uniform struck a false note', was uncomfortably aware that the politicians who knew that the future of their country was being debated 'were not thinking

in terms of France and her honour, but of their consti-
tuencies and their jobs'.

Back at the Hôtel Montré – where there was an unpleasant
whiff of burning as the less important papers were destroyed
– a message arrived from London. It asked simply what time
the French Cabinet was meeting. When Campbell told
London that it was due to start at 5 p.m., a second cable
arrived at about 4 p.m., asking Campbell to tell Reynaud
that Britain must be consulted as soon as any armistice terms
were received, and that 'you should impress on French
Government that in stipulating for removal of French fleet
to British ports we have in mind French interests as well as
our own, and are convinced that it will strengthen the hands
of the French Government in any armistice discussions'.

Obviously Churchill was still hoping that Campbell and
Spears could somehow still make certain that the Germans
did not get hold of the French fleet. Indeed, as both men felt,
'It was the only thing left to fight on the Bordeaux front.'

They found Reynaud 'more tired, certainly more difficult
and petulant', though Spears felt that he still hoped to carry
the day and 'I like to think he did, for he was plucky [and]
gallant to the extreme limit of his capacity'.

While the three men were discussing the future of the
French fleet, the telephone rang. Reynaud picked up the
receiver and 'the next moment his eyebrows went up so far
they became indistinguishable from his neatly-brushed hair'.

As Campbell and Spears watched, Reynaud shouted ex-
citedly, 'One moment, I must take it down.'

He picked up his short gold pencil with its extra-thick
lead. Spears pushed sheets of foolscap paper towards him,
and Reynaud started scribbling.

For a moment the others had no idea what was happening.
Then Reynaud began to repeat each word as he wrote it
down at de Gaulle's dictation. As one sheet of paper was
completed someone pushed another across to the French
Prime Minister. Spears became 'transfixed with amazement'
as Reynaud spelled out details of the momentous offer of a
permanent union between France and Britain.

Finally he stopped writing. He asked de Gaulle, 'Does he agree to this? Did Churchill give you this personally?'

There was silence as Reynaud listened intently. Then suddenly he started speaking in English. De Gaulle had handed the telephone to Churchill, who shouted into the phone, 'Hallo, Reynaud! De Gaulle is right. Our proposal may have great consequences. You must hold out. See you tomorrow!'

As Spears watched, Reynaud was 'transfigured with joy, and my old friendship for him surged out in a wave of appreciation at his response, for he was happy with a great happiness in the belief that France would now remain in the war'.

As Reynaud put the receiver down, he cried, 'I will die defending these proposals.'

The text of the declaration read:

At this most fateful moment in the history of the modern world the Governments of the United Kingdom and the French Republic make this declaration of indissoluble union and unyielding resolution in their common defence of justice and freedom against subjection to a system which reduces mankind to a life of robots and slaves.

The two Governments declare that France and Great Britain shall no longer be two nations, but one Franco-British Union.

The constitution of the Union will provide for joint organs of defence, foreign, financial, and economic policies.

Every citizen of France will enjoy immediately citizenship of Great Britain; every British subject will become a citizen of France.

Both countries will share responsibility for the repair of the devastation of war, wherever it occurs in their territories, and the resources of both shall be equally, and as one, applied to that purpose.

During the war there shall be a single War Cabinet, and all the forces of Britain and France, whether on land, sea, or in the air, will be placed under its direction. It will govern from wherever it best can. The two Parliaments will be formally associated. The nations of the British Empire are already forming new armies. France will keep her available forces in the field, on the sea, and in the air. The Union appeals to the United States to fortify the economic resources of the Allies, and to bring her powerful material aid to the common cause.

The Union will concentrate its whole energy against the power of the enemy, no matter where the battle may be.

And thus we shall conquer.

'This must be typed out at once so that you can have it for the cabinet meeting,' said Spears, helping to put the papers in order, before taking them into the nearby secretaries' room. One thing was vital – secrecy, to ensure dramatic surprise at the cabinet meeting.

To Spears' horror, Madame de Portes was standing in the middle of the secretaries' room, and as Spears handed the first sheet to the secretary she stood behind the man. He must have typed more quickly than she could read, for suddenly she held his arm to prevent him from turning the page until she had finished. Spears found it 'difficult to tell from her expression whether rage or amazement prevailed'.

Though Spears urged the secretary to hurry, Madame de Portes still tried to stop him from turning the second page. Spears had no business to interfere in what amounted to French affairs of state, but he was so angry that finally he pushed himself in front of the Countess, and in his impeccable French told the secretary curtly, 'This message must be typed without a moment's delay.'

As Madame de Portes read the last page, she stamped out of the room – to catch Baudouin, who was among the ministers gathering for the cabinet meeting which would be held next door. This was the moment when Reynaud's mistress did her lover the greatest disservice of all, for before the cabinet meeting started the defeatists knew the broad outline of the plan. Reynaud himself admitted later that spies told Weygand what was about to happen. He did not give the name of the informer, of the traitorous link between state and opposition. There was no need to; it was obvious.

To Campbell and Spears the rest of the afternoon and early evening was agonising, as they waited in the Montré while the Cabinet debated. They spent the interval talking over their hopes and fears. Spears, having watched Reynaud set off with a light step to read the declaration to President Lebrun, felt 'completely optimistic'. Not until the clock reminded him that the Cabinet had been sitting for over an hour did he have doubts, for 'if the Cabinet had accepted the British offer they would have done so enthusiastically, quickly, and we should have been told'.

When the Cabinet met at 5 p.m., Reynaud's mood was buoyant. He had no idea that Madame de Portes had told his enemies about 'the great secret'. Full of confidence, he slowly read out the text of Churchill's offer – and was immediately engulfed in an uproar of shouting, argument and cries of derision. For a moment Reynaud was stunned. He turned to President Lebrun and begged him to ask for silence. Then he read out the historic document a second time, adding that he had arranged to meet Churchill the next day to discuss the details.

'No need to go,' one deputy shouted. 'We have no intention of becoming a dominion of the British Empire.' When Mandel cried, 'Would you rather be a German district than a British dominion?' Ybarnégaray shouted back, 'Yes! Better be a Nazi province. At least we know what that means.'

Reibel, the sinister friend of Weygand, said that union with Britain would mean the complete destruction of France, which would become a vassal of Britain. Pétain went even further. Britain would soon be beaten, he said, so entering into a union with Churchill was like making 'a fusion with a corpse'.

When Reynaud managed to cry, 'I prefer to collaborate with my allies rather than my enemies,' he was howled down by politicians demanding an armistice approach to Germany.

Mandel acidly retorted, 'It is more and more evident that there are some ministers here who stand for war and some ministers who stand for peace.'

The suggestion of cowardice was aimed directly at Chautemps, and he knew it. Angrily he asked if Mandel were suggesting that some of the Cabinet were cowards.

'There are some Frenchmen driven to despair by their country's plight, who are trying to find a way out,' Chautemps added, and turning to Mandel said scornfully, 'Anyway, I don't need lessons from you.'

The rising tempers – almost on the brink of breaking out into physical fighting – was the signal to demand again the right to approach Germany and ask for Hitler's armistice terms. As Reynaud remembered later, 'I felt isolated. My position was weakened. I let the talk turn again to the question of an armistice.'

This tactical blunder was almost certainly influenced by an extraordinary interruption. One of Reynaud's secretaries opened the door of the cabinet room and placed a note in front of the Prime Minister. It was nothing more than a slip of paper, folded. Reynaud read it quietly. He knew the writing belonged to Madame de Portes. She had scrawled, 'I hope you are not going to play the role of Isabeau of Bavaria.' (It was a reference to Isabeau, consort of Charles VI of France, who in 1420 was instrumental at the Treaty of Troyes in making Henry V of England Regent of France.)

Reynaud crunched the message into a tight ball of paper. At this moment he received a second blow. Weygand, who was waiting in a nearby room, received a war report from General Georges. This should have been handed directly to the Prime Minister. Instead, Weygand told General Lafont, who was with him, to give it personally to President Lebrun, who, of course, had no executive power. It was unheard of for a serving officer to approach the President directly. In a dismal hushed voice, Lebrun read out the report:

5 p.m. Situation worse still. In the east, northern outskirts of Dijon and Saône front reached by enemy. In the centre,

numerous armoured columns heading for La Charité threaten encirclement No. 3 Group of Armies. Forest of Fontainebleau occupied. Supply situation for troops and retreating civilians serious. Manœuvring difficult on account of road-jamming and bombing of railways and bridges. Vital you make decision.

In the silence that followed, Lebrun blurted out, 'This is an appalling picture of the armies' position.'

It was enough to seal Reynaud's doom. Chautemps cried, 'It is impossible for the Government to leave France without asking the enemy to make his conditions known.'

'France's honour is at stake,' said Reynaud – but he was beaten, and he knew it. He looked at President Lebrun, who as head of state might have lent the weight of his authority to back him. But there was no hope there, though Élie Bois felt that Lebrun could have told the Pétainists, 'I will not have my name dishonoured. I am going to send a message to the country.' In fact Lebrun had the power to force the Pétainists to resign.

Without doubt Weygand's skilful direct approaches to Lebrun did much to swing the President of the Republic against Reynaud, against – even at this late hour – the possibility of a French 'Dunkirk' in which hundreds of thousands of men could have been evacuated to north Africa and the French fleet sent for safety to some distant port.

But in fact Lebrun was not influenced only by Weygand. He had decided that legally France had every right to break the 28 March agreement not to make a separate peace, because Churchill had refused to throw Britain's last fighter planes into the battle of northern France. He argued that, from the moment either Britain or France retained part of their forces for their own defence instead of risking them in common combat, they were released from the pact not to make a separate peace.

Normally the French Cabinet never voted – and no minutes were kept – but at this fateful moment some sort of rough count was apparently taken of those for and against the proposal to approach the enemy. Accounts vary as to the result, but the generally accepted one shows that the vote was 14–10 in favour of the defeatists.*

There was nothing left now for Reynaud but to declare his intention to resign later in the day. As the clamour ceased, as each man sensed the moment of climax, Reynaud announced, 'It is evident that a minority of the Cabinet shares my point of view. I think that I am not the man to ask for the armistice and to intervene with England to release France from her promises.'

It was the ignominious end of the great union proposal, and what horrified Élie Bois was that 'these fine Ministers virtually did not discuss a document which deserved either to be accepted with acclamation or to be examined in minute detail'.

Churchill wrote, 'Rarely has so generous a proposal encountered such a hostile reception.' (Many Britons shared Churchill's disappointment. 'What a shame,' Desmond MacCarthy, the noted critic, said to André Maurois, 'I would have been so happy to become a French citizen.')

It was not, however, the end of Reynaud, for he had not resigned, only announced his intention to do so. He assumed Lebrun would ask him to form a new government, and indeed, was so convinced that he would be returned to power later in the day that, as he wrote later, he had decided to tell Lebrun that when forming a new government he would demand the dismissal of Weygand.

So, having told the Cabinet that he wished to talk privately with the President, Reynaud summoned the cabinet ministers to meet again at 10 p.m. 'I wished to have them at hand in case M. Lebrun . . . entrusted me with the duty of forming a new administration.'

Among the first to see Reynaud after the Cabinet adjourned

* The fourteen were Pétain, Chautemps, Baudouin, Bouthilier, Février, Chichery, Queuille, Fossard, Ybarnégaray, Pomaret, Pernot, Prouvost, Julien and Rivière. The ten were Reynaud, Campinchi, Delbos, G. Monnet, Mandel, Dautry, Marin, Rio, Serol and Rollin.

was Biddle, to whom Reynaud described the position as 'heartbreaking'. Biddle found him utterly worn out, and cabled Washington at 9 p.m., 'He turned literally ashen grey in panic and you would never have known him to be the same man of two weeks earlier.'

Biddle also told Washington, 'I said that I assumed of course a French government would continue the fight from other shores even if metropolitan France was occupied by the German Army. He shrugged and looked away. I stressed the necessity for the continuance of a free government and the saving of the French fleet.'

At about the same time, Campbell and Spears received details of the meeting-place for Churchill and Reynaud the following day, and decided – perhaps out of anxiety – to go to the rue Vital-Carles. Sensing the moment of drama, a huge crowd had assembled. Troops had been rushed in to hold back the excited men and women, and Spears was delighted when 'they cheered the British car. This was surely the voice of the people expressing their desire to fight on.'

They walked into the empty, gloomy, pillared hall. It was 7.45 p.m. Almost the first person they saw was de Margerie, and without preamble he told them in flat tones, 'The Prime Minister is going to tell you that he is to resign.'

'What's that?' Spears exclaimed in astonishment.

In the same tone de Margerie repeated his words.

He showed the two Britishers into a room not normally used by Reynaud. They waited a few minutes, and then Reynaud walked in. He looked utterly exhausted. What was the cabinet reaction to the union proposal, Campbell wanted to know. Reynaud 'shrugged helplessly' and told him. Had Reynaud told the Cabinet he was meeting Churchill tomorrow?

'Yes,' said Reynaud. 'It made no difference.' Spears interjected, 'Have you actually resigned?'

'Not yet. But I intend doing so at the next cabinet meeting at 10 p.m.'

Spears, who had been brought up in France, who had known de Margerie since the First World War, felt 'stunned and suffocated', and a nausea rose like acid from his stomach to his throat. Campbell's first reaction was more that of a good ambassador. He must warn Churchill to cancel his trip – if there was still time.

He rushed back to the Montré, by now at sixes and sevens; the air was still heavy with the smell of burning. He asked for some scrap paper on which to draft an urgent cable. No one could find any. Finally, Anthony Nutting, an energetic young officer in Army Intelligence, resolved the shortage – by dashing out to the toilet, and returning with a supply of lavatory paper.

In London, Churchill, after a cabinet meeting lasting until 6 p.m., had dined early and left on the first stage of his journey – to Waterloo, where he was already seated in a train ready for the two-hour journey to Southampton to board a warship which, steaming at thirty knots, would reach the rendezvous by noon the following day.

His wife had bid him goodbye and returned home when his private secretary arrived breathlessly from Downing Street with a message from Campbell. It said simply, 'Ministerial crisis has opened. Hope to have news by midnight. Meanwhile meeting arranged for tomorrow impossible.'

There was nothing Churchill could do. 'I returned to Downing Street with a heavy heart,' he later wrote.

## 6. Night falls on Bordeaux

Around 8.30 p.m., Élie Bois was walking with a friend along the Cours de l'Intendance on their way to dine at the Chapon Fin. Almost opposite the rue Vital-Carles, a chauffeur-driven American car with whitewall tyres swung out recklessly, forcing Bois to pull his friend to safety. Bois looked up and caught a glimpse of Hélène de Portes, 'her face triumphant in the back seat'. To Bois it was an omen, and he whispered to his friend, 'She looks confident. That's bad for France.'

The two men sat quietly near the grotto in a corner of the restaurant. It was crowded. In the opposite corner near the serving-table Bois spotted the swarthy, bloated face of Laval. In the centre of the room he could see an English uniform. General Spears was dining with the British ambassador. Halfway through the meal an acquaintance approached Bois and said, 'It must be all up. The British colony have been told to register at the consulate for departure.'

Bois had no stomach for the rest of the dinner. He wanted to see Mandel. He walked quickly to the Prefecture, but when he arrived it was to find that all had changed. 'Strange door-keepers barred the entrance, roughly demanded entrance papers, flashed torches into faces, and asked questions rudely.'

'Mandel!' one man jeered. 'Your Mandel isn't a minister any more.' Somehow Bois managed to force a way through the mob which filled the hall and ante-room on the first floor and he soon discovered the identities of the new guards. They had been recruited by Laval's ally Marquet, in case Mandel resorted to violence – the last thing poor Mandel would ever do.

What sickened Bois most was the sudden realisation that the milling crowd resembled exactly 'the hurly burly of a peace-time political crisis'. Looking at them, feeling sick, he thought, 'a lot they care about France'.

Mandel was still in his room – and still hoping. 'The German terms will be so severe that the Government will have to collapse,' he declared.

'My dear Minister,' said Bois, 'I don't agree.' He was convinced that Pétain and his colleagues were 'caught in the toils' and could not escape the tragedy, even if they wished to. 'But they don't even want to,' he added sadly.

Back in the rue Vital-Carles, Reynaud – still hoping to form a new government – was doing his best to keep up appearances. Finally, he asked Biddle to come to see him.

'I know the United States can't do anything tangible for us,' Reynaud admitted, 'but for my sake *say* you will return at midnight. That will gain six hours for me, and during that time I might be able to persuade them to go to Africa.'

On his way out, Biddle stopped to have a word with de Margerie, who was more frank than Reynaud had been. Biddle cabled Washington that in all probability Reynaud would tender his resignation when the Council reconvened that night. As to who would head the new cabinet he could not say: there was great pressure by certain cabinet members to have Pétain head the new cabinet to ask for armistice terms.

It was true, not only of the Cabinet, but also of President Lebrun. As Biddle was returning to the embassy, Reynaud walked next door to see Lebrun. Reynaud felt it would have been a waste of time to reiterate arguments which Lebrun had heard at every cabinet meeting, so 'I went straight to the heart of the problem. Two policies were clashing: That of resistance which I myself embodied; and that of surrender which Pétain championed.'

It did not take Reynaud long to discover that, though Lebrun still wanted him to remain in office, he also believed that Pétain's policy was the right one for France. He was thinking, as he explained, of General Georges' report, and asked Reynaud, 'Who could remain impervious to such an appeal?'

'But I can't support the Chautemps proposal!' Reynaud was staggered. 'I cannot go on.'

'But yesterday I tried desperately to prevent you from resigning,' said Lebrun. 'I am asking you again to refrain from resigning today.'

Tragically, both sides – the fighters and the defeatists – had reduced their beliefs to oversimplified creeds, ignoring the unsaid thoughts behind a simple yes or no, questions that each side would have found embarrassing to ask. It was easy for Pétain to say, 'We have been beaten. You started the war. Now end it.' But would he dare to reveal his *real* thoughts? 'France is what I care about. I am not really interested whether Britain is invaded or not, even whether she wins or loses the war. I am thinking of France.' For that was the core of Pétain's philosophy.

Nor was it difficult for Reynaud to cry, 'France is not yet beaten, and honour demands that we fight on.' But it *was* difficult for him to say, 'I know that if we continue the war we will lose, and sacrifice our troops to support Britain; but we gave our word, and, if the Germans revenge themselves on the people of France, we must still fight, to keep our word.' Those were impossible words to speak to a nation almost defeated. Yet those were the hidden forces behind the struggle for power.

It was also tragic that at such a moment the President of France – like most Presidents of the 3rd and 4th republics – was such a vacillating, weak man, not evil like Laval, not misguided like Pétain, merely weak. (That afternoon Mandel had found Lebrun 'stretched out on a sofa, sobbing'.)

As he and Reynaud were talking, at about 9 p.m., the leaders of the two chambers arrived. Both the frail but magnificent Jeanneney and the more robust Herriot were patriots. They told Lebrun flatly that they were totally opposed to an armistice, and begged him to support Reynaud's decision to fight on from north Africa.

Since Reynaud had already indicated that he would resign, Lebrun in accordance with French parliamentary custom turned to Herriot and Jeanneney, and asked, 'Who, tomorrow?'

Both answered simultaneously, 'Paul Reynaud.' They thought that he must be asked to remain in power. Herriot remembered later that 'We mentioned no other name. Let it be clearly understood that neither M. Jeanneney nor I put forward the name of Marshal Pétain.'

Yet, having listened to the advice that he was constitutionally bound to consider, the worn out, defeated Lebrun told Herriot and Jeanneney 'in a tired voice' that he believed in the Chautemps proposal, 'that lives must be saved, that the battle was lost anyway'.

'In that case,' declared Reynaud, 'I can't form a government. If you want such a policy, go and ask Marshal Pétain.'

That one simple sentence, spoken perhaps without thinking by a tired, exasperated man, was perhaps the single most critical utterance by any statesman during the week France fell. For, had Reynaud remained silent, who knows whether the wise counsels of Herriot and Jeanneney might not have persuaded Lebrun to support Reynaud. Instead, it was Reynaud himself who suggested Pétain.

Why? What made him say something that would plague him for the rest of his life? The fact that he did say it is shown by printed records (including a letter from Reynaud to Pétain admitting it), but when one is reconstructing events from documents devoid of inflexion and emotion it is sometimes easy to ignore nuances that might affect even an apparently unambiguous utterance.

Reynaud using the same words *could* have been saying, in effect, 'If most people want an armistice, then Pétain is the man who bears the most illustrious name in France.' But, equally, Reynaud, staggered that his President should disdain the advice of parliamentary leaders, could have been saying, scornfully, 'Well, if you are going to sink as low as that, you might as well choose a senile old dodderer like Pétain.'

Many interpretations can be given to a simple phrase. Reynaud later told the author that the words were spoken in a sarcastic, disparaging voice. It seems the likeliest explanation. Louis Marin, a stalwart cabinet supporter of Reynaud, asked later, 'By what mystery and by what aberration the President of the Republic and the President of the Council, both hostile to the armistice, called to power the man whose first move, they knew, would be to ask for an armistice?'

Meanwhile, the cabinet ministers were gathering in Lebrun's outer sitting-room for the promised meeting at 10 p.m. But – with the usual French flair for the dramatic – the final cabinet meeting never took place. As the ministers stood there talking, Reynaud emerged from Lebrun's office. He walked straight through the crowd of ministers, crossing the room, stopping for one moment to say, 'Marshal Pétain is forming a government.' Then he banged the door behind him. He did not bother with the formality of handing in his resignation for it 'seemed to me a useless ritual'.

The ministers were flabbergasted. Louis Marin observed, 'None of us gave in our resignation. The Premier alone handed in the resignation of the cabinet without consulting his colleagues.'

As Reynaud closed one door, another opened. Lebrun walked out, looked around, stood quite still for a moment, then demanded silence. He said no word until the hubbub had died down.

'Gentlemen,' he declared, 'the Cabinet will not be meeting now. Excuse me for not having given you notice. I was unable to change Reynaud's mind. He insisted on resigning. But I ask you to remain with me. A new government is going to be formed by Marshal Pétain. A certain number of you will be called by the new President of the Council to become his collaborators. But I ask the rest of you to remain also. I want all of us to be united this evening in the same sentiment of sadness.'

Georges Monnet did not expect to be asked to serve under Pétain, but he and others among Reynaud's ministers stayed behind because they wished, as Monnet put it, 'to be witnesses of such a dramatic event'.

By now de Gaulle had flown back to Bordeaux, carrying the text of the plan for union with Britain. As soon as his plane touched down at Mérignac, he heard that Reynaud was threatening to resign. He did not blame Reynaud; he knew that the French Prime Minister had been catapulted into the leadership when it was too late and France was already on the eve of catastrophe. 'In reality,' de Gaulle wrote later, 'this annihilation of the State was at the bottom of a national tragedy. By the light of the thunderbolt the régime was revealed, in its ghastly infirmity, as having no proportion and no relation to the defence, honour and independence of France.'

Without hesitation, de Gaulle made up his mind; he would return to London. But first he had two things to do. He went to see Reynaud and told him he intended to fight on. Reynaud gave him 100,000 francs from the Government's secret fund. Then de Gaulle asked de Margerie to get passports for his wife and children, who were at Carantec, in Finistère, so that they could sail for Britain on the last destroyer to leave Brest.

De Gaulle realised that he would have to act quickly and carefully, for he had been warned that Weygand had again discussed with his crony Reibel the possibility of arresting him. It was too late now for the plane to take off; he would have to keep out of sight for the rest of the night.

Spears and Campbell dined as usual at the Chapon Fin. 'Of all the good dinners served us at the Chapon Fin,' Spears remembered, 'the one placed before us that night was the hardest to face.' Each dish was superbly prepared, but to Spears each tasted like 'cardboard served in sauces of sand'. But the food had to be eaten, for Campbell and Spears knew they were being watched by scores of people ready to draw deductions from their demeanour at the embassy table.

Campbell had promised to call on Reynaud, and with a face carefully devoid of any emotion he looked at his watch.

'It's just on ten o'clock,' he told Spears. 'I suppose we ought to be going.'

On the way they stopped to see Mandel, who was 'in a cold rage' and said, 'Il n'y a rien à faire avec ces gens là. When you are dealing with panic-ridden troops, only shooting will stop them.' Reynaud, he said, had lost all his authority, and as for Lebrun 'He's a poor man who just can't make up his mind to leave France.'

To Spears, it seemed all-important to have a word with Jeanneney, to whom the ambassador had shown the proposal for union with France. It was the first Jeanneney had heard of it 'and he immediately grasped the nobility and generosity of the gesture and was deeply moved'. Though Jeanneney seemed frailer than earlier in the day, they left 'this fine old man, a monument of rectitude' with a slight feeling of comfort.

In the house where Reynaud was staying, the imposing hall

was dark and seemingly empty. A dim light shadowed the columns and the wide staircase. To Spears it was like 'an ill-lit furniture repository' and he suggested that the ambassador wait in the hall while he went upstairs to see if anyone was around. Coming down again, he nearly bumped into an excited and distressed French major. Spears was now a little more used to the dark and he could make out the shadowy figure of two or three orderlies. In one corner the ambassador was talking to de Margerie. He walked towards them.

At that moment, in the eerie half-darkness, Spears heard an urgent whisper, 'General Spears! I must speak to you.'

To his astonishment Spears saw a tall figure flat against the column, 'shrouded in its shadow'. It was de Gaulle.

'It's extremely urgent,' de Gaulle whispered.

Out of the corner of his eye, Spears saw de Margerie open the door to Reynaud's study. Campbell, on the point of entering, had stopped, waiting for Spears.

'I can't now, the Ambassador and I are just going in to see the Premier.'

'You *must*!' insisted de Gaulle. 'I have very good reason to believe Weygand intends arresting me.'

Spears whispered to him to wait – stressing that he must stay exactly where he was, virtually hidden by the pillar. 'We shan't be long,' he whispered.

Inside the Prime Minister's study all three men stood. Reynaud was more reserved than usual, and made it clear that he did not want to discuss what had just happened. He was in fact going through a necessary formality. He reminded Spears of 'a producer giving an account of the last disastrous performance of a play to its backers. The curtain had been run down, it was over, he must think of his own plans.'

Spears searched his mind 'to think of anything that was worth saying or doing and found nothing, only a growing realisation that there were two worlds in that room and Reynaud had left ours'.

Reynaud apparently thought otherwise. Suddenly he

remembered the meeting with Churchill, planned for the morrow. What time would Churchill be arriving at Concarneau? he asked. 'I shall be glad to talk things over with him,' he told the British ambassador.

Spears was outraged at the idea of risking Churchill's life for 'a talk'.

'Tomorrow,' he said bitterly, 'there will be another government and you will no longer speak for anyone. The meeting has been cancelled.'

Spears had already written Reynaud off but, as far as Reynaud was concerned, Pétain had not yet formed a government and, as Reynaud wrote later, 'I was so convinced that I would resume power, that I put the question as to whether I could keep the rendezvous with Churchill next day.'

The ambassador felt the meeting had gone on long enough. He 'gestured wearily' to Spears, gave a polite 'Bonsoir' to Reynaud, and the two men left.

To all intents France had now capitulated. With the war all but over, with Pétain ready to form a government that would seek an armistice, Britain stood alone. Still stunned by Reynaud's illusions, Campbell and Spears walked out of the ex-premier's study. With the darkness throwing eerie shadows from the grey pillars, Spears looked anxiously for the tall figure whom he knew was awaiting him. De Gaulle was standing bolt upright, his back to a column, so that he could not be seen by anyone entering through the front door. He spoke briefly to Spears.

The ambassador had moved a few steps away. Spears beckoned him and they had 'a hurried conference' in the dimness of the almost empty hall. They obviously could not talk long in the hall, but at the same time Campbell did not advise taking de Gaulle in the embassy car. The lanky figure would attract attention; his presence in an official British car would be reported back to Pétain or Weygand in a matter of moments. The Hôtel Montré was only five minutes' walk away. Spears whispered to de Gaulle to take a chance and walk there. The two Britishers went ahead in their car.

Campbell went to his room. Spears waited in the deserted hotel lobby.

In a few minutes de Gaulle stooped and slid past the glass entrance-door. To the right of the hall was the old-fashioned salon, reached by steps lined with statues of semi-naked ladies. The men sat down on the red plush Empire-style chairs, while de Gaulle told Spears why he felt he must go to London immediately. He not only wanted to continue the fight – and that would be impossible in France – but he wanted above all to broadcast to Frenchmen, to appeal for continued resistance before the defeatists broadcast *their* message. Spears agreed, 'Every effort had to be made to help the solitary man prepared to take the only steps likely to rally French resistance.'

The only hope was for de Gaulle to reach Mérignac airport, which could soon be in Weygand's hands, and fly to Britain in the same aircraft which Churchill had lent de Gaulle to fly from London to Paris earlier in the day. One danger presented itself: the British crew had been told they would not be required to fly back to London before 9 a.m. the following day. Not only would it be difficult to round them up, but the facilities for taking off after dark were minimal. Then there was another problem: what would Churchill think? The British Prime Minister might not want to be encumbered with this Frenchman while still hoping to negotiate with the Pétain government for the future of the French fleet. Spears decided to telephone Churchill for his personal authorisation. He went into the next room, which was occupied by Henry Mack, the First Secretary, to get through to Downing Street.

There was an unexpected delay caused by a man who was important but who had played no role in the drama unfolding throughout the week – the Duke of Windsor. As Spears was on the point of unhooking the ancient 'ear-trumpet-like receiver' over Mack's bed, the phone rang. The Duke was speaking from Nice where he was marooned with the Duchess. Could Mack send a warship to pick them up? It was manifestly impossible. With 'suave but firm politeness'

Mack suggested that the road to Spain was still open, and the Duke set off by car.

Churchill came on the phone a few minutes later – and made it clear right away that he viewed the impending visit of de Gaulle with some apprehension. Certainly he did not want Spears to return.

'There is much to be done yet in France,' he growled, 'there are some important matters to be settled.' Spears of course realised that Churchill was referring to the French fleet, but Spears had a way with Churchill, who liked the bluff soldier unafraid to speak his mind. Lying on his back on Mack's bed, better to manipulate the short flex of the old-fashioned telephone, Spears replied, 'Let me bring de Gaulle back and report to you; there is much to say, and if you wish me to return, of course I will.' He added, almost as an after-thought, that he was going to ask Georges Mandel to fly to Britain too, and perhaps it was this almost casual suggestion that caused Churchill to change his mind, for he was a great admirer of Mandel. After a pause Churchill finally growled, 'All right.' He spoke in a tone that was 'not too pleased'. Then Spears heard the click as the British Prime Minister put the receiver down.

Spears arranged to meet de Gaulle at the Hôtel Montré at 7 a.m., with Lieutenant Geoffroy de Courcel, de Gaulle's aide-de-camp. Meanwhile Spears set off to see Mandel. As he drove towards the Prefecture through milling crowds, the dimmed street-lights were suddenly extinguished for an air-raid alert. The Prefecture was in darkness, but with the aid of a candle stuck in an inkwell Spears finally found Mandel's room, lit with several candles, and begged him to fly with him in the plane the following morning. Knowing that Mandel was deeply attached to Béatrice Bretty, the actress, Spears added tactfully, 'There are two places available.'

'Tomorrow – no,' said Mandel. 'I know that you fear for me because I am a Jew. Well, it's just because I am a Jew that I won't go tomorrow. It would look as if I was running away. Wednesday, perhaps.'

'It may be too late,' retorted Spears.

At that moment a door opened and Spears caught a glimpse of Mademoiselle Bretty's fair hair as she peeped round the corner. In a voice 'of slight urgency and pleading' she said, 'The trunks are packed, Georges.'

Spears was not sure whether or not Mademoiselle Bretty hoped to go to London or whether they were just going to get out of Bordeaux, but there was no point in staying. He rose to leave and his last words to Mandel were, 'Well, in London I hope – soon.' They never met again. *

Of the traumatic happenings on this fateful night, most of Bordeaux was mercifully ignorant. As when doctors wait until morning to break bad news to the relatives of a dying man, the people of France were given one last night of illusion.

No one seemed to grasp the enormity of the disaster about to descend on them. As James Lansdale Hodson was making for the coast, he stopped in a village where peasants and their families were sedately dressed in their Sunday best and Hodson felt that 'you could have thought the war a thousand miles away'.

Biddle found much the same thing when, as promised, he returned to the rue Vital-Carles to see Reynaud. It was too late to do anything, of course, but the refugees jamming the streets were excited by scores of rumours, including one that the United States had declared war on Germany, so that when the crowds sighted the American car many were certain that Biddle was on his way to convey the news to Reynaud.

As Biddle's driver tried to force a way through the Place de la Comédie, the press of men and women was so great that he had to stop. The people started to cheer the car, shouting, 'Vive les États Unis!' Biddle remembers that awful moment:

---

* What Spears did not know was that Béatrice Bretty was desperately anxious to go to England, and only appeared at that instant because she hoped her presence would sway Mandel. 'I had packed the bags ready to go to England,' she remembered later. 'General Spears had everything arranged and I tried my utmost to persuade Georges. But he was convinced that it was his duty to go to north Africa.'

'I sat there in that car and I had a lump in my throat, because I knew that we weren't going to do a damn thing.'

Some newspapermen already knew the worst. After a dreary and expensive dinner at the Splendide, Alexander Werth heard that Reynaud had resigned, and though 'nobody really knew anything definite... it all smelt pretty bad'.

By 10 p.m. the Splendide had been blacked out, and in the dimly lit front hall people exchanged gossip, fished for snippets of information. The hall was packed with couches, sofas and armchairs filled with drowsy and sleeping bodies. Werth groped his way into the street, determined to sleep in his car, one of hundreds that crowded the Place des Quinconces. Except for the dark shadows of the cars, the streets were empty; not a light showed from the windows in the houses.

To Werth it seemed inconceivable that people could sleep when their country was in its death throes, with German troops advancing everywhere, with Reynaud out of office, while 'an old, old man was taking the destinies of his country into his frail hands'.

Pétain might have been frail, but he knew what he wanted, as Lebrun discovered when he sent for him around 11 p.m.

Lebrun was, in his words, 'preoccupied with seeing to it that France had a government by the morrow'. He greeted the Marshal with, 'Well, now, form a government.'

Without a moment's hesitation Pétain opened his briefcase and pulled out a sheet of paper with a list on it.

'There is my government,' he said.

Lebrun was dumbfounded, and his immediate reaction gives perhaps a more revealing insight into his character than anything else he did or said during this tragic week.

'I remembered how difficult it had been during my eight years in office to constitute a government,' he said later. 'It had usually taken three or four days. But here I had one in a minute. I found that splendid.'

Chautemps was named Vice-Premier, Weygand Minister of National Defence, Darlan Minister of Marine. But when it came to the all-important post of Foreign Minister, which Laval hoped to fill, there was a hitch.

The corridors and rooms of the Prefect's house were crowded, and Weygand was waiting in the room next to Pétain's when Laval passed him on his way to meet Pétain. A few moments later Charles-Roux, Permanent Under-Secretary to the Ministry of Foreign Affairs, together with Baudouin, came into the room and told Weygand that Laval was insisting on being appointed Foreign Minister.

Horrified at the prospect of an anglophobe in power when Anglo-French relations were strained, Weygand asked to see Pétain immediately and privately, and implored him not to appoint Laval. 'Twice I returned to the charge, and a short time afterwards saw M. Laval reappear and walk straight across to the door without addressing a word to anyone.' Baudouin was given the post instead. Laval refused the Ministry of Justice, and so was omitted from the first cabinet.

So ended Reynaud's open struggle against Pétain and Weygand, perhaps summed up best by de Gaulle, at this moment waiting in hiding until daybreak. Reynaud, he said, 'was like a man who knows he must swim a river and who sees the other bank clear. But he was not strong enough to reach it.'

Reynaud had many faults, not the least being his deep love for the traitorous Hélène de Portes; but he had many good points too. So, for that matter, had Pétain and Weygand, who had brought dishonour on France. It is always easy, when sifting evidence, to make heroes white and villains black; this was not, of course, the case with French leaders during this tragic week. If Paul Reynaud was not whiter than white, neither were Pétain and Weygand blacker than black.

Apart from their bitterness towards the political régime of the Third Republic, and their pathological fear of revolution, apart from their narrow viewpoint, which never allowed them to envisage a global war, they never wavered from their conviction that Britain would either be beaten, or more probably would sue for an armistice. Pétain was convinced that Churchill only kept British fighter planes in England because they would give him a stronger bargaining power when it came to discussing peace.

Pétain and Weygand were sure that, if the renowned French Army could be thrashed ignominiously, the rag-tag and bobtail British troops would suffer a similar fate, so what was the point in wasting French lives when the final issue was a foregone conclusion? Pétain had told Bullitt bluntly that Britain would get better terms than France because her fleet, air force and empire were intact.

Pétain and Weygand never understood one fundamental truth: that the Luftwaffe was not yet the master of the skies. Nor was the German Navy master of the seas. All they could see, during this last weekend, was that Britain had refused to throw in her last fighter squadrons. How could one trust an ally who did not come to the help of a friend in distress? Much the same suspicions ran through the top echelons of the French naval command, specially among the historically minded who remembered that in 1793 the French royalists entrusted their fleet to the British at Toulon and when the British evacuated Toulon they had no compunction about burning the fleet.

Senator Tony Révillon, who was in Bordeaux, noted in his diary some of the prophecies flying around that weekend. Weygand's famous verdict, uttered on Saturday, took pride of place. He declared, 'In three weeks' time England's neck will be wrung like a chicken's.'* As Reynaud remarked later, 'Such prophecies were common currency in Bordeaux.' Charles Reibel told Révillon, 'General Weygand is sure that the British are incapable of resisting an invasion by the Germans.' That afternoon a colonel (whom Révillon does not name) rushed up to him and cried, 'Believe me, Senator, England will be put *hors de combat* in a few weeks. What's the use of continuing the war?'

Many French leaders felt that Britain would sue for peace, and Hitler – who repeatedly said that he had no quarrel with Britain – would give them terms so handsome that, while

---

* To which Churchill later made the famous reply, 'Some chicken!' And, when the laughter subsided, added, 'Some neck!'

France suffered the shame of defeat, Britain would emerge
as 'victor' – at least over France.

Baudouin's first task, around midnight, was to call Biddle
and Freeman Matthews to his office and tell them that the
French Army was 'completely smashed' and the slaughter
must end immediately. Carefully he stressed that if German
armistice terms were 'unworthy of the honour and dignity
of France' they would be broadcast to the French nation
to show Frenchmen everywhere why they could not be
accepted – a statement which, Matthews privately felt, 'was
complete applesauce'. And, when Baudouin continued that
this would help France to continue what he called the moral
struggle, Matthews remembers that 'we simulated a couple
of frigidaires and left no doubt as to our own views'. As far
as the future of the fleet was concerned – 'assurances which
were accepted with many grains of salt' – Biddle cabled the
State Department, 'He assured me formally that it would
never be surrendered to Germany.'

While Biddle cabled Roosevelt, Churchill in London was
trying to get through on the telephone to Pétain. For three
hours he sat hunched in his favourite armchair in the study
at Downing Street, as secretaries tried to get through the
tangled international lines. General Hollis, Military Secretary
to the Cabinet, stayed up to keep him company.

Around 2 a.m. the lines were finally cleared, and Churchill
spoke to Pétain. In all the words he spoke or wrote about the
fall of France, Churchill never divulged those he employed
as he begged France's new leader not to hand over the fleet
to Germany. Perhaps Churchill felt a trifle guilty at the
obvious anger he could not disguise, for he did not mince
his words. As Hollis remembered later, 'It was the most
violent conversation I ever heard Churchill conduct. He only
spoke so roughly because he felt that anger might sway the
old Marshal when nothing else would.'

But by then – though Churchill could not know it – all was

virtually over, and Pétain had already started the wheels of peace turning. Around midnight, on the Marshal's instructions, Baudouin sent for Señor Lequerica, the Spanish ambassador, who had been eagerly awaiting the moment when he could act as a go-between. Indeed, he had spent the evening with the President of the French Chamber's Foreign Affairs Committee, a defeatist called Mister, preparing 'procedure and forms of armistice'. So, the moment Lequerica entered Baudouin's room, he was able to say, 'Monsieur le Ministre, I was waiting for you to make this decision.'

Already he had stationed two attachés at St-Jean-de-Luz, on the Spanish frontier. As soon as he returned to his embassy, Lequerica telephoned them. A few minutes later they crossed into Spain and from Irun telephoned the message to Madrid.

So the most crushing defeat since Napoleon's campaign against Prussia in 1806 was completed. Now only Britain stood in Hitler's path.

## 7.  *The morning after*

Alexander Werth rubbed his eyes as a hot sun, slanting across the Place des Quinconces, woke him in the back seat of the car where he had slept fitfully through the night, one of thousands of refugees waking on the day of defeat.

He rushed over to the Splendide for a quick wash behind the hotel cloakroom, grabbed a paper, then settled down to coffee and *croissants* on the hotel terrace. The stark headlines in *Le Journal* read:

> *Pétain à la tête du Gouvernement*
> *M. Paul Reynaud a démissionné*

That was all. The rest of the newspaper was filled with inconsequential drivel, including the naïve statement that

'The regular air service between London and France will be re-established within the next few days.'

In front of the Hôtel Splendide traffic was already mounting on a morning that promised heat in a baking sun. The richer refugees were pulling out. There was a big trade in second-hand cars. One of Werth's friends sold hers for 20,000 francs, and immediately reinvested the money in jewellery and furs.

General Spears had risen earlier than Werth, and at 7 a.m. de Gaulle arrived. He did not say where he had spent the night in hiding, and Spears did not ask him. De Courcel was with de Gaulle, and shortly after half-past seven the trio set off for the airport at Mérignac – though not directly.

Still convinced that Weygand planned to arrest him, de Gaulle was determined to disguise his flight in case any official saw him and reported back. According to Spears he seemed afraid that the French commandant at the airfield had already received orders to prevent him flying to Britain.*

The car stopped first at the Ministry of War where de Gaulle, without leaving his seat, made a great play at arranging a large number of appointments for the rest of the day. While he made plans, the driver of the car kept the motor running just in case they had to make a dash for it.

The same drama was enacted at another building housing some War Ministry personnel. Only then did de Gaulle agree to make for the airfield, which they reached just before 9 a.m. As their car turned on to the bomb-pitted apron in front of the control room, Spears looked around in disgust. It was not a scene of pillage or destruction that made him angry, though Bordeaux had been bombed during the night. The

---

* In his memoirs de Gaulle dismissed his flight to England as being 'without drama', while de Courcel told the author that Spears' account was exaggerated. Yet it is hard to believe that Spears would distort the description of a historic flight by a leading political figure who was still alive at the time of writing. Spears' adventures during the week France fell were so exciting that he had no reason to embroider them. Spears *did* have an eye for colour, while both de Gaulle and de Courcel did *not* have an eye for colourful detail (as de Margerie remarked to the author). Perhaps each remembered what each wanted to remember.

airfield was 'filled with more flying-machines than I have
ever seen in one place, packed wing to wing as far as one
could see . . . offering a fabulous target'. Spears asked himself, 'Why were they not taking off for Africa? How long had
they been collected there like a great herd of flying sheep?'

Now they had to find the solitary British plane, and their
task was made more difficult because they could hardly
manipulate the car through the tightly packed lines of aircraft. Yet they needed the car because de Gaulle had piled
it high with luggage. At last they found it. There was an
agonising delay while the luggage was stowed. All seemed
ready, but then the pilot insisted that de Gaulle's heavy
trunk, filled with papers, should be lashed in case they ran
into bumpy weather. This was easier said than done, for
there was nothing to tie it with. De Courcel remembers that
he had to run off to find some rope; that took another precious ten minutes.

Still worried that he might be stopped if anyone saw him
get in first, de Gaulle insisted on playing one last scene.
When the luggage was stowed and the propellers turning,
Spears jumped into the aircraft. De Courcel followed him,
while de Gaulle, pretending to wave farewell, stood by the
plane. At the last second, at the very moment when the
chocks were pulled from under the wheels, de Gaulle leaned
forward, as though for a final handshake. With one mighty
heave Spears and de Courcel yanked him aboard as the pilot
revved up the engines and roared along the runway.

Within a few minutes they were over the sea and heading
for Britain. Soon, as de Gaulle remembered later, 'We flew
over La Rochelle and Rochefort. Ships were burning in the
harbours, set on fire by German planes. We went over Paimpont, where my mother was lying dangerously ill. The forest
was a mass of smoke from the blazing ammunition depots.'

When the plane landed at Jersey to refuel, de Gaulle and
Spears went into the R.A.F. canteen and ordered coffee.

De Gaulle took one sip, turned to Spears, with a grimace,
and said 'in a voice which indicated that without implying
criticism he must nevertheless proclaim the truth – that this

was tea and he had asked for coffee. It was his first introduction to the tepid liquid which, in England, passed for either one or the other. His martyrdom had begun.'

By the time de Gaulle reached London's Hyde Park Hotel, Pétain was putting the finishing touches to his first speech as premier, and by a strange circumstance most of the preparations for the broadcast were made by a young American woman who stood beside him in the studios as he addressed the nation.

Drue Tartière, the 'Charlie Chan' actress, watched 'every movement the old man made, and waited tensely for the words he was about to deliver'. The corridors in the Bordeaux radio station were crowded with personnel waiting near loudspeakers. Standing next to Pétain, Drue Tartière helped in any way she could as the old man fidgeted to find a comfortable position. He complained about the way the microphone was placed, and one of the studio hands rushed forward eagerly to help. The boy was apparently too slow for the impatient marshal, and Pétain's reaction was totally unexpected; as Drue Tartière watched, Pétain kicked him.

Then the old man stepped to the microphone and in a firm voice delivered his testament to the nation:

At the call of the President of the Republic I assumed, beginning today, the direction of the government of France.

I say that by the affection of our admirable army, which is fighting with a heroism worthy of its long military traditions against an enemy superior in numbers and arms, by the magnificent resistance with which it has fulfilled our duties to our allies, by the aid of the war veterans whom I am proud to command, by the confidence of all the people, I give to France my person to assuage her misfortune.

In these painful hours I think of the unhappy refugees who, in extreme misery, clog up our roads. I express to them my compassion and my solicitude.

It is with a broken heart that I tell you today it is necessary to stop fighting.

I addressed myself last night to the adversary to ask him if he is ready to seek with me, as soldier to soldier, after the actual fighting is over, and with honour, the means of putting an end to hostilities.

May all Frenchmen group themselves about the government which I head during these trying days and control their anguish in order to be led only by their faith in the destiny of the fatherland.

Drue Tartière never forgot the stunned moment in the studio as Pétain brushed against her and walked towards the door without a word. For a while, no one spoke. 'It took us some little time to grasp the meaning of what we had heard, but beneath the flattery and deception the news stood out brazenly. France had still been fighting, but Pétain, the new Chief of State, had decided to quit and was forcing the country along with him in that decision. I left the studio, filled with a sense of futility as well as despair. It was the same all over France.'

Emmanuel d'Astier was at St-Nazaire awaiting orders, and just before midday pushed open the door of a tiny bar which had become a meeting-place for the French Navy. The room was silent, the figures frozen in strange attitudes. The woman behind the bar was holding a bottle, 'arrested in the very act of setting it down'. D'Astier's second mate, a man called Guerin who was a bus conductor in civilian life, and 'who always stood with his knees bent as if on the platform of his bus', was as still as a waxwork in the Musée Grevin. A British officer, entering from a rear room, 'stood with his arm raised, not daring to let the box-wood curtain fall'.

D'Astier looked at the faces of his friends, 'attending a funeral'. He did not hear a word Pétain spoke, did not even recognise the voice, he was so stupefied. The silence was broken as Guerin smashed his glass on the floor and cried, 'We have been betrayed!'

It was then that d'Astier and many of his comrades

decided that they, anyway, would fight on – either from abroad or by forming a resistance movement.

West of St-Nazaire, James Lansdale Hodson, the British writer, was waiting at Brest to board a boat for England. Like many others, he at first thought Pétain's appointment meant the French would fight on – and was appalled as he listened to the broadcast while standing on the balcony of the Hôtel des Voyageurs. Below him three women were crying, 'wiping their eyes with their fingers like those do in extremity of grief, past caring for appearances'.

Pétain's voice seemed to tremble, and as the broadcast ended 'a French naval officer stared at us blankly. He looked stricken and appalled.'

While Hodson waited in a local café for orders, one of his fellow travellers went to the bank and miraculously managed to change all his French money into sterling. When another offered to pay for drinks with English money the waiter waved the offer aside with the words, 'You'll need that in England.' Hodson said to him, 'We'll go on with the fight.' The waiter replied, 'Of course we will,' as though France had not capitulated. When Hodson reached the quay, his last memory of France was a pretty girl waving goodbye and giving him a cheerful thumbs-up sign.

Near Bordeaux Gordon Waterfield was also waiting for a ship, and stopped for lunch on his way to the docks. The girl who served at his table was 'gay and charming' – until someone told her of Pétain's speech, then, 'she burst into tears and served the rest of the meal red-eyed and sobbing'.

Like Waterfield, Werth was driven out to the docks, and waited until a launch arrived to ferry the passengers to their ship, the *Madura*. Werth carried his luggage from the car to the water's edge.

He too had his last thoughts. 'Nearly everyone is weeping. To leave France, and to leave it like this, is hard.'

Zena Marshall left on the same ship – with Gussy smuggled in a basket as she sat in the launch. Others were also relieved to go. Marguerite de Gelabert already had her exit visa and her Spanish transit visa, so she crossed the frontier

at Hendaye without incident. From Spain she made her way
to Italy, where her son was born.

Back in Bordeaux there was a shocking incident at the
Chapon Fin, where Georges Mandel was lunching. He had
finished the main course and the dessert had just been placed
before him when a hand touched his shoulder from behind.
Mandel turned – to face a colonel on the *gendarmerie* who
asked him impassively, 'Monsieur, please follow me.'
Mandel asked, without any show of emotion, 'May I
please be allowed to finish my cherries?'
'No, monsieur, follow me,' said the gendarme. Mandel did.
His arrest was the work of a newcomer to power, the rabid
anti-Jewish Raphael Alibert, whom Pétain had given a lowly
rank outside his cabinet. Alibert ordered Mandel's arrest
solely on the hearsay of a journalist he never named, who
told him Mandel was planning a *coup d'état*.
Lebrun, aided by Herriot and Jeanneney, secured Mandel's release later in the day, and Pétain, who had no knowledge of the affair, offered Mandel his apologies in front of
Alibert, who could hardly contain his rage. 'That Jew is the
main enemy of the new régime,' he shouted as he stormed
out of Pétain's office.

Drue Tartière decided to stay in France, but it was a sad
afternoon. Her work finished for the day, she sat on the terrace of a café in the Place de la Comédie with a friend, the
artist Marie-Louise Bosquet. They held each other's hands
and wept together as they watched the last French planes
flying low over the city, almost shaving the rooftops, dipping
their wings in a farewell salute before flying across the
harbour – and on to England.
Like many people Drue Tartière could not at first accept
the fact that this was the final curtain. Together with others
who refused to believe the war was over, this American girl
discussed moving the French radio propaganda machine to
Martinique. She put the plan to Charles Pomaret, the newly
appointed Minister of the Interior. All the Radio Mondiale

wanted, she urged him, was 'transportation and the guarantee of a sum of money sufficient to enable us to continue shortwave propaganda for France'. But Pomaret was understandably nervous, and either would not, or could not, help them.

Many British refugees were still on the road, including the two sisters Frances and Joan Kay. Frances had changed her plans after reaching Lyons. With the Germans advancing to the south-west, this resourceful girl decided to bypass Bordeaux and make for St-Jean-de-Luz, where she hoped either to find a ship or cross into Spain over the bridge at Hendaye.

She had parted company with Consul and Mrs Ledger, found another bicycle and by now had reached Toulouse. Early on the same day a packed refugee train from Bordeaux jolted into the main station at Toulouse; out stepped sister Joan Kay, who had not the faintest idea where sister Frances was.

Joan had been given the name of a French family in Toulouse whose daughter had worked in the Chamber of Commerce, and with whom she hoped to stay for a while, but apart from trying to find it her immediate concern was her luggage. She had lost it in the chaos on the train. She spent hours trying to find it, but in vain. Finally she gave up, and set off to find her contact.

She was walking along the rue de Metz, towards the bank of the Garonne, when she saw a strangely familiar figure cycling towards her. 'I watched her coming and suddenly realised it was Frances. It was such a shock, I could hardly believe it. Until that moment I had no idea where she was or what had happened to her.'

Joan stopped in her tracks; at the same moment, Frances saw her sister and nearly fell off her bicycle. So great was the shock that they were almost covered in embarrassment. 'We did not hug or kiss.' Joan remembers saying 'something idiotic' like 'Hello! What are you doing here?'

Frances blurted out, 'What are *you* doing here?'

They talked on the pavement though, as Joan remembers, 'I can't recall that we said anything very dramatic, we just chatted.'

After they had swopped stories of their adventures, Frances said she had to be on her way. They wished each other luck, and Joan remembers the sudden feeling of loneliness as Frances cycled off, 'leaving me so stunned by the incident that at first I wasn't sure it had really happened'.

Frances pedalled on, finally reaching the coast near St-Jean-de-Luz, from where she was evacuated on one of the last British ships to leave France. Joan decided to remain in France, for all her closest friends lived there and were making for Toulouse. So the sisters did not meet again until after the war.

The sense of tragedy was as deeply felt by Americans, even though they were not involved in the same way as the British. Thousands of Americans fervently agreed with Thomas Jefferson that 'France is every man's second country.'

To Dynevor Rhys, listening in his Paris apartment to Pétain's 'skeletal voice', it was like waking up 'at the crisis of a terrible nightmare, only to find that it wasn't a nightmare after all, but for real. I had left America to live in freedom in what I believed to be the most wonderful country in the world. And now it was a nation in slavery.'

William Shirer felt much the same. A neutral American correspondent who roamed the world, he returned annually to Paris 'on some kind of an assignment or pretext', and was heartbroken as he walked the streets on 'one of those lovely June days, bright and sunny under a cloudless sky that had often made life seem so wondrous in this ancient and beautiful metropolis'.

Almost the only people he saw were German soldiers gaping like tourists. Virtually all the shops were closed, the windows of apartments shuttered. It reminded Shirer of August when Paris empties for the holidays.

As he walked the almost silent streets, Shirer asked himself how it had all come about, how this great empire, perhaps the most civilised power in Europe, with one of the world's greatest armies, had gone down 'to utter military defeat, leaving its citizens, who had been heirs to a long and glorious history, dazed and then completely demoralized', their country prodded into absurd surrender by 'an 84-year-old, nearly senile marshal, a legendary hero of the First World War, aided and indeed prodded by a handful of defeated generals and defeatist politicians'.

To Shirer it seemed 'beyond the power of the mind to grasp'. Not even the German generals he talked to had expected it.

To the French themselves it was equally incomprehensible. Jacques Maritain, the Catholic philosopher, felt it had to be 'a humiliation without precedent of a great nation', while the French historian Professor Marc Bloch of the University of Paris confessed, 'It was the most terrible collapse in all the long history of our national life.'*

This was true, yet Freeman Matthews was right in thinking that the ordinary and bewildered French people greeted the end with apathetic relief. 'The war was over for them and the millions of refugees that jammed the roads could return home. Nothing else mattered for the moment,' he wrote.

In London, on Monday evening, Churchill talked briefly on the radio.

'The news from France is very bad and I grieve for the gallant French people who have fallen into this terrible misfortune,' he said. 'Nothing will alter our feelings towards them or our faith that the genius of France will rise again. What has happened in France makes no difference to our actions and purpose. We have become the sole champions now in arms to defend the world cause. We shall do our best to be worthy of this high honour. We shall defend our island home and with the British Empire we shall fight on unconquerable until the curse of Hitler is lifted from the brows

* Professor Bloch, a Jew, became a hero of the French resistance until he was arrested, brutally tortured, then shot by the Gestapo on 16 June 1944, only a few weeks before liberation.

of mankind. We are sure that in the end all will come right.'

Mollie Panter-Downes summed up the atmosphere in London in a cable to the *New Yorker*, 'For once the cheerful cockney comeback of the average Londoner simply wasn't there. The public seemed to react to the staggering news like people in a dream, who go through the most fantastic actions without a sound.'

There was still evidence of the blind optimism that always seems to prevail in Britain during crises. When Lieutenant Ivan Foxwell reached Sherstone, his home in Gloucestershire, he was astounded at the indifference. During drinks with a neighbour, Charles Treymane, who lived near Badminton, someone rushed in and announced (incorrectly) that the Germans had invaded the Isle of Wight. An alarmed Foxwell immediately thought about rejoining his unit, but none of the other guests seemed interested. 'Anyone for more martinis?' asked the host.

Foxwell felt that anything happening more than five miles from an English village was too remote to comprehend but, 'if Badminton had been invaded, everyone would have been rushing for pitchforks and scythes'.

The fall of France produced a curious sense of relief that had nothing to do with apportioning blame. Rather was it the instinctive feeling, common to all: 'Well, at least we know where we are.'

As the people of Britain went to bed on Monday night, knowing the country was unprepared for the expected invasion, that the Luftwaffe would soon be roaming the skies over London, all were cushioned by an emotion which none explained more succinctly than King George VI, when he wrote to his mother, 'Personally, I feel happier now that we have no allies to be polite to and to pamper.'

# The Price

THOUGH the armistice terms were harsh enough to arouse howls of rage in the Allied camp and tears of despair in France itself, they were in fact far more lenient than they might have been. This may seem a curious remark in view of the fact that Frenchmen would for the next four years be listening to the tread of the jackboot, or for the Gestapo's knock on the door in the night. But most historians agree that the terms could have been even more harsh.

The ostensible leniency was not due to any change of heart by Hitler, who was at his headquarters near Sedan when the French request reached him. Before replying, Hitler arranged to meet Mussolini at Munich on Tuesday, the eighteenth. Hitler knew exactly what he wanted. As German documents prove conclusively, his greatest desire was to reach an immediate agreement with Britain, so that he could have a free hand in the east. With this in mind, he decided on what he thought of as a stroke of genius. He would occupy only half of France. This would prevent a united France from rebelling or co-operating with England, but would instead create two Frances, in conflict with each other.

Though his army had hardly been in action, Mussolini arrived in Munich with grandiose ideas for the Italian occupation of a large part of France, to say nothing of Corsica, Tunis and several strategic areas in the French African colonies.

Hitler pooh-poohed all his demands, and the Italian dictator could only fortify his public image by announcing that Ribbentrop had promised him that after the war Italy would receive Nice, Corsica, Tunisia, Algeria, Jibuti, and British Somaliland.

Not until the Wednesday morning did Hitler inform Pétain that he would meet the French plenipotentiaries on 21 June in the Forest of Compiègne.

This was the moment of shame for France. Hitler had deliberately planned it. For it was here, on 11 November 1918, that Germany had suffered her ultimate shame, when Marshal Foch dictated peace terms in his private railway coach.

When the French armistice delegation, led by General Huntziger, arrived on Friday, they could hardly control their shock. Foch's historic railway carriage – long since relegated to a museum – had been returned to the forest by German engineers, and rested on the rusty railway lines which had been cleared of more than twenty years' undergrowth. Hitler was in uniform, with the Iron Cross over his left breast. Goering carried his jewelled baton and was flanked by the German High Command, eager to watch the cunningly contrived moment of revenge.

Fifty yards away William Shirer was watching the scene through binoculars. Hitler's expression, he wrote that night, was 'afire with scorn, anger, hate, revenge, triumph'. For a moment the Führer stood waiting, 'then he swiftly snaps his hands on his hips, arches his shoulders, plants his feet wide apart. It is a magnificent gesture of defiance, of burning contempt for this place now and all that it has stood for in the twenty-two years since it witnessed the humbling of the German Empire.'

Silently, the Frenchmen followed him into the railway coach. Hitler sat in the chair Foch had used in 1918, raised his arm in the Nazi salute, and permitted an underling to read out a list of British and French crimes against the Fatherland.

Then came the armistice terms. Germany would occupy

French territory north of Tours from the west coast to the east, plus a strip down the western coast to the border of Spain, thus neutralising the Atlantic seaboard. The area covered more than half the country. France would have to pay the astronomical cost of occupation. The fleet would be collected in specified ports and disarmed. French prisoners of war would remain in Germany until the actual peace treaty was signed, though German prisoners would be released immediately. The terms also included the infamous clause that the French must immediately hand over all German subjects in France (their names being supplied by the Gestapo). This was directed mainly against Jews who had fled Germany, and resulted in an almost immediate wave of suicides.

When the French protested, they were curtly told that no discussion would be permitted. These were the terms, and they had to be accepted as they were or rejected.

So, in a forest glade where once France had sealed a victory for freedom, all Pétain's pitiful promises of 'peace with honour' flew out of the window of an old railway coach.

No sooner had the French delegation left than Hitler ordered the entire site, which had been turned into a commemorative park, to be levelled to the ground. The historic railway carriage was sent to Berlin (only to be destroyed in an R.A.F. raid).

Meanwhile Reynaud, who had fought so hard to avoid France's humiliation, had moved into Hélène de Portes' double room at the Hôtel Splendide. His mistress had taken out an insurance in case he was not recalled to lead the nation.

She had extracted a promise from Baudouin; it was not difficult, for these two had a hold on each other. Baudouin had always been able to count on Madame de Portes to further his career, not only because they were both pro-German, but also because she needed him. Baudouin was a Catholic convert with great influence in Italy and the Vatican, and Madame de Portes felt that he was perhaps the only man who could arrange for the divorces necessary before she and Reynaud could marry.

Since Baudouin couldn't be certain that Reynaud would not be recalled, particularly if the German terms proved to be too harsh, he readily agreed to persuade Pétain to appoint Reynaud ambassador to Washington. In this he had no trouble since Pétain, Laval and Weygand regarded the move as a brilliant way to get rid of a troublesome rival who still commanded great respect in France.

On Tuesday, the morning after Pétain's speech, de Margerie went to the Splendide to see Reynaud. The lovers had no sitting-room, so the two men sat in the bedroom. The bathroom door was open and de Margerie could hear the sounds of gurgling water and splashing as Madame de Portes took her bath. Through the open door she shouted advice as they talked. 'What is he saying?' she asked in her 'usual shrill voice'. In fact Reynaud was saying that the prospect of going to Washington excited him. De Margerie had the impression that Reynaud was looking forward to a minor role in which he would have nothing to do but obey his government's orders.

He was also pleased that two old colleagues from the Treasury, named Dominique Leca and Devaux, had been appointed to help him, and were already preparing to leave, Leca as financial attaché, Devaux as head of the French Purchasing Committee. Both, according to the American, Thomas Kernon, had been appointed at Madame de Portes' request.

On Saturday, 22 June, Leca and Devaux set off, with the diplomatic pouch, for Madrid, from there they would leave for Washington. Nobody envisaged any problems. They had diplomatic immunity, their papers were in order. But Madame de Portes 'did not count', as Kernon put it, 'on the lack of gallantry of the Spanish authorities'.

As they crossed the frontier, the Spanish customs officers briskly ordered them to open their trunks. A blazing argument lasted an hour as the French diplomats refused. But in

the end the Spaniards simply ignored their protests, forced
the baggage open and searched it.

Inside they found the vast personal wealth of Madame de
Portes – a large amount of currency, hundreds of thousands
of pounds' worth of bonds, and a hoard of jewels. Alas, they
found something else – two million dollars in gold. In vain
Leca and Devaux insisted that some of the money came from
secret funds, earmarked for propaganda use in the United
States. The sceptical (and pro-German) Spanish notified
Pétain. The gold was sent back to France; so were the diplomats, and Reynaud's appointment was cancelled.

Reynaud swore that he knew nothing about the contra-
band suitcase, but feared that the over-zealous Leca or
Devaux had taken the money from the secret government
funds without his knowledge, in the hope of handing it over
to Reynaud when he reached Washington. He told Bullitt
later: 'It's going to be most difficult to prove that I had
nothing to do with it. But I gave Leca no orders to do what
he did. As for the gold and jewels, they belong to the Countess.'

Knowing that Reynaud was an honest man, one must take
his word for it – though two million dollars is a lot of money
for a *bourgeois* girl from Marseilles to accumulate.

No one questioned the honesty of Leca or Devaux, both
men of impeccable records, or suggested they were abscond-
ing with the money for themselves. The evidence seemed to
narrow down to two possibilities: they were smuggling the
money out of France as a patriotic gesture to save it from
the Germans; or one of them was the cat's-paw of a lady
whose admiration for the Nazis did not include leaving gold
in their care.

The lady in question could have answered the question
in a moment had she been arraigned, even informally; but it
was not to be. Within a week Madame de Portes was dead.

She and Reynaud had lunched in an isolated restaurant in
the spectacular Gorges du Tarn, in the mountains north of
the Mediterranean town of Sète. One report said that they
spent some minutes in anxious conversation as they finished

their meal. It looked 'as though they were trying to decide something, but couldn't'.

What were they talking about? Why were they so anxious? Was Madame de Portes guilty – and afraid? After all, Sète was barely a hundred miles from the Spanish frontier at Le Perthus. Did she want to bolt? Or was this a lovers' quarrel, with an angry Reynaud upbraiding his mistress for using his name to smuggle a fortune out of France? Reynaud has never spoken on the subject.

The talk ended. Reynaud paid the bill. They got into the car. It seems that Reynaud was driving. The car was loaded with baggage, and he swerved on a sharp bend. The suitcases fell over, on top of them in the front seats. Reynaud jammed on the brakes too quickly. He lost control. The car careered off the road and, as he tried to pull it back, it hit a tree head on. She was killed instantly, and Reynaud was so badly injured that for several weeks he lay critically ill in hospital at nearby Montpellier.

Madame de Portes' life had been stamped with the inexorable quality of a classic Greek tragedy – the *bourgeois* girl who married into the aristocracy, then chose a brilliant, budding politician as her lover and patiently intrigued until she promoted him to the summit of a political career, only to cause his downfall by the same determination that had helped him rise to the top.

The accident, following so closely on the Spanish gold scandal, all but ruined Reynaud. As Robert Murphy, the American diplomat, felt, 'What appeared to be irregular personal behaviour, occurring in the midst of national tragedy . . . had a profound effect in 1940 upon those Frenchmen like Marshal Pétain, who had contended for years that the Third Republic's politicians were not merely weak but were morally rotten.'

Lying in hospital at Montpellier, his head bandaged, one eye closed and bloodied, Reynaud was convinced he would soon be thrown into prison. He wrote to Bullitt of his hopes to have married Hélène de Portes and of her desire 'to continue the struggle for France'. He had obviously been in much pain as he penned the letter, for it is hard to decipher the words, but one can make out certain phrases, 'I will carry out her wish . . . but I have need of friends such as you – so few – to help me.'

Even with Reynaud out of favour (and out of action), could anything have been saved from the shipwreck? Could leaders who wanted to go to north Africa – men like Herriot and Jeanneney – have gone? They tried to. They persuaded Lebrun to go, and actually set off to board a vessel at Le Verdun with Pétain's blessing – only to be stopped at the last moment by Laval, who saw the dangers of a rival government.

One man might have been able to make Pétain countermand Laval's orders. Freeman Matthews believes that Bullitt, who had considerable influence with the old marshal, thanks to the dormant might of the United States, could have persuaded Pétain to think again.

Yet, after France was defeated, the man who so often declared his undying love for France, who stayed in Paris to save the capital's honour, seemed strangely reluctant to help. Matthews tells how 'the pleadings of the President and Secretary Hull to get him [Bullitt] to stay and bolster and influence Pétain's Vichy Government were of no avail'. At first Bullitt, taking advantage of the delay in communications, pretended that cables from the State Department never arrived, until finally he agreed to travel from Paris to Vichy. On the way he stopped at La Bourboule, in the Massif Centrale, where the embassy staff from Bordeaux was awaiting orders, and met Freeman Matthews, who had always disagreed with Bullitt's decision to remain in Paris. Bullitt's very first question denoted his anxiety.

'Do you think it would have made any difference if I had been at Bordeaux?' he asked.

'Yes, Mr Ambassador,' Matthews replied without hesitation, 'I think it might, with your close and friendly relations with all the key figures and the very high regard they have for you. You might have swayed them at critical moments.'

Matthews had in mind 'the possible move of the government to North Africa'. Bullitt 'made no comment'.

It is tempting to wonder whether after the anguish, the exhortations, the recriminations, the charges and counter-charges, the French demand for an armistice did not, after all, turn out to be for the best. Was France better off than if she had fought on? And, for that matter, did it harm the Allied cause?

If Hélène de Portes had used her influence to bolster Reynaud in his determination to go to north Africa, how different those dark years of occupation might have been. For at the moment of her doom France had three great assets: a powerful navy, unscarred in battle, backed by a huge merchant fleet; a mighty empire with a million men at arms; and to run that empire at war she had more gold stashed in the United States than any other country in the world outside America.

No one can over-estimate the role the empire might have played. Indo-China lay astride the Japanese path to Singapore. Syria lay astride the British lifeline to India. French North Africa could have been the launching pad for early liberation, instead of becoming a desert graveyard for the bones of men and the carcases of tanks.

When Churchill engaged in what he called 'ghostly speculation', he was convinced that, had France remained in the struggle, the war would have been shortened. Apart from the Far East, he believed that the British and French fleets could have controlled the Mediterranean, where so many lives were lost, and that Malta, instead of being 'a care and peril', would have been an aggressive base for unceasing attacks on Italy, Libya and Tripolitania.

Yet the historians G. and W. Fortune, in their excellent book *Hitler Divided Europe,* ask a pertinent question, 'Had France refused to sign an armistice and the Government gone to North Africa . . . could anything have been done by the Allies to prevent the total occupation of North Africa by Germany in the autumn of 1940?'

Perhaps not, though Churchill felt that if Hitler had attacked north Africa he could not have launched the Battle of Britain.

Pétain, of course, regarded the French defeat as only the first round in Hitler's war effort, and expected British resistance to end soon afterwards. But, more important, he saw in defeat his opportunity to rid France forever of the danger of Communist revolution and the corruption which had stigmatised its politics for so many years.

After Bullitt met the Vichy leaders in July, he reported to Washington:

> The impression which emerges from these conversations is the extraordinary one, that the French leaders desire to cut loose from all that France has represented during the past two generations, that their physical and moral defeat has been so absolute that they have accepted completely for France the fate of becoming a province of Nazi Germany. Moreover, in order that they may have as many companions in misery as possible they hope that England will be rapidly and completely defeated by Germany and that the Italians will suffer the same fate. Their hope is that France may become Germany's favourite province – a new 'Gau' which will develop into a new Gaul.

Under Pétain, France was down, but not out. The emasculated Unoccupied France was preserved as an entity, with its own government (of sorts) and administration; and, though half of France was under the lash of the Gestapo, Pétain *did*, for all his faults, keep France in being. To the end he believed, rightly, that if France had fought on the entire country would have been occupied.

Instead, Pétain kept in the back of his mind that in June 1940 Germany held two million French prisoners of war and that the only way to free them was to stop fighting. His belief that he could treat with Hitler as man to man was based on a childlike simplicity, backed by an adult vanity that was truly awesome. He never did get all the prisoners back – Hitler kept thousands as hostages – but, by the end of 1942, 750,000 French soldiers had reason to thank Pétain for their release.

The hopes of his brave new world never materialised. They were the idealistic dreams of an old man who simply could not believe that, once the fighting stopped, the Germans would still execute 29,660 French hostages in France before the country was liberated, and who was putty in the hands of wily politicians like Laval.

Over 'the other France', the darkness of occupation by a detested foe descended like a black curtain, blotting out the faintest chink of light, the smallest ray of hope. Hapless victims of a line drawn casually across a map, the people of Occupied France needed more than any others inspiration and comfort to sustain them in the dreariness, the degradation, the oppression of total defeat.

Inspiration soon came in the ringing tones of de Gaulle; and magnificent it was. But to the victims of a fearful plague the clinical promises of eventual recovery are not enough. They need the comforting pat on the back of the family doctor, the consoling words of the village curé, urging them to be in good heart during the pain that will follow, but promising them in homely words that they will recover. In short, they need a friend.

The people of Occupied France found that friend in Winston Churchill, the English bulldog who never uttered a word of reproach for what had happened. He warned the British to be careful in their judgments of the French. He pointed out that since their only salvation lay in following the advice of 'the illustrious Marshal Pétain . . . very little choice was offered to the masses'.

He never forswore his love for France* and never put

* In 1945 the author lunched with Churchill on his first post-war visit to Paris as a private individual. As he looked at the other people in the restaurant – some raising their glasses in silent toasts – Churchill turned to me and grunted, 'It is a country without parallel. There could never be another France.' There were tears in his eyes as he spoke.

them out of his mind, during even the darkest days. In October, during the German blitz on London, he broadcast to them.

His French – of which he was so proud – was not of the best, and his words were not those of a man employing lofty phrases but rather the homespun talk of a friend who has dropped in for a chat.

All over France people listened. In Vaucresson, Iris Schweppe heard the voice on the radio which her mother, as a German, had the right to keep. Dynevor Rhys heard it in his apartment, and reflected, 'Extraordinary, he makes one feel proud of France, not ashamed.' Henri Malherbe listened under a blanket in his small apartment, and afterwards paraphrased an old saying when he told his wife, 'While there's Churchill, there's life.' The bombs were crashing down on London, as Churchill spoke.

'Français!' he cried. 'C'est moi, Churchill, qui parle!' And then, still in French, he carried on, 'For more than thirty years in peace and war I have marched with you, and I am marching still along the same road.' He told them of the Blitz. Deftly he inserted a shaft of humour: 'We are waiting for the long-promised invasion,' he boomed. 'So are the fishes.' He promised his French friends that Britain would 'never stop, never weary and never give in'.

And finally, like a father giving comfort to an adopted family he loves, Churchill told them quietly, 'Good night, then: sleep to gather strength for the morning. For the morning will come. Brightly will it shine on the brave and true, kindly upon all who suffer for the cause, glorious upon the tombs of heroes. Thus will shine the dawn. Vive la France!'

# What Happened to Them

ASHWORTH, JAMES. Was interned until V.E. Day. After the war worked with the author for eight years in Paris. Ashworth died in Le Touquet while this book was being written. His daughter Jenny lives in Nice.

BEAUREPOS, KITTY. Murdered by the Germans. See p. 236.

BULLITT, WILLIAM C. United States ambassador to France from 1936 to 1941, then President Roosevelt's special representative in the Near East and a special assistant secretary of the Navy. He died in the United States in 1967.

CHURCHILL, SIR WINSTON. Britain's wartime prime minister lost office in 1945 but was premier again from 1951 to 1955, when he retired. Knighted in 1953, he died in 1965.

COURCEL, GEOFFROY DE. De Gaulle's aide, who escaped to Britain with the General, has had a distinguished diplomatic career, and is now at the Quai d'Orsay, Paris.

DARLAN, ADMIRAL FRANÇOIS. He was an anti-British member of the Vichy Government after the fall of France but ordered the end of French resistance to the Allied invasion of north Africa in 1942, a month before he was assassinated.

FOXWELL, IVAN. Became a famous film producer of, among others, *The Colditz Story, Tiara Tahiti, The Quiller Memorandum.*

GAULLE, GENERAL CHARLES DE. He returned from virtual retirement in 1958 during the Algerian troubles to become prime minister again and, later in the year, first president of the Fifth Republic. He resigned in 1969 after defeat of his referendum proposals for reform. He died a year later.

GELABERT, GABRIEL DE. Was sent to Buchenwald after the Germans discovered he had organised the escape of twenty-seven British fliers. He survived, later was divorced from the Countess, and now lives outside Paris.

GELABERT, MARGUERITE DE. Divorced the Count (see above) and in 1954 married Noel Barber.

HERRIOT, ÉDOUARD. The Radical-Socialist President of the French Chamber of Deputies was arrested by the Pétain government and taken to Germany after showing hostility to collaboration. After the liberation he was elected President of the National Assembly from 1947 to 1954 and opposed German rearmament. He died in 1957.

HULL, CORDELL. America's Secretary of State under Roosevelt and an advocate of maximum aid to the Allies retired in 1944 and received the Nobel Peace Prize. He died in 1955.

JEANNENEY, JULES. Pro-British President of the Senate. Despite the observations of many witnesses in this book that he looked frail, and moved only with difficulty in 1940, this gallant Frenchman lived until 1957 when he died aged ninety-three.

KAY, FRANCES. Now married to the artist Sam Rabin, and lives near Poole, Dorset.

KAY, JOAN. Remained in France. Now lives outside Paris.

LEBRUN, ALBERT. The last president of France's Third Republic relinquished his powers to Pétain in 1940 but was arrested by the Gestapo and interned. He died in 1950.

MACKWORTH, CECILY. This brave British nurse returned to France, married a Frenchman and still lives there.

MARGERIE, ROLAND DE. After a distinguished political career, retired and now lives on the Left Bank in Paris.

MARSHALL, ZENA. Became famous as a film star, now lives in London.

PÉTAIN, MARSHAL PHILIPPE. The man who became head of the Vichy State in 1940 was charged with treason after the liberation, sentenced to death but the sentence was commuted to life imprisonment on the Île de Yeu. He died in captivity in 1951.

REYNAUD, PAUL. The French Premier at the time of the fall of France was imprisoned by the Germans during the war.

After 1945 he married again, returned to politics, was a delegate to the Council of Europe in 1949, lost his seat in the French Chamber of Deputies in 1962, and died in 1966.

RHYS, DYNEVOR. Returned to America at the end of 1940, but came back to Paris after the war and still lives in the same apartment, though he has sold his photographic business.

ROMMEL, FIELD-MARSHAL ERWIN. His successes in France were equalled by those in the north African desert. For condoning the July plot to kill Hitler he was offered the choice of suicide or a court martial and he poisoned himself.

ROOSEVELT, FRANKLIN D. Died at Warm Springs, Georgia, where he had gone for treatment, three weeks before the German surrender in 1945.

SCHWEPPE, IRIS. Now lives in London, and is still working in photography.

SHIBER, ETTA. Wrote a book about her adventures (see Select Bibliography) and returned to live in America.

SPEARS, MAJOR-GENERAL SIR EDWARD. The British Premier's representative to the French Premier in 1940, head of the British mission to General de Gaulle from 1940 to 1942 and then a member of the Middle East war council. Was created a baronet in 1953 and died in 1974. He was the author of several books, including *Assignment to Catastrophe* which covers the fall of France, and the classic *Liaison 1914*.

TABOUIS, GENEVIÈVE. Over eighty, she still works as a columnist and also broadcasts three times a week. Lives in Paris.

TARTIÈRE, DRUE. Wrote a book about her experiences (see Select Bibliography). Her husband was killed in the war, and she is now believed to be living in the United States.

WEYGAND, GENERAL MAXIME. The commander of the French armies at the time of the collapse became a prisoner of the Germans and retired into obscurity after the war. He died in 1965.

# Select Bibliography

## DOCUMENTS CONSULTED

*Britain*
Prime Minister's papers, May, June, July 1940, Public Record
    Office.
Cabinet documents and reports, Public Record Office.
Foreign Office minutes and documents, Public Record Office.
Reports from General Spears to War Cabinet, London, Pub-
    lic Record Office.
Reports from Lord Hankey to Prime Minister, Public Record
    Office.
B.B.C. Monitoring Service.

*United States of America*
State Department files on the Second World War.
Private papers of United States Ambassador H. Freeman
    Matthews.
Papers collected by the Council on Foreign Relations, New
    York (various).

*France*
Revue Défense National (various).
Revue d'Histoire de la Deuxième Guerre Mondiale (various).
Revue Historique de l'Armée (various).

## SOME BOOKS CONSULTED

Amery, L. S., *My Political Life,* 3 vols (London: Hutchinson,
    1953–5).

Amouroux, Henri, *La Vie des français sous l'occupation* (Paris: A. Fayard, 1961).

Angèli, Claude and Gillet, Paul, *Debout, Partisans!* (Paris: A. Fayard, 1970).

Arenstam, Arved, *Tapestry of a Débâcle from Paris to Vichy: a book of contacts* (London: Constable, 1942).

Armstrong, Hamilton Fish, *Chronology of Failure: the last days of the French Republic* (New York: Macmillan, 1941).

d'Astier de la Vigerie, Emmanuel, *Seven Times Seven Days* (London: MacGibbon, 1958).

Attlee, Clement, *As It Happened* (London: Heinemann, 1954; New York: Viking, 1954).

Auren, Sven, *Signature Tune* (London: Hammond, 1943).

Avon, Anthony Eden, Earl of, *The Reckoning* (London: Cassell, 1965; Boston, Mass.: Houghton Mifflin, 1965).

Balbaud, René, *Cette Drôle de guerre: Alsace-Lorraine, Belgique, Dunkerque (26 août 1939–1er juin 1940)* (New York and London: Oxford University Press, 1941).

Barlowe, D., *French Officer's Diary (23 August 1939–1 October 1940)* (London: Cambridge University Press, 1942; New York: Macmillan, 1943).

Barnett, Corelli, *The Swordbearers: supreme command in the First World War* (London: Eyre & Spottiswoode, 1963; New York: Morrow, 1964).

Barros, James, *Betrayal from Within* (New Haven, Conn.: Yale University Press, 1969).

Baudouin, Paul, *Private Diaries (March 1940 to January 1941)*, trans. Sir Charles Petrie (London: Eyre & Spottiswoode, 1948).

Beccles, Gordon, *Dunkirk and After* (London: Hutchinson, 1940).

Benoist-Méchin, Jacques, *Sixty Days that Shook the West* (London: Jonathan Cape, 1963; New York: Putnam, 1963).

Bloch, Marc, *Strange Defeat* (New York: Oxford University Press, 1949).

Bois, Élie, *Truth on the Tragedy of France* (London: Hodder & Stoughton, 1941).

Boothe, Clare, *Europe in the Spring* (New York: Knopf, 1940). Published in Britain as *European Spring* (London: Hamish Hamilton, 1941).

Bryant, Sir Arthur, *The Turn of the Tide* (London: Collins, 1957; Garden City, New York: Doubleday, 1957).

Bullitt, William C., *For the President: Personal and Secret*, ed. Orville H. Bullitt (London: André Deutsch, 1973).

Butler, J. R. M., *Grand Strategy*, vol. II, *September 1939–June 1941* (London: Her Majesty's Stationery Office, 1956).

—, *Lord Lothian* (London: Macmillan, 1960; New York: St Martin's Press, 1960).

Chandos, Oliver Lyttelton, Earl of, *Memoirs of Lord Chandos* (London: Bodley Head, 1962; New York: New American Library of World Literature, 1963).

Chapman, Guy, *Why France Collapsed* (London: Cassell, 1968).

Charles-Roux, François, *Cinq Mois tragiques aux affaires étrangères (21 mai–1er novembre 1940)* (Paris: Plon, 1949).

Churchill, Winston, *The Second World War*, vol. II, *Their Finest Hour* (London: Cassell, 1949). Published in the United States individually as *Their Finest Hour* (Boston, Mass.: Co-operation Publishing Co./Houghton Mifflin, 1949).

Davis, Forrest and Lindley, Ernest K., *How War Came, an American White Paper: from the fall of France to Pearl Harbor* (New York: Simon & Schuster, 1942). Published in Britain as *How War Came to America: from the fall of France to Pearl Harbor* (London: Allen & Unwin, 1943).

Divine, Arthur D., *The Nine Days of Dunkirk* (New York: Norton, 1959; London: Faber, 1959).

Downing, Rupert, *If I Laugh* (London: Harrap, 1941).

Draper, Theodore, *The Six Weeks' War: France, May 10–June 25, 1940* (New York: Viking, 1944).

Du Cros, Janet Tessier, *Divided Loyalties* (London: Hamish Hamilton, 1962).

Farre-Luce, Alfred, *Journal de la France, mars 1939–juillet 1940* (Paris: De Trevoux, 1940).

Fontaine, Peter, *Last to Leave Paris* (London: Chatterson, 1941).

'Fortune, G. and W.', *Hitler Divided France: a factual account of conditions in occupied and unoccupied France . . .* (London: Macmillan, 1943).

Freeman, C. Denis and Cooper, Douglas, *The Road to Bordeaux* (London: Cresset, 1940; New York: Harper Brothers, 1941).

Friedländer, Saul, *Prelude to Downfall: Hitler and the United States, 1939–41* (London: Chatto & Windus, 1967; New York: Knopf, 1967).

Fuller, J. F. C., *The Second World War, 1939–45: a strate-

*gical and tactical history* (London: Eyre & Spottiswoode, 1948; New York: Duell, Sloan & Pearce, 1949).

Gafencu, Grigoire, *The Last Days of Europe: a diplomatic journey in 1939* (London: Muller, 1947; New Haven, Conn.: Yale University Press, 1948).

Galland, Adolf, *The First and the Last: the rise and fall of the German fighter forces, 1938–1945* (New York: Holt, Rinehart & Winston, 1954; London: Methuen, 1955).

Gaulle, Charles de, *The Call to Honour, 1940–1942* (London: Collins, 1955; New York: Viking, 1955).

—, *The Speeches of General de Gaulle*, 2 vols (London and New York: Oxford University Press, 1942–3).

—, *Vers l'Armée de Métier* (London: Hutchinson, 1946).

Ghebali, Victor Yves, *La France en guerre et les organisations internationales, 1939–1945* (Paris: La Haye, Mouton, 1969).

Gillois, André, *Histoire secrète de français à Londres* (London: Hachette, 1973).

Goebbels, Josef, *The Secret Conferences of Dr Goebbels, 1939–43* (London: Weidenfeld & Nicolson, 1970; New York: Dutton, 1970).

Goutard, Adolphe, *The Battle of France, 1940* (London: Muller, 1958; New York: Washburn, 1959).

Greenwall, H. J., *When France Fell* (London: Wingate, 1958).

Habe, Hans, *A Thousand Shall Fall* (New York: Harcourt, Brace, 1941; London: Harrap, 1942).

Harrisson, Tom and Madge, Charles, *War Begins at Home* (London: Chatto & Windus, 1942).

Hart, B. H. Liddell, *Current of War* (London: Hutchinson, 1941).

Hodson, James Lansdale, *Through the Dark Night: being some account of a war correspondent's journeys, meetings, and what was said to him, in France, Britain, and Flanders during 1939–1940* (London: Gollancz, 1941).

Horne, Alistair, *To Lose a Battle: France 1940* (London: Macmillan, 1969; Boston, Mass.: Little, Brown, 1969).

Hull, Cordell, *The Memoirs of Cordell Hull* (New York: Macmillan, 1948).

*I Was Lucky to Escape: twelve true stories of refugees and war-time escapes* (London: Lindsay Drummond, 1940).

Ironside, Edmund, *The Ironside Diaries, 1937–1940*, ed. Roderick Macleod and Denis Kelly (London: Constable,

1962). Published in the United States as *Time Unguarded: the Ironside Diaries, 1937–1940* (New York: Mackay, 1963).

Jeanneney, Jules, *Journal politique, septembre 1939–juillet 1942* (Paris: A. Colin, 1972).

Joulie, Michel, *La Vie politique d'Édouard Herriot* (Paris: Max Leclerc, 1962).

Jucker, Ninetta, *Curfew in Paris: a record of the German occupation* (London: Hogarth Press, 1960).

Kennedy, Gen. Sir John, *The Business of War* (London: Hutchinson, 1957; New York: Morrow, 1958).

Kernan, Thomas, *France on Berlin Time* (Philadelphia: Lippincott, 1941). Published in Britain as *Report on France* (London: John Lane, 1942).

Keun, Odette, *And Hell Followed . . . A European Ally Interprets the War for Ordinary People like Herself* (London: Constable, 1942).

Langer, William L., *Our Vichy Gamble* (New York: Knopf, 1947).

— and Gleason, S. Everett, *The Challenge to Isolation, 1937–1940* (New York: Harper Brothers, 1952).

— —, *The Undeclared War, 1940–1941* (New York: Harper Brothers, 1953).

Langeron, Roger, *Paris, juin 1940* (Paris: E. Flammarion, 1946).

'Lania, Leo', *Darkest Hour: adventures and escapes* (Boston, Mass.: Houghton Mifflin, 1941; London: Gollancz, 1942).

Leasor, James, *War at the Top: based on the experiences of General Sir Leslie Hollis* (London: Michael Joseph, 1959). Published in the United States as *Clock with Four Hands: based on the experiences of General Sir Leslie Hollis* (New York: Reynal, 1959).

Le Verrier, Madeleine G., *France in Torment* (London: Hamish Hamilton, 1942).

Liebling, A. J., *The Road Back to Paris* (Garden City, New York: Doubleday, 1944; London: Michael Joseph, 1944).

McCallum, R. B., *England and France, 1939–1943* (London: Hamish Hamilton, 1944).

Mackworth, Cecily, *I Came out of France* (London: Routledge, 1941).

Maritain, Jacques, *France, My Country, through the Disaster* (New York: Longmans, Green, 1941).

Maurois, André, *Battle of Flanders* (London: John Lane, 1940).

—, *Tragedy in France* (New York: Harper Brothers, 1940). British edition published as *Why France Fell* (London: John Lane, 1941).

Murphy, Robert, *Diplomat among Warriors* (Garden City, New York: Doubleday, 1964).

Novick, Peter, *The Resistance versus Vichy: the purge of collaborators in liberated France* (London: Chatto & Windus, 1968; New York: Columbia University Press, 1968).

Pangé, Jean de, *Mes Prisons* (Paris: Desclée, de Brouwer, 1945).

Panter-Downes, Mollie, *London War Notes, 1939–1945* (New York: Farrar, Straus & Giroux, 1971; London: Longman, 1972).

Parkinson, Roger, *Blood, Toil, Tears, and Sweat: the war history from Dunkirk to Alamein, based on the War Cabinet of 1940–1942* (London: Hart-Davis MacGibbon, 1973; New York: Mackay, 1973).

'Pertinax', *Les Fossoyeurs* (New York: Editions de la Maison Française, 1943).

Philip, Percy J., *France in Defeat* (London: Muller, 1941).

Rebatet, Lucien, *Les Décombrés* (Paris: De Noël, 1942).

Révillon, M. M. Tony, *Mes Carnets (juin–octobre 1940): documents et témoignages pour servir à l'histoire* (Paris: O. Lieutier, 1945).

Reynaud, Paul, *In the Thick of the Fight, 1930–1945* (London: Cassell, 1955; New York: Simon & Schuster, 1955).

Rhodes, Anthony, *Sword of Bone* (London: Faber, 1942; New York: Harcourt, Brace, 1943).

Rommel, Erwin, *The Rommel Papers*, ed. B. H. Liddell Hart (London: Collins, 1953; New York: Harcourt, Brace, 1953).

Roosevelt, Franklin D., *The Roosevelt Letters*, ed. Elliott Roosevelt, 3 vols (London: Harrap, 1949–52). Published in the United States as *FDR: his personal letters*, 3 vols (New York: Duell, Sloan & Pearce, 1947–50).

Rossi-Landi, Guy, *La Drôle de guerre: la vie politique en France, 2 septembre 1939–10 mai 1940* (Paris: A. Colin, 1971).

Rouchaud, Martine, *Journal d'une petite fille 1940–1944* (Paris: Gallimard, 1945).

Rowe, Vivian, *The Great Wall of France: the triumph of the Maginot Line* (London: Putnam, 1959; New York: Putnam, 1961).

St John, Robert, *Foreign Correspondent* (Garden City, New York: Doubleday, 1957; London: Hutchinson, 1960).

Sartre, Jean-Paul, *Iron in the Soul* (vol. III of *The Roads of Freedom*) (London: Hamish Hamilton, 1950). Published in the United States as *Troubled Sleep* (New York: Knopf, 1951).

Sheean, Vincent, *Between the Thunder and the Sun* (New York: Random House, 1943; London: Macmillan, 1943).

Sherwood, Robert E., *White House Papers of Harry L. Hopkins: an intimate history* (London: Eyre & Spottiswoode, 1948–9). Published in the United States as *Roosevelt and Hopkins: an intimate history* (New York: Harper Brothers, 1950).

Shiber, Etta, *Paris Underground* (London: Harrap, 1944).

Shirer, William L., *Berlin Diary: the journal of a foreign correspondent, 1934–1941* (New York: Knopf, 1941; London: Hamish Hamilton, 1941).

—, *The Collapse of the Third Republic* (New York: Simon & Schuster, 1969; London: Heinemann, 1970).

Sington, Derrick and Weidenfeld, Arthur, *Goebbels Experiment: a study of the Nazi propaganda machine* (London: John Murray, 1942; New Haven, Conn.: Yale University Press, 1943).

Smith, Denys, *America and the Axis War* (New York: Macmillan, 1942; London: Jonathan Cape, 1942).

Snyder, Louis L., *The War: a concise history, 1939–1945* (New York: Julian Messner, 1960; London: Robert Hale, 1962).

Spears, Sir Edward, *Assignment to Catastrophe*, 2 vols (London: Heinemann, 1954; New York: A. Wyn, 1954).

Tartière, Dorothy and Werner, M. R., *The House near Paris: an American woman's story of the traffic in patriots* (New York: Simon & Schuster, 1946; London: Gollancz, 1947).

Templewood, Viscount, *Nine Troubled Years* (London: Collins, 1954).

Thompson, Laurence, *1940 – Year of Legend, Year of History* (London: Collins, 1946).

Tuchman, Barbara, *August 1914* (London: Constable, 1962). Published in the United States as *The Guns of August* (New York: Macmillan, 1962).

—, *The Proud Tower: a portrait of the world before the war, 1890–1914* (New York: Macmillan, 1966; London: Hamish Hamilton, 1966).

Vansittart, Sir Robert, *Roots of the Trouble* (London: Hutchinson, 1941).

'Vercors', *The Battle of Silence* (London: Collins, 1968; New York: Holt, Rinehart & Winston, 1969).

Viorst, Milton, *Hostile Allies: FDR and Charles de Gaulle* (New York: Macmillan, 1965).

Vomécourt, Phillippe de, *Who Lived to See the Day: France in Arms, 1940–1945* (London: Hutchinson, 1961). Published in the United States as *An Army of Amateurs* (Garden City, New York: Doubleday, 1961).

Waterfield, Gordon, *What Happened to France* (London: John Murray, 1940).

Welles, Sumner, *The Time for Decision* (New York and London: Harper Brothers, 1944).

Werth, Alexander, *Last Days of Paris: a journalist's diary* (London: Hamish Hamilton, 1940).

Weygand, Maxime, *Recalled to Service* (London: Heinemann, 1952; Garden City, New York: Doubleday, 1952).

— and Jacques Weygand, *Role of General Weygand: conversations with his son* (London: Eyre & Spottiswoode, 1948).

'Weymouth, Anthony', *Journal of the War Years, 1939–1945, and One Year Later*, 2 vols (Worcester, Mass.: Littlebury, 1948).

—, *Plague Year, March 1940–February 1941: being the diary of Anthony Weymouth* (London: Harrap, 1942).

White, Dorothy S., *Seeds of Discord: de Gaulle, Free France and the Allies* (Syracuse, New York: Syracuse University Press, 1964).

Williams, John, *The Ides of May: the defeat of France, May–June 1940* (London: Constable, 1968; New York: Knopf, 1968).

Wilmot, Chester, *The Struggle for Europe* (New York: Harper, 1952; London: Collins, 1952).

Woodward, Sir Llewellyn, *British Foreign Policy in the Second World War* (London: Her Majesty's Stationery Office, 1970).

# Index